Kalman Silvert

For Shone and Barb,

With fond memories
and hopes, for us, the Red Sox
and the world.

Oct 2008

Kalman Silvert

Engaging Latin America, Building Democracy

edited by

Abraham F. Lowenthal
Martin Weinstein

LYNNE
RIENNER
PUBLISHERS

BOULDER
LONDON

Published in the United States of America in 2016 by
Lynne Rienner Publishers, Inc.
1800 30th Street, Boulder, Colorado 80301
www.rienner.com

and in the United Kingdom by
Lynne Rienner Publishers, Inc.
3 Henrietta Street, Covent Garden, London WC2E 8LU

Library of Congress Cataloging-in-Publication Data
A Cataloging-in-Publication record for this book
is available from the Library of Congress.
ISBN: 978-1-62637-555-0 (pb)
ISBN: 978-1-62637-554-3 (hc)

British Cataloguing in Publication Data
A Cataloguing in Publication record for this book
is available from the British Library.

Printed and bound in the United States of America

The paper used in this publication meets the requirements
of the American National Standard for Permanence of
Paper for Printed Library Materials Z39.48-1992.

5 4 3 2 1

Contents

Acknowledgments

The editors and other contributors express appreciation to all who helped make this publication possible: those who wrote reminiscences on Kalman Silvert published in the *LASA Forum*, those who provided interviews about Silvert for our chapters, Peter S. Cleaves and Louis W. Goodman for their editorial and strategic suggestions; and Ronald G. Hellman for hosting a working session at City University of New York. We also thank Henry Silvert and Benjamin Silvert for their important assistance.

We are especially grateful to the Ford Foundation and the Latin American Studies Association (LASA) for generous support that has expedited this publication and made it available to key supporters as part of the association's fiftieth anniversary celebration, as well as to all LASA members at an affordable price.

We thank Lynne Rienner for her personal commitment to this project and her skillful guidance and the anonymous reviewers whose suggestions helped us improve the manuscript. We also thank Linda Miele for her invaluable assistance in the production of the manuscript.

We thank each other for a warm and collegial experience, a true labor of love. We thank our significant others, especially Jane Jaquette and Ruth Weinstein, for their many contributions.

Our greatest debt, of course, is to Kalman H. Silvert, our teacher, mentor, colleague, and friend and a pioneer in our chosen profession. We trust that this book will allow Kal's many contributions to be more widely appreciated and serve as a continuing inspiration.

Prologue

Kalman Silvert: An Appreciation

Ricardo Lagos

I do not remember exactly when first I met Kalman Silvert because one begins to know a social scientist of his stature through his writings and the references of colleagues. I do know that it was sometime between 1971 and 1973, when I was secretary general of the Latin American School of Social Sciences (FLACSO). In that capacity, I received an invitation from Kal Silvert to participate in a seminar at the Rockefeller Foundation's conference center in Bellagio, Italy, that Silvert had organized.

I was asked to make a presentation on the development of the social sciences in Latin America. Silvert opened the discussion, inviting us to discuss two points that had emerged in the opening session of the conference. The first was that the social sciences are never completely autonomous, nor should they be completely inverted to look at themselves or be completely integrated with other institutions. Rather, it is a question of nuances (and not of absolutes) in favor of one aspect or another. The second point was that social sciences are never completely national or international, but to a certain degree there is a continuum between both. What is done on a national level slips invariably into the international arena and vice versa.

This way of creating a seminar on social sciences as a system integrated by autonomous and complementary aspects, national and international, illustrates the way Kal Silvert understood the development of the social sciences and how and to what extent they could come to constitute a system within international affairs. Was there a cultural specificity to social sciences, or were they based on universal qualities, as Max Weber argued? Could we infer valid norms for everyone, or is it necessary to pass norms through the filter of regional or national realities?

1

Taking these questions as a point of departure, I initiated the debate about social sciences in Latin America, alluding to three periods that we could observe in the development of regional social sciences: the most traditional period, when it was somewhat less than professional at best; the scientific period, which I attributed to the contact Latin American social scientists had with what they learned in Europe or the United States; and finally the period of the beginning of the 1970s, of dissatisfaction because such a large portion of mainstream social sciences applied more to the realities of the developed world of the United States and Europe and therefore had to pass through the filter of Latin American reality to see how much was applicable.

Put another way, I observed a kind of intellectual dissatisfaction with the capacity for real transformation of knowledge imported from so-called first world countries to confront our reality. It was precisely on this point that Silvert's perspective proved so illuminating and constructive. I believe that he accepted the post of senior social science program advisor at the Ford Foundation largely because from there he could influence the construction of a perspective that was at once global and regional. With this perspective, it would be possible to explore whether social sciences could have the ability to help explain different realities.

In this seminar in Bellagio I met and came to perceive the human qualities of Kalman Silvert as I came from Chile, which in 1973 was profoundly divided. Chile was then torn between the project of constructing a socialist society through a democratic process—something that had never been achieved—and those who strongly opposed this project. Obviously the division of Chilean society also reached the social sciences, and therefore the theme of the autonomy of social science was at the crux of the discussions, not just for Chile but for many countries in the 1970s. Silvert knew quite a bit about these themes because of his lengthy stay in my country during the 1960s.

In 1975, Silvert decided to continue the conversations of Bellagio, now with a plan that he was carrying out within the Ford Foundation and with the support of other academic entities. For that project he chose to bring together a strong nucleus of social scientists who had the opportunity to study his drafts and comment on them in extensive day-long meetings throughout a year in New York. We had, if I remember correctly, some ten meetings. At that time, after the Chilean coup, I was a visiting professor at the University of North Carolina, Chapel Hill; from there I traveled once a month to the meetings, which began punctually at 11 at the headquarters of the Council on Foreign Relations on Park Avenue. Another colleague was Osvaldo Sunkel, who was then at the University of Texas, Austin. The seminar was an illuminating experience; Silvert organized those meetings and pushed for probing discussions on key points.

During those years I became acquainted with another facet of Kalman Silvert. From the Ford Foundation, he hurriedly organized a seminar in Lima in October or November 1973 to see how Ford could collaborate and help respond to the fall of the democracies of the Southern Cone, of which Chile was unfortunately the prime example—how the foundation could help keep alive scientific thought under these adverse circumstances.

I recall with strong emotion his role in the Ford Foundation, which was indispensable in supporting and helping many scholars leave their country in the face of grave danger. The role that Peter Bell played was also fundamental; he was the representative of the Ford Foundation in Chile at the time of the coup and was urged by the foundation to abandon the country, but he stayed for a while to take charge of these important efforts. This began a difficult period because several people in the foundation lacked understanding, but with Silvert's help the foundation came to realize the necessity of maintaining the flame by supporting autonomous and critical thought during the authoritarian period.

Argentina joined the "club of the dictatorships" in the Southern Cone in March 1976, and Silvert's programs gained strength because he became the leader within the Ford Foundation in carrying out two tasks—helping social scientists leave their countries when necessary, and supporting those who stayed so they could continue their intellectual work, which had been abruptly interrupted by the military intervention and the military's atavistic scorn for the academy and intellectualism in general. Some critical programs began to develop in Chile and the Southern Cone: CIEPLAN and FLACSO in Chile, the DiTella Institute and CEDES in Argentina, and CEBRAP and other centers of research in Brazil. Silvert's role as an eminent intellectual behind these efforts was enormous. Because it was possible for the Ford Foundation to take the leading role on this path, many doors were opened. His ability to engage the president of the foundation at that time, McGeorge Bundy, was decisive.

I have no doubt that in many sectors of Latin America, especially those with an ideology that today we would classify as neoliberal, there was opposition to the approaches that were being formulated by the Ford Foundation with Silvert's influence. But when I see what was accomplished during his nine years at the foundation, I feel tremendous respect for how he managed to maintain and support autonomous intellectual work in the Southern Cone during the worst moments of the dictatorships.

From the Latin American Council for the Social Sciences (CLACSO) in Buenos Aires, I directed, jointly with UNESCO, a program to strengthen postgraduate programs in the social sciences in Latin America. I worked on this task from June 1975 to the middle of 1978. I traveled intensively to the different centers of investigation of Latin America, exploring the possibilities of having a few modest projects to start postgraduate programs of study and also some research projects. I recall seminars held in Costa Rica about reshaping the curriculum for graduate study in economics. Here, too, the support of the Ford Foundation was essential. Thanks to the foundation, relationships were formed with the United Nations Program for Development and international financial institutions. In all of that, Silvert played a tremendously effective role, both from the intellectual point of view, and because of his commitment to support those who were in trouble, at a time when the dictatorships considered the social sciences dangerously subversive. Later, the Ford Foundation's example helped stimulate support of social science research by other agencies: the International Development Research Centre of Canada, the Swedish International Development Agency, and the various German political foundations, as well as many nongovernmental organizations from the Netherlands, Belgium, and France.

In the context of all these efforts, many concrete issues were raised, such as how to help social scientists leave their countries after dictatorships initiated persecutions. I remember the number of seminars that were organized in Argentina so that Chilean scientists could be invited to attend as a more expeditious way to leave Chile. At a later stage, programs were developed to send professionals back to their countries when that was possible, organized by the World University Service (WUS) of Canada and the United Kingdom.

In the case of the United Kingdom, the minister of cooperation of that time, Judith Hart, approved an important program of cooperation with the government of Salvador Allende in 1973. Once the coup took place, the British government decided that these resources would be channeled to generate postgraduate scholarships so that Chileans could continue their studies in England. This became a program of enormous significance. Subsequently another eminent social scientist, Dudley Sears of the United Kingdom, organized a program from England to help those Chileans who wanted to return to Chile and be integrated into local research. In 1978, when I was able to return to Chile to work with the United Nations, Dudley asked me to organize a subsidiary of the

WUS in Chile to support the return of the social scientists. Many of those who returned with the initial support of the WUS were able to continue until the end of the 1970s with the support that they were given by the Ford Foundation. This was a combined effort, made from distinct angles, but in those angles the presence, thought, and actions of Kalman Silvert were decisive.

I have often thought that when one talks of relatively successful cases of countries in the postdictatorship stage, to a great degree Chile's success and that of the Southern Cone countries were due to Silvert's interest and important work in recovering democracy, which had such a positive impact on the transitions of the 1980s and 1990s. He understood the need to maintain social thought in very difficult conditions to help scholars think about how to prepare for the postdictatorship stage. That helped make possible the influence of social scientists in the different processes of Latin America's democratic transitions. The principal advisers of those who led the democratic transitions included many people who had participated in the meetings that Silvert and other social scientists organized, social scientists who also understood that the commitment to social sciences was also a commitment to human rights. Was this insight at the very core of Kal Silvert? Did he take this approach in part because of the horrors of World War II?

We owe a great deal to Kalman Silvert. Among other things, we owe him gratitude for the affectionate welcome he and Frieda gave to many of us in their apartment in the Village. I think that they were among the first to introduce a spacious and sizable loft in those old apartments by knocking down walls. That is something that Silvert knew how to do: knock down the walls of intransigence so that the ideas that produce thought could flow through the debris, for he had the unshakeable conviction that it was possible through thought to improve the societies in which one lived. He also had the conviction that the man of action must have, first, a set of ideas to carry out action. Without ideas and vision, action is sterile.

Silvert's push to create a Latin American Studies Association was a consequence of his conviction that such an association would bring together ideas, concepts, and policies between the North and the South of this American hemisphere. He was correct.

All of us, both intellectuals and practitioners, owe a great deal to Kal Silvert. He was an intellectual in the broadest sense of the word, one of those who leave a mark through thought and capacity to deal with the historical moment with fascinating lucidity, in his case precisely when the dictatorships were emerging. Thanks to him, social sciences reclaimed their relevant role in Latin America in recovering democracy, and then, with democracy recovered, to help develop reasonable social policies that had at their core the dignity of the human being. That was Silvert's great message—that knowledge should serve to make all human beings equal in dignity.

1

Silvert's Wide-Ranging Contributions and Legacy

Abraham F. Lowenthal and Martin Weinstein

Kalman Hirsch Silvert (1921–1976) was an eminent scholar and teacher and a leader in the pioneering generation of US social scientists who focused attention on Latin America during the Cold War years. He published eleven books on topics ranging from the political system of Guatemala to the nature and future of democracy, education and social change, nationalism, and the changing role of religion and religious institutions. He crafted numerous insightful essays on the history, politics, culture, and institutions of Latin America and on the dynamics of Western Hemisphere relations; many of these essays are collected in his classic volume, *The Conflict Society,* and others were published in *Essays in Understanding Latin America.*

Silvert's writings, his close colleagueship with others, especially Latin American social scientists, and his strong influence on, within, and through the Ford Foundation helped him become an important shaper of Latin American studies in the United States and throughout the Americas. He was one of the principal architects of the Latin American Studies Association (LASA), working closely with Howard Cline of the Library of Congress, Bryce Wood of the Social Science Research Council, Richard Morse of Yale University, and Richard N. Adams of the University of Texas. Together they framed LASA's aims, charter, and procedures and secured the support necessary to launch the association, with Silvert serving as its first president in 1966. Silvert was a key bridge and community-builder between social scientists in Latin America and the Caribbean and those in the United States.

In his years at the Ford Foundation, Silvert helped secure the foundation's indispensable support for a number of independent social science institutions that carried out critical inquiry in Latin America during its years of authoritarian repression. These centers helped preserve and invigorate the values of individual human rights and democratic governance, and they trained a generation of scholars and practitioners. They also provided life-saving havens for Latin American social scientists, often exiled from their home countries, many of whom became leaders in rebuilding democracy in the region.

Silvert maintained a continuing intellectual exchange with scholar-activists, mainly from Latin America. Several of these social scientists have credited their dialogues with Silvert for helping them move from rigid Marxism to a deep appreciation of the values and institutions of democracy. Silvert also learned from them, particularly about structural obstacles to Latin American development and the often domineering role of the United States in the hemisphere. Above all, Silvert was an extraordinary teacher and mentor, whose instruction, advice, and example inspired and shaped the careers and contributions of many, including the contributors to this volume.

Kalman Silvert is recognized by LASA at each International Congress when it awards the Kalman H. Silvert Prize for lifetime contributions to Latin American studies. Some twenty-four outstanding scholars from Latin America, the United States, and Europe have thus far earned the prize, LASA's highest distinction, forever linking Silvert's name with high accomplishment in the illumination of Latin American and Caribbean realities. Yet few of the more than 12,000 members of LASA today know who Kalman Silvert was, how he earned this recognition, or how relevant his multiple contributions are to contemporary issues, challenges, and opportunities. Silvert's scholarly contributions have rarely been cited in recent years.

Latin American studies have been developed by new generations of scholars, each more deeply grounded in a specific discipline than was Silvert's generation of area studies experts. Silvert's discipline-building and institution-nurturing contributions, in the Ford Foundation and beyond, are known only to a dwindling number of those who experienced them firsthand. Silvert's reflections on the strengths and vulnerabilities of democracy and on the role of education and social change are in some ways even more relevant today than when he wrote, but they are rarely discussed. Only senior colleagues can still bring to mind the unique features of Silvert's big personality and the charisma he exuded in many different contexts.

This gap between Silvert's significance in building Latin American studies and the low profile of his lasting reputation has motivated this volume. We have prepared it in part out of deep respect and appreciation of a shared mentor. We have also done so because we believe that Silvert's life and work provide relevant insights and important inspiration that can help LASA and its members make their own contributions over the next fifty years.

As the chapters in this volume suggest, Silvert's career continues to be relevant for today's Latin Americanists, and indeed for all students contemplating a career in international affairs. Silvert viewed the world broadly in its political, economic, cultural, and historical dimensions, and his work was multidisciplinary long before that became fashionable. He understood that individuals are shaped by values, and he therefore sought to discern and respond to the values held by students, associates, political leaders, and social groups. He commended those who were empathetic, democratic, and humanistic, and he confronted those who were self-serving, exploitative, or autocratic and those who rationalized evil.

Silvert maintained collegial relations with many peers, even those with whom he did not agree on questions of theory or policy. He was able to exert authority, even when lacking the formal levers of power, through persuasive argumentation and by developing a network of allies. His mentoring relied less on providing explicit advice than on asking probing questions that others eventually answered themselves. He argued that the United States could best defend its own legitimate national interests by pursuing foreign policies that took into account and respected the underlying interests of other countries and peoples. Although he was a serious researcher and scholar, Silvert knew that his long-term contribution rested as much on the persons he trained, inspired, and assisted in the development of their own careers.

The lessons that emerge from this volume relate to each part of Kalman Silvert's legacy: how to exercise leadership as a thinker, a teacher, a mentor, a practitioner, an analyst, an adviser, a change-maker, a colleague, a friend, and a citizen, mobilizing the full range of one's talents to pursue noble objectives.

A Brief Biographical Sketch

Kalman Silvert was born in Bryn Mawr, Pennsylvania, on March 10, 1921. He earned all his degrees at the University of Pennsylvania. During World War II, he served in a US Army Air Force Intelligence unit in North Africa from 1942 to 1945, using the knowledge he acquired of Swahili and Arabic. He had begun his studies at Penn in anthropology, but completed his master's and PhD in political science after the war. Awarded a Pennfield Scholarship to do doctoral field work in Chile, Kalman wrote his dissertation on the Chilean Development Corporation (CORFO).

In retrospect, Silvert often remarked that he became a Latin Americanist in part because his department at Penn wanted him out of the way; as a Jew, he would not have been hired as faculty, as the top graduate student traditionally was, because of anti-Semitic prejudice at that time. Silvert's choice to focus on Latin America may well have been partly accidental, but he quickly became deeply attached to and rooted in the region.

From 1948 to 1960, Silvert taught at Tulane University, with frequent research stints in Latin America, both in the Southern Cone (especially Chile and Argentina) and Meso-America, especially Guatemala. Early in that period, he began his association with American Universities Field Staff (AUFS), first as a staff associate and then as director of studies. The AUFS appointment gave him the time and resources to spend long periods in Latin America, which enriched his research and extended his networks. These stints also enabled Kal and his wife, Frieda, to arrange extensive physical therapy for their oldest son, Henry, who had suffered catastrophic injuries in an automobile accident in Mexico.

In 1962, Silvert became professor of government at Dartmouth College. Several of his students, including some of the contributors to this volume, began their studies of Latin America there under his influence. During his time at Dartmouth, Silvert continued his leadership role in the AUFS. He also became an influential adviser to the Ford Foundation, beginning in 1959 when, as a consultant, he helped articulate and design the foundation's new program for the region.

Silvert moved to New York in 1967 to become program adviser in the social sciences for the Office of Latin American and Caribbean Affairs at the Ford Foundation. During his years there, he had a decisive influence on its program and grants in Latin America and eventually helped reshape its approaches in Asia and Africa. He became professor of politics at New York University, where he directed the Ibero-American Center and conducted legendary salons in his large apartment near campus.

During his time in New York, Silvert was active in the Council on Foreign Relations, the American Assembly, the Brookings Institution, the Center for Inter-American Relations, the Commission on United States–Latin America Relations (the Linowitz Commission), the Social Science Research Council (SSRC), and LASA. Perhaps most important, during the period of authoritarian repression in much of Latin America, Silvert took a leading role working with the Ford Foundation, the SSRC, and others in rescuing Latin American intellectuals, helping some develop independent research centers in their own countries, and placing others in positions outside their own countries. He was intensely involved in rescuing Argentine colleagues from the brutal repression after the March 1976 coup and in helping scholars from throughout the Southern Cone. Silvert suffered a fatal heart attack in 1976 while driving back to New York from his beloved Vermont home to continue this work.

A Personal Note

Both of us had the privilege of knowing Kal and Frieda Silvert and of enjoying their friendship and mentorship. In 1967, while Weinstein was working in Mexico City on his master's thesis for NYU, he met Kal Silvert for the first time. He had learned that Silvert would be moving to New York in the fall to assume his joint positions at NYU and the Ford Foundation. Weinstein went over to the foundation's offices to see Silvert. Silvert said very little as he mostly listened to Weinstein talk about his thesis and his plans to become a Latin Americanist. In retrospect, Weinstein felt that he tried too hard to impress Silvert.

When Weinstein took his first classes with Silvert at NYU, he quickly learned how much he did not know. Silvert agreed to be Weinstein's dissertation adviser and encouraged him to go to and write on Uruguay. As Weinstein began his teaching career at William Paterson University, he became closer to Kal as a friend and junior colleague. He fondly recalls his discussions—sometimes at the salons in the Silverts' apartment—on subjects ranging from US politics to the increasingly dire situation in the Southern Cone and the overall state of the social sciences. After Kal's death, Weinstein became very close to Frieda and her sons.

Silvert's passing left a hole in the graduate program at NYU. Weinstein was asked to teach some of Silvert's courses; he did so for more than two decades, always thinking about Kal's teaching style, scholarship, ethics, and humor. These qualities continue to inspire Weinstein today.

Lowenthal, while taking an intensive Spanish course at Harvard in the summer of 1963, to facilitate concentrating his continued studies on Latin America, audited Silvert's summer course on the government and politics of Latin America. They talked several times and began an extended mentor/student relationship that continued as they became colleagues in the Ford Foundation, the Council on Foreign Relations (where Silvert nominated Lowenthal for membership), and the Linowitz Commission in 1974.

Lowenthal vividly recalls many encounters with Kal, including a long walk on Lowenthal's first day in Buenos Aires, when Silvert pointed out the views and neighborhoods he loved best; a stimulating dinner in the Silverts' Vermont home; a seminar in Princeton; a session of the Linowitz Commission when Kal jumped in to administer emergency care to Samuel Huntington after Sam went into diabetic shock; and many conversations about Ford Foundation programs, Latin American politics, and inter-American relations. Lowenthal consulted Silvert in developing the proposal in 1976 to establish the Latin American Program at the Woodrow Wilson Center. They were scheduled to meet in New York in mid-June to develop the proposal in detail. Unfortunately, Kal passed away days before that meeting was to take place. Sadly, Lowenthal was called on to substitute for Silvert at the Hearings of the Joint Economic Committee of Congress less than two weeks later.

As Lowenthal testified,

> Kal Silvert infused data with meaning, related statistics to people, and linked politics and economics. He reported on the sad state of democracy in the Americas, and speculated on the reasons why democracy was everywhere in crisis. He considered the profound consequences and implications for the United States of recent events in Latin America....An authority on many of the individual countries of the region, Kal was able to speak Spanish with most of the different accents of the Americas.
>
> He knew and felt the politics of the region with a depth of understanding and insight that few in this country could match. As a social theorist, Kalman Silvert learned from his analysis of nation-building in Latin America much that he showed to be relevant to democracy's troubles in the United States as well. An inspiring teacher, Kal Silvert trained a whole generation of scholars to ask meaningful questions, to probe, to practice empathy and to focus always on the connection between theory and data.
>
> An imaginative, creative executive of the Ford Foundation, Kalman Silvert did more than any other single individual to strengthen the capacity of Latin American social scientists and social science institu-

tions to carry out their work, in surroundings that were far from supportive. As the first president of the Latin American Studies Association, Kal worked with scholars from many disciplines and many different countries to forge a profession and to infuse it with scholarly and ethical norms and standards.

Above all, Kal was an uncommonly warm and empathetic human being, one who merged his professional and personal concerns into a coherent whole, a person who was hard at work in the final days of his life helping victims of repression in Argentina, as he had helped many others with many challenges before. We shall miss Kalman Silvert more than any of us now realize.

This volume expresses our shared conviction that Kalman Silvert's commitments and contributions remain highly relevant today. We hope this book will help new generations gain from his legacy.

2

Silvert's Probing and Committed Scholarship

Christopher Mitchell

Over a span of almost twenty-five years, Kalman H. Silvert produced a body of scholarship on politics, especially in the Western Hemisphere, that was diverse in theme and geographic focus, as well as probing (empirically, theoretically, and ethically). He carefully sifted evidence to help explain societies from the Southern Cone to Central America and the Caribbean. His scholarly output was remarkably consistent in its terms and cumulative in its development.

This chapter reviews nine of Silvert's principal books—or book-length essay collections—in the approximate order of their publication. The volumes range from detailed analyses of Guatemalan law and politics in the 1950s to trenchant critiques of US political leaders in the Watergate era. Through these works, Silvert presented a coherent model of the operations of power in Latin American societies, together with a clear account of how and why Latin American politics differ from their analogs in other cultural areas of the world. He also offered insights of lasting value on inter-American relations, as well as a set of ethical standards to orient the pursuit of scholarship and citizenship. The assessment concludes by outlining some of the ways that Silvert's scholarship, his values, and his many organizational activities helped to strengthen social science research and intellectual exchange in the Americas.

Assessing Silvert's Scholarship

A Study in Government: Guatemala, stemming from an academic year of field research in 1952–1953, is concerned with "the organization and

15

functioning of the Guatemalan government, and...the implications of the reasons for such functioning" (Silvert 1954, p. ix). The volume is concise, commencing with an examination of Guatemala's 1944 revolution, before turning to portraits of the executive, congress, the judiciary, and political parties at the national level.

One of the volume's central theses, presented as a clear but not assertive framework, is that the Central American nation was experiencing a "growing Westernization." In particular, Silvert writes, "nationalism is being adopted in Guatemala, as elsewhere, as the value which will serve to gain that social cohesion at home which will also allow the government to operate externally as a more powerful unit" (pp. 92, 93). Earlier in the text, he had defined nationalism as "a social value which elevates loyalty to the state to a supreme position" (p. x).

A second and related assertion in the book deals with the regime established there for a decade, following the 1944 overthrow of dictator Jorge Ubico. Silvert writes that "three fundamental aspirations...greater freedom of social choice, nationalism, [and] democratic mechanisms...[were] behind the revolution" (p. 28). Although the post-Ubico government was not democratic, he continues, its links with leftist politicians and political ideas were not part of its essence, and "the legislation which has been adopted is in large measure politically neutral" (p. 93).

A Study in Government can be seen as transitional in political science form and method, moving beyond a then-conventional focus on constitutional provisions to analyze political behavior, using diverse data and tools. Silvert's constitutional analysis is carried out with a more critical eye than was often the case in political studies of Latin America during the 1950s. In parsing the provisions of Guatemala's 1945 constitution, he sought to grasp the revolutionary (or reformist) leaders' intentions, not merely summarize the text. In his investigation, he evidently read extensive debates held among the basic document's drafters and interviewed fifteen members of the Constituent Assembly. The book is sprinkled with tabulated data on population, ethnic divisions, party representation in congress, sources of gross national product, and governmental budgets. Silvert also uses the fairly abundant anthropological literature on Guatemalan society, while criticizing that scholarship for failing to distinguish adequately among urban and rural cultural groups, as well as between Ladinos and Indians (pp. 61–63).

Almost a third of the text is devoted to the structure and problems of departmental and local government—a very unusual element in Latin American national political studies, even today. Although much of this material provides dry coverage of numbers and pay rates of local elected officials, Ladino/Indian relations, and minor court verdicts, Silvert also finds local evidence of union activity and agrarian reform efforts "designed to foment...nationalism" (p. 61). Engaged in a determined empirical hunt, Silvert evidently conducted research in all six of the municipalities—some of which were quite isolated—that were included as case studies.

Silvert set ambitious goals for his analysis of politics in Guatemala. The book's preface announces a "purpose...to take the assembled facts of the matter and to try to treat them as a problem in government, with relation to the general questions which confront students of politics everywhere" (p. ix). He was not asserting generalizations based on a single case, but was proposing comparative categories and relationships to be tested through politically oriented research in "underdeveloped areas." Within less than a decade, Silvert organized just such a project on a global scale, which was published as the edited volume *Expectant Peoples*.

Silvert's 1954 book notably underestimated the latent political power of conservative social forces in Guatemala, including landowners, foreign investors, and elements of the military. The major political party opposing President Jacobo Árbenz was depicted as isolated and inept, "dreaming of dramatic Hollywoodesque rescue by the Marines" (p. 55). Though Silvert noted "a complete absence of relevant data on this score," he speculated that Guatemala's army might be reluctant to turn against Árbenz, due to post-1945 indoctrination, improved pay and benefits, and mobilization of new pro-regime organizations (p. 30). However, a far greater burden of responsibility falls on US policymakers. Within a month of the completion of Silvert's manuscript (and probably before its publication), they helped cause Árbenz's overthrow by sponsoring a cross-border invasion from Honduras and El Salvador, after which the Guatemalan military abandoned Árbenz. Washington officials could and should have informed themselves far better before embarking on one of the twentieth century's most baneful political intrusions, whose negative effects still echo loudly today.

In the late 1950s, Silvert lived in Chile for approximately a year and then for an equal time in Argentina, as a correspondent in the American Universities Field Staff (AUFS). The field staff was sponsored by a coalition of North American universities and colleges. Scholars and journalists dispatched to nations on many continents by the AUFS filed letters, roughly every three weeks, on "current developments" in their countries of residence. These sometimes lengthy texts were duplicated and widely distributed by an AUFS office in the United States and were later reissued in bound volumes. Under this program, between August 1956 and November, 1957, Silvert published eighteen letters totaling 203 pages from or about Chile, and fifteen letters, totaling 175 pages, centering on Argentina and hemispheric politics, mostly written in 1958, but some as late as 1963 (American Universities Field Staff, 1957 and 1966). These letters make for informative and enjoyable reading. In preparing them, Silvert dove with his customary vigor into a wide array of themes, including Chile's social structure and Chileans' attitudes toward class status; the etiquette of bringing imported household goods through Chilean customs; the organization, politics, and pedagogy of the University of Buenos Aires; and tensions between an Argentine industrialist and the US firm that acquired his company. The letters' tones vary from the seriously analytical to the informal and even playful, and some are enlivened by Silvert's own pen-and-ink sketches or his hand-drawn statistical charts. Numerous disciplines take part in the mix, notably sociology, history, and economics as well as political science.

Silvert's caution in assessing data, skepticism about received wisdom or doomsday scenarios, and thoroughness in reasoning toward a conclusion (which sometimes came across as sheer complexity) are all present abundantly in the AUFS letters. At times he delighted in plunging his readers directly into the intricate details of his "raw" data. He reprinted the details of the complex D'Hondt system of proportional representation that was then used in Chile, explaining the counterintuitive, even somewhat perverse outcomes it could produce. In a letter that made up thirty-four pages, he translated a lengthy speech by an Argentine prodemocracy general, adding forty-seven footnotes to explain the historical references and subtly coded political points through which the officer's central message found expression. In an extended and notably courteous exchange of letters with the head of the University of Chicago's economics advisory group at the Catholic University in Chile, Silvert more than held his own as an advocate of Chile's import substitution policies (though he also faulted national policymakers for combining tariff protection with local monopoly, tending to boost prices to the consumer).

A present-day critic enamored of disciplinary rigor might well deride Silvert's AUFS letters as a prime example of "soak and poke" methodology: the allegedly unsystematic collection of random data in a purportedly vain pursuit of significant generalizations. However, Silvert was quite systematic; he carefully amassed information on at least half a dozen themes within and surrounding the realm of politics: class power and status, parties, elections, higher education, proindustrialization policies, and military intervention. During his very active sojourn in the Southern Cone, he also developed generalizing and synthesizing theories on which he drew for the following two decades.

Silvert's model of competition among political parties and interest groups in Latin America is a prime example of this pattern. In a letter titled "Elections, Parties, and the Law," he described in detail the assortment of seventeen parties that competed in Chile's congressional elections that year (AUFS, 1957). The letter arrayed the rival parties on a single scale, basically moving from right to left. By 1961, a briefer and more theoretical essay asserted that Latin American parties and interest groups tended to compete along *two* right–left scales, distinguished from each other by the "basic question of whether one is a modernist or a traditionalist—the two great universes of political thought in Latin America" ("Political Universes of Latin America," AUFS, 1956, p. 3). Silvert had evidently elaborated and deepened his theory as he reflected on data from his fieldwork. He continued to use this revealing two-scale model, embracing traditionalist as well as modern dimensions, up through his last (posthumous) publications.

Another instance of Silvert's use of varied data as a pathway to enduring insights is provided by the AUFS essay with which he concluded his year in Chile, titled "Coda." Seeking to sum up his research-based perceptions of Chilean politics and society, he drew for inspiration on a text (originally relating to the Caribbean and Meso-America) by Aldous Huxley. The British writer emphasized the irrevocability and pain, as well as the benefits, of any society's leap from tradition to modernity. In his travel book *Beyond the Mexique Bay* (1934), Huxley had written:

> The advance from primitivism to civilization, from mere blood to mind and spirit, is a progress whose price is fixed; there are no discounts even for the most highly talented purchasers. . . . When man became an intellectual and spiritual being, he paid for his new privileges with a treasure of intuitions, of emotional spontaneity, of sensuality still innocent of all self-consciousness. . . . In practise…it [is] psychologically impossible to return the new privileges or be content with the primitivism that has been paid away for them. . . . Human Bondage, in the words of Spinoza, is the price of Human Freedom. The advantages of the first state (and Human Bondage has many and substantial advantages) are incompatible with those of the second. We must be content to pay, and indefinitely to go on paying, the irreducible price of the goods we have chosen. (quoted in "Coda," AUFS 1957, p. 4)

Silvert interpreted these passages to mean that "the irreducible price for 'intellect and spirit' is that individuals must *be* 'intellectual and spiritual'" (p. 5, Silvert's emphasis). Relating these ideas to Chile, he remarked:

> If I have one reigning, high-level impression, it is that Chileans live in a wrenched, twisted society. (p. 3) . . . As I see it, Chile is in a crisis of values and not of institutions. The society as such is not organized to pay the price of the progress for which an irrevocable down payment has been made. (p. 5) . . . [Reigning Chilean social attitudes] seem to me to demonstrate that the down payment, the discarding of primitivism, has been well and fully made, but that the continuing payments have been forgotten, many of the privileges of that older situation of Human Bondage still being held dear. (p. 7)

The reader can tell that in this letter Silvert is straining to quarry revealing concepts from a mass of information and impressions—and in at least two later publications he returned to Huxley's formulation to describe the mechanics and cost of societal transformation. These were some of the spiny fruits of his Southern Cone research.

In the AUFS letters, three additional strands were added to Silvert's scholarly fabric, each combining empirical interest and analytic skill. He became a well-informed observer of Latin American social sciences, from experience as scholar and teacher (the latter in at least Chile, Argentina, and Uruguay). As of the late 1950s, he was still keenly aware of a lack of reliable data on society and its changes in Latin American countries, stressing gaps in institutional strength. Reviewing Chile's situation, he wrote: "All too often Latin American social science work has been hortatory and forensic. The development of trained specialists, the building of adequate plant, and the provision of respectable libraries, all of which are quite far progressed in Chile, are most hopeful signs in a country which knows little about itself in an organized fashion" ("Truancy and Illiteracy: Chilean Sociology Moves toward Quantification," AUFS 1957, p. 5). Following an extended political, pedagogic, and intellectual anatomy of the University of Buenos Aires, only the discipline of history emerged from his description as solidly present and well served in Argentina. Political science hardly existed, he wrote, and whereas some scholars in the social sciences published prolifically under difficult circumstances, little original data were gathered and much of the (perhaps too extensive) literature was simply speculative ("Other People's Classrooms," AUFS 1957, pp. 7–8).

Silvert also showed a growing mastery of international themes, etching out an approach to inter-American relations that took account of domestic politics and society and the "chessboard" of rivalries among states ("The Meeting of North and South: Comments on Problems of Hemispheric Relations," AUFS 1966, p. 1). That essay, written in 1961, also includes a prescient insight into the possibility of harsh regimes that only began to appear five years later:

> The grave danger of a failure to link social, political, and economic development is that the unilateral fortifying of economic factors is likely to lead to the imposition of greater political force than Latin America was ever capable of before. The repression, if "successful," will give us authoritarianisms of the Right; if "unsuccessful," we shall have authoritarianisms of the Left. In either case these internal decisions will affect hemispheric relations at their roots. (p. 8)

Finally, Silvert propounded a pithy account of the often fraught relations between social science disciplines and area studies. In a 1963 comment on a panel at the American Political Science Association (APSA) convention, he maintained that area specialists cannot collect data without theories to guide them, and that disciplinary theories that have never been exposed to data from underdeveloped areas can't be considered scientific. "The moral is not only that we cannot be so far apart as advertised, but also that we continue to need each other," he observed ("Area Studies and Subject Areas: A Comment on Specialists, Generalists, and Disciplinarians in Foreign Area Studies," AUFS 1966, p. 4).

The same year that he addressed APSA, Silvert published the edited volume *Expectant Peoples: Nationalism and Development* (Silvert 1963), a major effort to use area data to clarify, test, and elaborate a mainstream disciplinary concept—nationalism—with links to comparative politics and international relations. All of the dozen contributors to this nearly 500-page book were AUFS correspondents, drawing on deep experience in Africa, Asia, the Middle East, and Latin America. The central aim of *Expectant Peoples* was "to view the processes of total development through the lens of the formation of the nation-state" (p. 7). Defining nationalism as "the acceptance of the state as the impersonal and ultimate arbiter of human affairs" (p. 19), the contributing authors profiled the varied roles this emerging social and political attitude (which had so impressed Silvert as a key variable in Guatemala) were playing in the drama of development on a global scale. In Saudi Arabia, for example, nationalism had gained a foothold only ten years earlier, and (perhaps given the absence of a colonial past) Saudi nationalism was described as moderate and "practical" (p. 93). Indonesian nationalism had moved over the previous fifty years through "self-generating, self-realizing, and self-defeating phases"; President Sukarno's charisma and nationalistic symbols had left the nation "bewitched" (pp. 175–76). In Japan, a chauvinistic elite-imposed nationalism in the nineteenth century had given way to disastrous ultranationalism in the twentieth; more conservative contemporary political leaders were seeking to blend nationalism and democracy (pp. 398–426).

Silvert's introduction and conclusion to this volume make up his most detailed published elaboration of nationalism's meanings. He noted that the existing literature properly identified four aspects: nationalism as formal juridical concept, as symbolic concept ("language, dress, food habits...the symbols of a common heritage"), as ideology, and as social value. This last facet of the notion, which was usually most salient to Silvert, was described as "that norm defining the loyalty due to fellow citizens and to the mandates of the state...tacit consent...and the internalized 'feeling' of national community" (p. 18). "What we are suggesting," he wrote, "is that nationalism as a social value has been the major cohesive force to date within each separate modern society, and that its existence in underdeveloped areas is a necessary part of the process of development" (p. 26).

Silvert recognized that tensions existed among the varied aspects of nationalism, e.g. if nationalist ideology were used to justify authoritarianism, and thus to limit the growth of the empathy implicit in nationalism-as-social-value (p. 32). In his own contribution to *Expectant Peoples*, an essay called "The Costs of Anti-Nationalism: Argentina," Silvert argued that the values of the Argentine nation-state had not been sufficiently accepted within the total population to absorb the social stresses imposed by industrialization and social mobilization (pp. 352–53). Part of the responsibility lay with the Peronist government (1945–1955), under which "Argentine nationalist ideology was restricted largely to attacks on foreign countries...and to mystical glorification of the nation, but devoted itself little to the task of assuring the relative position of the state as the supreme social institution" (p. 364).

Argentina's "antinationalism," Silvert asserted, was an example of a more generalized pattern of "Mediterranean political thought and practice" characteristic of Iberia and some Latin American societies. In this political configuration, including what Silvert called syndicalism and falangism, "an innate distrust of the state coupled with the direct representation of economic and occupational interest in the government are destructive of party strength, erode pluralism, and deny the sweeping grandeur possible to enlightened political action" (p. 359). A syndicalist regime, "a complication of the idea of hierarchical order of medieval society," was marked by a simple and stolid relationship between the state and society, with only six or eight "institutional pillars created to become the fasces, so to speak, of quasi-modern traditionalism" (pp. 359, 360). Silvert revisited this formulation many times in his later writings as a major component of his working model of domestic politics in Latin American nations. Falangism, syndicalism, and related governmental forms represented projects to make the "traditional" scale of interparty competition hegemonic over the "modern" array of contenders for power.

Silvert's concluding essay in *Expectant Peoples* effectively performs the central summarizing and thought-provoking roles of such a symposium text. While rejecting any rigid "stage" theories of social development, he notes that the assembled studies offered "at least partial confirmation that the developmental process is a total social occurrence intimately involved with the emergence of the nation-state" (p. 428). A "search...for human richness," beyond the simple desire for greater wealth, appeared to drive the embrace of "Western development" in tandem with nationalism (p. 434). Interestingly, Silvert also speculated on the possible relationship between development (almost equivalent to nationalism) and freedom (which sometimes implied democratic practices). On evidence provided by the volume's case studies, he hypothesized that while nationalism was probably "a necessary but insufficient condition for democracy," enough freedom "to make the most rational decisions needed" might be "a functional requisite for *self-sustaining* development" (p. 435). Freedom/democracy, if it materialized within a nation, might be a vital factor in preventing developmental stagnation or failure.

The Conflict Society: Reaction and Revolution in Latin America (three editions: 1961, 1966, and 1968) is a very significant work that would be easy to underestimate. Silvert wrote all the essays in this volume; many had been published or circulated earlier, and some are innovative essays that appear nowhere else among Silvert's works. Eight of the seventeen chapters originated as AUFS letters and are only very modestly revised; one more essay reported on a small-*n* survey conducted for the Guatemala study, and one included most of the Argentina chapter from *Expectant Peoples*, plus some added data on the social origins of Argentine political leaders. The seven new chapters, plus the choice and sequencing of the older texts, trace out an analytic arc that constitutes an important moment in Silvert's scholarly evolution.

The first two chapters sum up Silvert's portrayal of Latin American political dynamics while notably elaborating some earlier views on the embeddedness of Latin American underdevelopment in historical and intellectual patterns. He stresses the central role played by nationalism, reiterates his two-scale model of intergroup competition, and contrasts modern with traditionalist societal attitudes. Turning to "what makes Latin America unique among underdeveloped areas," Silvert profiles the region as "for all practical purposes, an offshoot of late medieval Western culture in the process of making an adjustment to modernism" (*Conflict Society,* 1966 edition, pp. 6–7). Latin American intellectual and political leaders are described as playing influential and, in comparison with other world regions, unusual roles in this adjustment. Accepted accounts of worldwide social and political development, in Silvert's view, assumed that economic changes alter occupational patterns, followed by a modified social hierarchy and, finally, by political phenomena. In Latin America, however, "one of the manners in which social change has occurred...is along the following line: change of ideology in Europe, carry-over to Latin America and readaptation by local intellectuals, translation of the notions into political terms, change in the political institution, and then a political attempt to implement economic and social policies" (p. 8).

Almost 100 pages later, Silvert returns to the theme of intellectuals' actual and potential roles in Latin American societies. His main vehicle is an essay titled "*Ariel* and the Dilemma of the Intellectuals," originally filed with AUFS in 1958. This chapter studies and explicates the Uruguayan writer José Enrique Rodó's short book *Ariel* (1900), an attack on North American ideas and values that enjoyed widespread currency in Latin America. Silvert asserts that many Latin American intellectuals lack the necessary support of a fully integrated national society and world outlook to contribute to a global discourse, and not simply consume some of the ideas generated by already-developed nations. "Objection [to North American society] is not enough," he continues.

"The politicalized Latin American intellectual has his task clearly presented to him. If he is to justify the goodly measure of leadership and respect he now has, he must begin to speak in terms of *specific* wants, *specific* programs, and *specific* capabilities. To do so, he must learn techniques of research to find out what is possible to satisfy what he thinks is desirable. He must leave his ivory tower and dirty his intellectual hands, finding solutions within himself and within his society" (p. 142, emphasis in original).

In a closely reasoned chapter entitled "American Academic Ethics and Social Research Abroad," Silvert places in perspective the scandal triggered when "Project Camelot" was fully revealed in 1965. Camelot was a research venture based at American University in Washington DC, seeking potential causes of internal revolt in at least six Latin American nations, and speculating on policy options to redirect or check those pressures. In efforts to launch this ambitious $6 million undertaking in Chile, a US professor concealed Camelot's funding by the US Department of the Army, a ruse that quickly failed. Camelot was widely viewed in Latin America as an effort at antirevolutionary intervention under the guise of social research; the Chilean government protested and the comparative study collapsed.

Kalman Silvert probed the broader causes and lessons of Project Camelot, asserting that it was rooted partly in a longstanding neglect of Latin America as a subject area by US universities and scholars, just when the region "became a lucrative and thus intellectually attractive field after the Cold War came to the Caribbean" (p. 144). He contended that universities' underinvestment in Western Hemisphere studies—especially in political science—had created a dearth of well-trained and highly principled researchers. Since few "prestige" departments of political science included senior specialists on Latin America, not many excellent graduate students in the discipline saw an opportunity for (or future professional advancement from) the scientific study of power in Western Hemisphere countries. Until larger stores of first-rate scholars and research achievements on Latin America were developed in the United States, it would be difficult to develop investigators able to strike the correct balance in examining legitimate policy questions, and in handling justifiable government financing. Official funding as such might be reasonable, he maintained, but "the peculiar attribute and unique scientific virtue of the university-affiliated social scientist is his freedom. Once abridged, for whatever reason, then the people relying on his objectivity are in serious danger of accepting a misrepresented product" (p. 151).

Finally, *The Conflict Society*'s next-to-last chapter is a new text called "Peace, Freedom, and Stability in the Western Hemisphere." Here Silvert revises and deepens his account of the relationship between, on the one hand, freedom (closely related to but not identical with democracy), and, on the other, development. At the end of *Expectant Peoples* he had depicted freedom/democracy as a constructive result that may flow from development, which might help the latter process become self-sustaining. Now he goes further, embracing the thesis that "the direct fomenting of freedom is…a meaningful policy concern." (For this alteration he credits "Bernard Rosenberg, Professor of Sociology at the

City College of New York, who on a beach in Piriápolis, Uruguay, destroyed my own facile belief in this fallacy [that underdeveloped lands cannot be democratic] and pushed me into thinking about the functional relationship between freedom and development" [p. 257]).

Once again, intellectual leaders are presented with opportunities and responsibilities:

> Development is neither unilineal nor automatic. The choices of men and their ability to translate those choices into action constitute one of the determinants of whether the process will be expeditious and immediately fruitful or nasty, brutish, savage and corrupt, or perhaps even a total failure. ...Viewed in this fashion, freedom is at least as intrinsic to the development process as is occupational specialization, capital investment, or industrial urbanization. . . .
>
> Full development is not merely a state of existence; it is also a process, a means of organizing change so that further development can proceed without breakdowns. It is in this dynamic sense that stability is essential to development, stability not of being, so to speak, but of becoming. (p. 259)

This emphasis on freedom and democracy as vital policy goals is a critical breakthrough, which gave Silvert's analysis of Western Hemisphere politics moral strength, empirical accuracy, and temporal flexibility that were not present—or were far less prominent—in some other contemporary political science models. Other aspects of his paradigm bore considerable resemblance to elements in, for example, Charles W. Anderson's model in *Politics and Economic Change in Latin America* (1967). Anderson peopled Latin American political life with "power contenders"—rival interest groups ranging from the highly traditional (landlords, many church hierarchies) to more modern entities such as the military, diverse political parties, and popularly oriented student groups and labor unions. Anderson posited that once interest groups, militating for political influence, demonstrated a "power capability" (an effort in which they might use varied resources), they would be admitted to the circle of accepted participants. Older contenders, he asserted, were not discarded, which gave Latin American politics the character of a "living museum" of political rivalries. Democracy was not adopted as a highly valued goal in Anderson's theory.[1]

Buttressed with a commitment to freedom and democracy as explicit policy goals, Silvert's analysis was considerably better prepared than other models to address the wave of harshly repressive authoritarian governments that took power in the Southern Cone between 1964

(Brazil) and 1976 (Argentina). Not only had he foreseen that some political takeovers might not stint on violence, he had also prepared an ethical framework from which to critique what came to be known as "bureaucratic-authoritarian regimes." In addition, his two-scale paradigm gave adequate emphasis to the deeply rooted character of Latin American traditional values, even in Southern Cone societies. Models such as Anderson's could not explain why some military-led governments sought to eliminate and even exterminate left-wing "power contenders," nor could they offer the guidance for current analysis and future action that were embodied in Silvert's philosophical embrace of freedom. If a demonstration were needed of the vital role of (conscious or unconscious) political values in political science, this conjuncture would surely provide it.

Given Silvert's increasing concentration on human agency in moving societies toward "full development," it is logical that his next book was *Man's Power: A Biased Guide to Political Thought and Action* (1970). This concise work, comprising just over 160 pages, is his most focused effort at a broad-gauge theory of politics—an endeavor, as he writes at the book's outset, "to explore the relation between constraints and freedoms in the human political condition" (p. xxiii). The formulations presented here, on what political action is, can, and should be, inform the great bulk of Silvert's writings in the remaining years of his career.

Silvert introduces and describes the four basic "elements of politics": value systems, "the potential power or effectiveness of individuals in groups" (including social-class power), individuals' institutional locations, and their personal characteristics. The text provides a nuanced view of social class, describing it as a very important category that must be analyzed with care. The author asserts that class power is potential rather than automatically exerted: it must be transmitted via institutions in most instances. At times, Silvert adduces Latin American examples to illustrate his points, just as he draws on Western European history and on aspects of politics in locales as diverse as Vietnam and Nigeria for other clarifying examples.

Silvert distances his philosophical position emphatically from what he calls "homeostatic," tension-related models of social behavior, whose recent roots he traces to Jeremy Bentham and other Utilitarian thinkers. Less categorically, he critiques Marxist approaches that picture class conflict and class consciousness as absolutely central. Silvert finds notably greater validity in the concepts advanced by Max Weber and Ernst Cassirer, whose ideas he described (in a later book) as drawing on the idealism of Immanuel Kant. Summing up the interactions among his "elements of politics," Silvert asserts that

> the necessary and sufficient conditions for a satisfactory social expla-
> nation are the sum of these factors: what makes choices possible, plus
> the effective exercise of choice or the routine following of custom and
> habit, or a mixture of conscious choice and custom. (p. 54)

> At the risk of indulging in the vice of sentimentally longing for social
> freedom, I am, of course, moving toward positing the possibility, even
> necessity, of a rational voluntarism in many areas of the social order.
> (p. 55)

The highest objective of society, and government within it, is not to produce stability or equilibrium, as "homeostatic" philosophies would assert, but to pursue "a politics of human enrichment" (p. 161). Stirred by Weber's and Cassirer's ideas that men and women experience and create social reality through perception and communicate it by creating symbols, Silvert asserts:

> To be human is good, to be more human is better. The more sensitized
> a person is to the symbols of others in his own time and place, to the
> symbols of others in his own time and different cultures, and to the
> symbols of others across all social time and space, and the more that
> person can assist others to such a richness of symbolic understanding,
> the more human he is and, so, the better he is. The human purpose of
> social organization is to promote humanness in this, its most meaning-
> ful sense. (p. 150)

Education, Class and Nation: The Experiences of Chile and Venezuela, a book Silvert wrote jointly with Leonard Reissman, a Cornell University sociologist, was published in 1976, shortly before Silvert's death. This complex work, Silvert's first monograph based on field research since the volume on Guatemala, had gestated in varied forms for almost twenty years. As the title implies, it examines the role of education in influencing—perhaps transforming—social attitudes and values toward the class system and the national community in Chile and Venezuela. The work was designed to test some of Silvert's most central assertions, especially on the key developmental role of nationalism. *Education, Class and Nation* was rooted in a research project (begun but not completed with Frank Bonilla) in the early 1960s, which was not formally published. Collaboration on this final form of the study with Reissman began in 1965, and research and drafting lasted until late 1974; Reissman died before publication.

This volume rested on rigorously empirical bases, including a survey of more than 9,300 people, almost equally divided between the two nations. Four groups or cohorts were interviewed in each country: elementary school pupils, secondary school students, parents of students at both levels, and teachers in all the schools that were surveyed. (Political resistance in both nations, stimulated in part by Project Camelot, prevented the authors from interviewing more than a small number of university students.) Respondents answered approximately eighty questions on their social and educational backgrounds and their attitudes related to "the five grand institutions: the family, religion, education, the economy, and the polity" (p. 23). Alternative answers were categorized as "traditional" or "modern," and each cohort's perceptions of the institutions were tallied and displayed. The survey's findings were clear: with a few minor exceptions, all the groups in these nations displayed declining traditional attitudes and increasingly modern ones in relation to the family, religion, the polity, the economy, and education, in that order (pp. 25–30).

Moreover, when Silvert and Reissman examined the detailed views of the four cohorts that made up the pattern just described, the differences among groups' perceptions tended to confirm the authors' expectations about the roles played by education and the state. In both Chile and Venezuela, the most consistently traditional perceptions were voiced by elementary school pupils, followed by the group of parents; the next most modern attitudes were displayed by teachers, whose modernity was in turn exceeded by that of secondary-level students. Education, the coauthors argued, emerged as a major catalyst for more modern attitudes and values. The least traditional views on social institutions were voiced by members of the group most recently exposed to considerable education: the secondary school students. They likely had adopted more modern ideas most rapidly, as they advanced from the more tradition-bound elementary school years. Parents' greater traditionalism was interpreted as stemming from their generally more limited exposure to schooling, while the modernity evinced by teachers (second highest among the groups surveyed) might have been tempered by their greater age compared with their students (p. 30).

Silvert and Reissman read considerable significance into the intermediate level of modern perceptions that were garnered by the Chilean and Venezuelan polities. "We should expect," they wrote, "that…inherent ambivalence about ends and means will place any institution pretending to decisive power somewhere in the middle range of all other feelings about other institutional activities. That result is precisely what we found" (p. 30). The state's claim of "a legitimate authority to use its coercive power in the resolution of intra and inter institutional conflicts" (p. 29), in turn, made its policies toward education into a vital stake in determining the speed and secure status of national development. Partly to discuss that dimension, Silvert and Reissman include substantial chapters on the ideas and political pressures that shaped educational policy in the two nations studied—Chile in the nineteenth century and Venezuela in the twentieth.

Their other findings provided empirical and/or conceptual reinforcement for ideas that Silvert had put forward earlier. The research design deliberately avoided assigning any composite "traditionalism" or "modernity" score to individuals (pp. 24–25); instead, Silvert and Reissman collected and reported respondents' differing (often less than mutually consistent) perceptions of different institutions in society. This image of ideological dispersion and change meshed with the idea of development-as-process that Silvert had propounded since at least 1966. In addition, the detailed survey results provided data to support the existence of two scales of left–right distribution of views among respondents—an important element of Silvert's working map of intergroup competition in Latin America. The survey data also indicated that greater exposure to education—resulting, in all likelihood, from "pronational" state policies—tended to efface that "bimodal distribution of responses" (pp. 57–62, quoted at p. 59).

Kalman Silvert was not only satisfied that *Education, Class and Nation* had been completed after such lengthy toil; he also evinced notable fulfillment at its publication. The volume fully elaborated and in many aspects substantiated contentions that he had pursued for most of his scholarly career. It also led him and Leonard Reissman to emphasize, in conclusion, that "freedom is the master theme of this study;" that subject had "intruded itself willy-nilly, forced into consideration by the nature of our findings and the evolution of our theoretical understanding" (p. 173). Education, both for individuals and for national societies, was found unequivocally to "promote humanness," the goal that Silvert had come to exalt as the highest purpose of social organization.

Silvert's next book, *The Reason for Democracy*, is (as he states in the text repeatedly) basically a polemic centered on American politics, with broader implications. Vexed by "our present political hollowness" (1977, p. 26), for which he asserted that conservatives and liberals shared responsibility, he set out to recall Americans to a truly democratic path. Specific spurs to his argumentation included governmental misconduct and deception revealed by the Watergate scandal, pervasive dishonesty in the framing and defense of Washington's policy in Vietnam, and the concealed US subversion of Chile's socialist-led government (1970–1973) documented in 1975 by a select committee of the US Senate.

Deliberately omitting a specific, crisp definition of democracy (to "analyze it, break it into parts, fondle its pieces...would shatter its essence," p. xiii), Silvert extols "the classically Liberal state...designed to ensure *all* citizens in their equal status." That model of the state, whose origins Silvert attributes to Rousseau and Locke, had been too far replaced by "the corrupted Liberal state [which] seeks only to ensure all citizens in the equal application of laws, which are the fallout of the interplay of special interests" (p. 24). Squarely targeted as responsible for this institutional and moral decline are the classical liberals' "Utilitarian successors" (chiefly Jeremy Bentham and James Mill), who substituted mechanical interest balancing for a richer, equally shared political community. Mainstream economists and "pragmatic" contemporary politicians had, in Silvert's view, adopted simplistic utilitarian concepts and values all too thoroughly (p. 26). Marx (though he had "little to say about the state in itself") at least recognized "the unrealized ideal of Liberalism—the community of universal membership" (pp. 25, 35).

The power that Silvert attributed to a corrupted liberal state draws attention to a vulnerable point in his outlook on politics: nationalism-as-social-value was subject to being crowded aside, in the world of political practice, by nationalism-as-ideology and nationalism-as-symbolic-concept. Racism, contempt for the poor, and in-group exclusiveness were too often served by nationalist activists. Silvert recognized and deplored such misuses of nationalism, and his calls to suppress them in the name of true democracy placed greater stress on "a responsible community of universal membership" (p. 42) than on insightful leadership by intellectual or other elites. He was especially acerbic in challenging the authors, including Samuel P. Huntington, of the 1975 report to the Trilateral Commission, *The Crisis of Democracy.* The trilateralists asserted, Silvert observed, that "the troubles of the 1960s were an evidence of a 'democratic distemper'—of too much democracy!" (p. 61).

> Huntington thinks the government is giving more than ever; I think society and the government are in many ways giving us less — less frankness, honesty, meaningful involvement, and for many, less work, less dignity, less hope. I think of limits as I do the banks of a canal; Huntington thinks of them as the four walls, ceiling, and floor of a cell. Huntington explicitly rejects Al Smith's maxim that when democ-

racy is in trouble we need more of it; I explicitly accept that proposition. (pp. 82–83)

Silvert sums up his extended argument by reasserting his belief that at the roots, US society stood at a juncture where it vitally needed democracy in its best, most vigorous form. The rapid pace of social, economic, and technological change had made possible lopsided innovation, with adjustments in some sectors unmatched by modifications elsewhere. Though "social life is becoming unhinged...nothing should be more joyously hailed...just that much more room for reason and choice is available, that much more grist for the democratic mill" (pp. 69–70). Both democracy and science were needed to address urgent social and political problems, and Silvert argued that they shared a vital intellectual style and moral commitment to the toleration and indeed embrace of uncertainty, wedded to necessary action. "If we deliver ourselves over to a society dedicated to affirming the truth of a master certainty," he wrote, "we must bid farewell to respect for the uniqueness of our personalities—and to democracy" (p. 100).

Before his death, Silvert chose and placed in sequence the fifteen texts that are included in *Essays in Understanding Latin America* (1977); the volume was published posthumously with a graceful foreword by Joel Jutkowitz. Most of the essays were originally prepared as journal articles, chapters in other symposia, or reports for organizations including AUFS and the Commission on United States–Latin American Relations (often known as the Linowitz Commission). They constitute valuable, skillful elaborations and applications of concepts Silvert had honed in earlier research. Of special interest are his treatments of democracy as a political and scientific value, US priorities in Western Hemisphere diplomacy, and Cuba's revolutionary political and social regime.

The chapter "In Search of Theoretical Room for Freedom" is introduced perfectly by its title. Pursuing a priority he had taken up more than a decade before, Silvert asserts that the social sciences have taken few steps to integrate democracy as a goal in their analyses of Latin American societies. Economists, demographers, political scientists, anthropologists (with a few honorable exceptions), and sociologists all paid far too little attention to "the classical concepts of tyranny, human rights, civil liberties, democracy *in its ethical sense*, and justice" (pp. 63–65, quoted at 65). The then-innovative dependency school of analysis, stemming largely from the work of Latin American sociologists and economists, is also described as falling short in its handling of democracy, since it focused on the absence of power rather than on how best to use it.

Silvert was unflinching in submitting all parties to the same standard. He observes that the shortcomings of social scientists in theorizing about democracy have cast a shadow over the laudable efforts by Latin Americanists (and other citizens and groups) to mitigate the injuries suffered by colleagues harassed by authoritarian governments in the hemisphere since the mid-1960s. "Whatever our overt expressions of assistance may be in the cases of violations of academic freedom, we have neglected to think about the relationship between academia and its needs and the rest of the society caught in the processes of profound transformation. We have not assisted in the task of asking whether freedom is merely for the academic and thus academic for everyone else" (p. 57).

Silvert's chapter in the Linowitz Commission's report, reprinted here, focuses on the utility for North American foreign policy of attaining a grasp of Latin American domestic politics. In a well-grounded and well-specified essay, he crisply summarizes concepts based on his decades of research: two "fundamental areas of political clash" have emerged in Latin America, he wrote: "between nation and class at the level of total social organization and…between sacred and secular legitimation within the formal state" (p. 162). Using these two clarifying optics, Silvert sorts Latin American societies into four groups, ranging from "the most complete *social* (not *political*) nations" (Cuba, the Southern Cone omitting Brazil) to "countries with harsh class divisions…and little growth in access to national institutions" (most of Central America, poor Andean states, Haiti, and the Dominican Republic) (pp. 164–65).

Silvert goes on to suggest that a more acute understanding of marked differences among Latin American societies might have dissuaded US policymakers from launching the 1961 Bay of Pigs invasion against Cuba's revolutionary government. The operation was modeled on the 1954 US maneuver against President Árbenz in Guatemala, "one of the most fragmented of Latin American countries." However, the intervention failed because it was ill-suited to topple a government in Cuba, "a country socially ready for nationhood" (p. 165).

He broadens his policy advice in straightforward terms, easily communicable to decisionmakers: "I should like to suggest an overarching criterion: to the extent to which we may pursue policies to influence Latin American countries to change in any direction, we should always seek to increase the ability of Latin American polities effectively to make ever-broadening sets of choices" (p. 169).

Essays in Understanding also provides an impressive and in retrospect heartwarming glimpse of Silvert in an unfamiliar role: as a Caribbeanist. The essay "Frames for the Caribbean Experience," originally written for an American Assembly volume edited by Tad Szulc, is a sophisticated and balanced overview of a region notoriously difficult to summarize. Few writers who had spent far more time focusing on the Caribbean could have captured as well as he did the common traits and local nuances of societies in that zone.

Kalman and Frieda Silvert spent two weeks in Cuba in the summer of 1974, at a time when North American scholars seldom visited the island. Their jointly written report on their experiences and impressions appeared first as an AUFS letter, and it has the relaxed intellectual openness of Silvert's dispatches from the Southern Cone almost twenty years earlier. There is the same cheerful analytic doggedness ("the very determination of the frame within which Cuba fits is a harshly troublesome theoretical problem," p. 80), and the same clarity and civility in offering opinions. The Silverts came to view Cuba as going through something like a massive national experiment with "open enrollment," with the attendant leveling and social service advances, but also a certain growth of provincialism since so many persons of modest previous training and experience were being empowered. They also regretted the loss of urbane values in urban Havana, a city stripped of the disorder that comes with capitalist roles and competition. Nostalgia and admiration blend as one imagines the Silverts tinkering with these ideas, as they sat on the wall that surrounds the Bay of Havana.

Kalman Silvert's Impact on Inter-American Social Science

Comprising more than 1,500 printed pages published over more than two decades, Kalman Silvert's scholarly output was notably wide-ranging in themes and locations. He drew attention to the importance of nationalism in Latin America and other regions and propounded methods for understanding the modes and structures through which individuals and societies act politically. Through subtle analysis he applied the concepts of tradition and modernity, and explored the influences exerted by class interests and education. He developed a consistent (but not rigid) conceptual repertoire, which he refined in cumulative fashion, developing and interrelating his ideas. He expounded an ethical commitment to freedom and democracy which bound together the empirical and analytical aspects of his scholarship. He also focused deeply on diverse societies within the Western Hemisphere, embracing the Southern Cone, Central America, and parts of the Caribbean.

Even with these notable strengths, Silvert's pattern of scholarly performance is not the sort that we routinely associate with the major, internationally recognized academic he was. His publishing career did not feature a groundbreaking empirical finding that reoriented the research of many other investigators, nor a transformational reinterpretation of existing data. Instead, as a scholar Silvert was a profound generalist—a relatively rare variety of researcher but one that may have uncommon impact if the historical and disciplinary moment is opportune.

From the outset of his scholarly career, Silvert displayed and refined a set of deeply held precepts as an intellectual and a social scientist. He embraced empiricism, an open-minded search for reliable data using modern research techniques. He was steeped in social theory, especially the sweep of Western political and social thought from the Renaissance through Lévi-Strauss and Chomsky. He eagerly sought information and ideas from all relevant disciplines, while asserting as a matter of course that each discipline's central tenets should evolve in the light of evidence from all world areas. Silvert's dedication to human freedom—a value that he saw manifested, albeit imperfectly, in efforts toward democracy—made him resistant to state influence on scholarship. He also expressed intense compassion for the trying aspects of human experience, especially the often wrenching costs and travails brought on by development.

Silvert's initial influence—guided by these profound principles—was exerted from the mid-1950s through the mid-1970s, a period of rapid change in both social conditions and the social sciences in the Western Hemisphere. Many Latin American nations experienced noteworthy economic growth, especially early in this era, combined with unprecedented urbanization and rising political participation. Political régimes controlled by military forces often alternated with civilian governments based on limited suffrage. The United States—represented by diplomacy, investment, trade, aid, and government agencies both open and secret—had long wielded extensive hemispheric influence. It now tended to link its priorities in Latin America and the Caribbean with its newer and global Cold War concerns.

At this same juncture, social research expanded and evolved in Latin America and the United States. Growing ranks of intellectuals and scholars clustered in Latin American cities, employed or empowered by universities, international organizations, non-profits, and state development agencies. The relatively new academic field of Latin American regional studies simultaneously took root in North American and European universities, eventually including the most prestigious institutions. These research-related changes not infrequently had to contend with states' interests and the possibilities of politicization and constraint. In Latin America, political pressures on social research tended to be more overt (and sometimes violent), while they were subtler and less recognized in the United States. There, the widely accepted norms of an anti-Communist era worked to encourage the pursuit of stability and the tacit avoidance of dissenting themes or theses. For example, financial and institutional support for Latin American studies in the United States, from both public and private sources, increased notably following the Cuban revolution of 1959. Implicitly, the disturbance of long-established distributions of hemispheric political power was often defined as problematic.

Through his writings at this historical moment, Kalman Silvert influenced social science on Latin America in two principal ways: by undercutting rigid and ideological models, and by endorsing democracy as a value and a policy goal. Comparative political studies were taking leave of dry institutionalism, adopting more behavioral models. As this change took place, Silvert's scholarship acted to deflect or discourage the adoption of monistic paradigms, which might well have brought with them excessive political inflections or concealed ideological interests. His precepts emphasized and encouraged pluralistic analyses, marked by the provisional commitments that set science apart from ideology.

The flavor of Silvert's discriminating theoretical critiques is provided by a passage from *Essays in Understanding Latin America* (1977):

> Even political scientists have not devised a way of theoretically seating the idea of democracy, or the possible centrality or marginality of civil liberties and respect for human rights, in the processes of contemporary social change in Latin America. Pluralist theories of competing interest groups are but a variant of homeostatic theorizing; "civic culture" approaches are usually and justifiably accused of American ethno-centrism, but they also do not treat democracy as more than a convenience for the better lubrication of the system; political-party studies simply beg the democratic question; and some political scientists bluntly assume the inevitability or even the desirability of authoritarianism in developing states, and leave the matter at that. (p. 64)

It was not simply that Silvert resisted Project Camelot as well as the repression of intellectuals and institutions in nations including Argentina and Chile. Perhaps more significantly, he shunned the two-dimensional formulae purporting to summarize political dynamics in "Latin America" (jumbled together as a whole) that were all too readily at hand from the late 1950s into the mid-1960s. Beyond the standard self-justifications offered by authoritarian governments and corporate interests, those analytic clichés included the Pan-American myth and the later-appearing duality of "reform or revolution," which was often the official Kennedy-era US viewpoint. Kalman Silvert was also skeptical of oversimplified Marxist models and assumptions, as we have seen. Importantly, he advocated maintaining the connection of empirical social science to the core disciplines, and this dedication helped serve as a bulwark against researchers' bias or stasis.

Beyond offering lucid critiques of more limited or tendentious analyses of Latin American societies, Silvert influentially embraced the values of democracy and human freedom. In contrast to many contemporaries who lauded contrasting goals including equilibrium, development, or revolution, he pointed the way to a process that would broaden human liberty, in accord with the ideals of Rousseau, Kant, and Locke. Silvert considered even nationalism—which he urged, with limited success, as a mainstay category for comparative politics—to be a necessary but not sufficient condition for democracy. In the decades following his death, the trajectories of both political events and political analysis in Latin America increasingly harmonized with Kalman Silvert's democratic values. Postauthoritarian régimes sought legitimacy through regular elections; human rights were endorsed (and sometimes even partially attained) by citizens and societies in all areas of the hemisphere; political science executed a multifaceted reorientation to study transitions to democracy.

Silvert's effect on social science, stemming from his scholarship, was reinforced by his developmental and institutional efforts. We have seen his clearly articulated view of Latin American intellectuals' influential roles in society; that doctrine brought to center stage the task of expanding and strengthening the ranks—and the prominence—of Latin American social scientists. Through his undertakings via US foundations and additional channels that are related in other chapters of this book, Kalman Silvert contributed to pluralism, empiricism, and scholarly independence in the emerging international social science on Latin America and the Caribbean. Analytic diversity and the pursuit of "human richness" were both advanced through this line of action. Just as importantly, Silvert worked to institutionalize collegial international efforts. Through structures including the Latin American Studies Association, durable forums were established for interchange and joint endeavors among autonomous individual scholars. These routinized debates created settings in which new social-scientific ideas were able to thrive. Within political science, the most conspicuous fruits of this process were the analysis of "bureaucratic-authoritarian" régimes, and the many-sided study of transitions to democracy (e.g., electoral studies, decentralization processes, the analysis of civil society and its links with politics, and many others).[2]

Kalman Silvert's intellect, energy, gregariousness—and luck, of course—assisted him in exerting such a notable impact on the growth of social science. Specific strands in his scholarship fitted him well for the task that his theories helped to specify: furthering academic and institutional development in Western Hemisphere countries. His focus on nationalism, and his multiform definition of that social value, gave him an interest in a priority recognized (and likely to be reinterpreted) in every locality. He wore his open-mindedness, by this token, on his sleeve. In addition, his adherence to a philosophical tradition that he traced from Rousseau through Kant to Weber and Cassirer provided him with a theoretical ground independent of both Marxism and of Utilitarian models. This circumstance perhaps freed him to assist communication among many analytic and ideological schools in the Western Hemisphere. Silvert's philosophical allegiances—chosen for deep scholarly and moral reasons—may have helped prevent his being perceived as too linked with an unexamined North American liberalism in Latin America, or as too radical in the United States.

Finally, in calling for enhanced scholarship on Latin American politics within US universities, Kalman Silvert's appraisal was discriminating, and his timing was fortuitous. Exactly because too few resources had been devoted to the hemispheric subfield, opportunities existed for widespread advances. Within five years of Silvert's 1966 essay on Project Camelot and the North American academy, at least seven of the eleven front-rank political science departments he took to task in that chapter had made what proved to be long-term appointments on Latin America. All those scholars, plus an additional half-dozen at other excellent US institutions who launched careers in the early 1970s, made enduring contributions to Western Hemisphere social science. Even if most were not direct students of Kalman Silvert, this new generation had been exposed to his persuasive orienting ideas, and they plied their craft in a scholarly world that he did much to create.

Notes

1. See especially pp. 87–114. Later in his argument, Anderson observes that "democratic process is peculiarly appropriate to the requirements of development in Latin America," but avoids basing this assertion on "the inherent superiority of the values of the Western democratic tradition." Democracy, instead, is viewed as assisting development by best supplying information and public feedback needed for intelligent choice among policy alternatives (pp. 372–73). Martin C. Needler's contemporaneous volume, *Latin American Politics in Perspective* (1963) does argue that only restructuring on the basis of "popular sovereignty and juridical and social equality" can bring stability and peace to Latin American politics (p. 39), but the construction of democracy is not well integrated in his model, which focuses on interest groups. Needler gives substantial credit for several instances of democratic advance in Latin America to the efforts of "creative statesmen" such as Uruguay's José Batlle y Ordóñez and Colombia's Alberto Lleras Camargo (p. 179).

2. In related disciplines, the successful role of LASA as a growth medium for new approaches is illustrated well by the range of "program tracks" that were included in the Association's 2009 International Congress held in Rio de Janeiro. Fully thirty-five substantive themes were explored by congress participants; in the social sciences (in addition to variants of the long-standing disciplines) these included "Afro-Latin and Indigenous Peoples," "Citizenship, Rights and Social Justice," "Gender, Sexualities and LGBT Studies," "Latin American Diasporas," and "Violence and (In)security."

3

Silvert's Approach
and Methods

Daniel H. Levine

Kalman H. Silvert participated vigorously in academic life in the United States and Latin America, founded programs and institutions, and launched many careers, including mine. He helped build intellectual and practical bridges across cultures and developed organizations to carry that vision forward. As a teacher and mentor, he inspired his students and colleagues by word and example, pointing them to research and teaching that underscored the importance of empathy, combining ideas with institutions, and looking beyond the national level to see how things worked in different contexts.[1] He was also a scholar—one of the first to take the study of Latin American politics beyond general historical reflections and insist on analytical rigor and comparative insight. Comparative analysis was central to his point of view.

As a scholar, Silvert made contributions of note as editor and contributor to numerous symposiums organized with American Universities Field Staff (AUFS) and promoted, encouraged, and at times rescued important academic institutions and figures in Latin America. Apart from his early work on Guatemala (*A Study in Government: Guatemala*, 1954) and the book he coauthored with Leonard Reissman (*Education, Class and Nation: The Experiences of Chile and Venezuela*, 1976), Silvert wrote mostly essays and commentaries, sometimes very extended essays, as in the case *The Reason for Democracy* (1977).[2] The relative absence of extended empirical work makes it difficult to judge how well the ideas that undergirded Silvert's scholarship may serve now and in the future as guides to research and analysis. This is the task before us.

Silvert was firmly rooted in Enlightenment values of rationality and freedom. He was also deeply influenced by thinkers like Ernst Cassirer

41

and Max Weber, who stressed that human action was value laden and complete understanding required seeing how values emerged, gained a foothold, and worked their way into regular patterns of behavior. Like many social scientists of his time, he was influenced by theories of modernization and development (Packenham 1977). Central to these theories was the concept of a transition from tradition to modernity, polar ends of a dichotomy connected by the "great transformation" (Silvert acknowledged borrowing the term from Karl Polanyi's classic work [Polanyi 1957]), otherwise known as modernization, development, or sometimes the "development process." This transition is characterized above all by the growing convergence of rationality and freedom in the process of building societies that value and manage inclusiveness, complexity, and diversity without tearing themselves apart.

Silvert's position differs from Polanyi and others who stressed the economic foundations of development. For him and his collaborators, the modernization process was ultimately about the institutionalization of individual and social capacities for empathy in broadly inclusive communities capable of sustainable change and tolerance of diversity. Working toward this end state is what modernization and development are all about. Although they acknowledged that there is no common set of stages through which all countries must pass, at the same time they insisted that stages *could* be identified and that the transition was measurable.

The preceding brief sketch conveys the core of a highly optimistic view of human possibilities, achievable through the "development process." Despite setbacks and conflicts, in this view of the world all good things can and do go together. Silvert was concerned with development and modernity for moral, practical, and theoretical reasons, and he had firm views on the best way to study the process. His moral bias in favor of the modern is very clear. Modern societies were likely to be freer and more rationally organized—more tolerant places in which to live. In practical terms, he thought he saw a way to get there, through the inculcation of values of empathy and skills of connection that would allow individuals to see beyond their own ascriptive connections (family, region, religion; gender is not mentioned) to a larger social unity, the nation.

The unity of a modern society can only be constructed around shared secular and rational values and the vehicle Silvert identified for these values was common adherence to the nation-state as the ultimate arbiter of secular dispute. He devoted much of his scholarly career to exploring the conditions that might make this work. In theoretical and methodological terms, he strove for a dynamic understanding of change that would combine ideas with institutions and a method that would reach across and within nations. An initial statement of these goals can be found in the programmatic volume *Expectant Peoples: Nationalism and Development* (EP; 1963), which lays out a particular understanding of nationalism along with an elaborate set of propositions and hypotheses concerning how this may look and evolve at different points in the transition to modernity, the successive "stages" of the development process.

The best method for achieving a valid and reliable understanding of these processes is one that combines ideas and institutions and looks across and within communities. These ideas provided the basis for Silvert's *Education, Class and Nation: The Experiences of Chile and Venezuela* (ECN; 1976) coauthored with Reissman. This ambitious, multination, multilayered study examined how education and educational institutions can work to generate and sustain the values and commitments the authors believed to be central to modernity.[3]

In this scheme of things, secularization is the necessary counterpart of the transition to modernity, and secular rules of the game are the sine qua non of modern society. "Religion in a modern setting," Silvert wrote, "must somehow come to terms with a pluralistic society if the necessarily absolutist beliefs of religion are not to destroy the equally necessary relativistic beliefs of societies dedicated to the institutionalization of change" (Silvert 1966, 7). As a set of institutions, beliefs, and practices, religion is conceived in static terms, unlikely to change itself and certain to act as a drag on the process, when not engaged in active resistance. Silvert's position on religion and secularization provides an underlying motif in all his work but is the explicit focus of only one book, the conference volume *Churches and States: The Religious Institution and Modernization* (CS; 1966).[4] This book is often overlooked and is not included in Chris Mitchell's otherwise excellent review of Silvert's scholarship. I give separate attention to it here because of the intimate relation between secularization, modernization, and modernity in the whole body of his work.

The working theory of secularization that developed in the late nineteenth and early twentieth centuries (defined as the progressive, desirable, and inevitable decline and privatization of religion in the face of enlightenment) dominated social science thinking for a long time and was integral to concepts of modernization (Casanova 1994). The problem is that this theory, and the expectations it generated, have not fared very well. In the years since Silvert died, waves of innovation in religion in Latin America and around the world have exploded the notion of religion as necessarily static and resistant to change, and in any case doomed to long-term extinction with the advance of modernization. These developments have opened new lines of inquiry. For these reasons, secularization is an important part of the puzzle left by Silvert's work.

Concepts and Theories

The unity and focus of Kalman Silvert's scholarship is built around a compact set of concepts: tradition, modernity, modernization and development, transitions and stages, nationalism and the nation-state, rationality, and secularization. These go together and influence one another as they are expressed in individual and collective behaviors and enshrined in institutions. They come as packages, but for analytical purposes I consider them separately. What follows is based on close reading of three books that give us a clear sense of the evolution of core concerns and issues: *Expectant Peoples* (EP; 1963), *Churches and States* (CS; 1966), and *Education, Class and Nation* (ECN; 1976).

Tradition and modernity are ideal types, opposite ends of a continuum. Like all ideal types, these are not descriptions of any particular reality but provide models or outlines of possibilities. All real situations are mixed: the point is to grasp the dynamic of movement from one end of the continuum to the other and understand what behavior looks like at any point along this dimension. At its heart, this movement is a progression from ascription to choice, individual and social isolation to inclusion, coercion to authority freely given.

> We should be explicit in defining the core of what we mean by "modernism." Certainly all modern societies have created attitudes, social devices, and traditions which permit orderly institutionalized change; they also assume, in one or another degree, that public decision must be secular, empirically derived, and subject to empirical change. The self sustaining nature of change, supported by appropriate values and by other social institutions as well as by the state, is probably the most important single characteristic of modern society. (EP, pp. 4–5)

The end point is clear—modernity. The question is how to get there. This is what modernization, development, or sometimes the "development process" are all about. The general vehicles for enabling and enhancing this movement are nationalism and the nation-state.

Nationalism is intrinsic to the development process because "it discharges a strategic function in a particular kind and phase of change, and [that] as has been said, part of its nature remains structurally as well as functionally unchanged everywhere it appears" (EP, pp. 8–9). Silvert deploys the concept of nationalism as a shorthand for a syndrome of attitudes, loyalties, and understandings and commitments that made it possible to hold a diverse community together without breakdown. Consistent, gradual expansion of the community identified as belonging to the nation is central to this process. This view draws on the Enlightenment story of European (above all French and perhaps English) history, which saw nation-states expand, capturing roles and powers from church and nobilities to build secular institutions unified around the common identity of belonging to a nation.[5] Silvert devoted much of his intellectual effort to describing and explaining similar processes at work around the world.

The growth of nationalism and the nation-state is not just a matter of creating institutions that cast a broader net of power and capacity. It is also, and more importantly, about the creation and diffusion of values that reinforce coherent and inclusive identities. The construction of effective and inclusive values and the broad diffusion of a capacity for empathy ("the emotional condition of modernism," EP, p. 27) are critical. Silvert's working concept of modern values privileged empathy, a sense of personal and group autonomy, and placed at the heart of the process rationality and acceptance of change and what we might today label diversity. "Nationalism, in a certain sense, is the institutionalized power reflection of 'empathy' both constituting requirements of the ability to follow a modern style of life. This primary function of nationalism is an unavoidable aspect of development and indeed may itself be used as an operational definition of social and political development" (EP, p. 24). The emergence and consolidation of these values is what made the process self-sustaining.

This inverts standard accounts of economic and political change. Referring to Polanyi's influential work on the Great Transformation, he writes,

> We have chosen to shift the subject on its axis, and to examine the changes introducing modernism in light of the relations between the attitudes, values, ideologies, and the public behavior of individuals, and the social institutions to which they both cede and concede power by extending to them or investing in them their loyalties, expectations, and obedience. The positive function of nationalism is to order the set of relationships, thus building reasonable expecta-

tions and security patterns into the greater complexity which is social modernism. (EP, p. 20)

All good things go together in this view, which paints an almost utopian picture of the national community. The working assumption is that the process extends itself progressively in a rationalizing and inclusive process. This is preferable, it is assumed, to one that is dogmatic and closed. But what of nation-states that are dogmatic and closed? These are dealt with by what is almost a trick of definition. They are dismissed as somehow caught in an "incomplete transition." The term suggests clear expectations of movement along a linear path from tradition to modernity. Silvert rejected models of development that involved a unique, one-size-fits-all path for change. In the conclusion to *Expectant Peoples*, he wrote,

> We have concerned ourselves with the development of certain social relations; our evidence allows us to say only that the presumed connection between development and the nation holds throughout all the studies, *but not that there is a fixed progression of stages for developing these relations*—the growth of the social elements and relations involved in total development must follow very different roads from country to country. (EP, p. 430, emphasis in original)

This statement notwithstanding, Silvert and his collaborators repeatedly affirm that there are defined and measurable stages to the process and point to transitions that are incipient, incomplete, partial, or full, with elaborate specification of what to expect at each point.[6] The transition to a consolidated modernity is not automatic, nor is it without conflict. There are lags and resistances, and some particular detours and blockages that can undermine change or turn it in pathological and self-destructive directions. The specifics vary from case to case, but several sources of resistance are especially prominent in Silvert's work: religion, corporatist politics (identified with elements in Iberian tradition), cultural failure and elite betrayal.

The depiction of religion is perhaps best described as dogmatically antidogmatic, and has much in common with nineteenth-century anticlericalism and French *laïcité*. Silvert puts the case succinctly: "Man's freedom from the stigmata of religious ascription is another one of those painfully won victories over the accidents of birth that inhibit persons from adjusting their individual social abilities to the general social need and their own preferences" (CS, p. 219). The separation of church and state is conflated into a general separation of religious beliefs and affiliations from broader social and cultural life. There is no provision for regular interchange between religion and society, and the very idea of religion itself as a potential source of change is absent. "It will not do," Silvert writes, "for students of contemporary religion to close their eyes to the status quo character of religious institutions through much of history—religious institutions are prone to isolate themselves from the immediate and proximate, to set the eyes of the believers on otherworldly concerns, and to organize the life of the church around a complex of absolutes of a supra worldly status" (CS, p. vii).

Within the overall question of religion and modernization, Silvert was particularly concerned with church-state conflict, or its equivalent in traditions that do not have easily identifiable churches.[7] He understood this above all as a struggle to determine the values that would give order and meaning to political and social life.

> To the extent to which religious institutions insist on their right and duty to proclaim a truth basis for general social relations, they are on the same terrain as the nation state with its claims to overriding temporal authority. The coincidence of church state conflict and modernization thus requires no elaborate theoretical explanation. The general pattern of resolution of the conflict is also quite clear. (CS, pp. 216–217)

The extended conflicts over power and property that have played so central a role in church-state issues over the centuries have little place here. The stress is on separation as a necessary step in the establishment of rational (read: secular) values as the organizing principles of national identity. Thus,

> It is not historically "necessary" [then], that the resolution of church state conflicts in modernizing societies take a given, single path. But if the way of effective separation is not followed, then the entire development process is confounded by the resultant confusion between absolute and relative truth, religious and secular authority and sanction, the socially universal as opposed to the religiously universal. Judging social patterns by dogmatic prescription impedes that self correction without which change becomes tortured maladjustment instead of enthusiastic exploration. (CS, p. 218)

There are problems here. It is assumed that as institutions, religions legitimize and benefit from the status quo, while maintaining themselves somehow in isolation from more general currents of change brought by modernization (and, we might add, globalization, communication, and the like). The truth is that in social and cultural terms, religion is an empty vessel and has been filled in different periods and traditions with the most varied meanings. Religious ideas and institutions have been identified with everything from Prohibition to abortion, from liberation theology or the experience of the civil rights movement in the United States to monarchies, Buddhist pacifism to militant monks leading armies in Sri Lanka, right-wing evangelicals and "the Tory Party at prayer" (how one wag described the Anglican Church). The proper metaphor is not isolation and otherworldliness but continuous and often conflict-charged interchange between what we call religion and what we label society and politics. Not walls but porous membranes connect them, and the traffic is constant and moves in both directions.

Silvert's general stance on religion was framed by a narrative of secularization that predicted a progressive and inevitable privatization and disappearance of religion, seen as desirable. These expectations have not fared well. The only part of the world in which the conventional secularization story holds up is Western Europe. In much of the rest of the world, particularly in the global South, religions are flourishing and diversifying at a dizzying pace, competing vigorously for members, resources, and public voice. They have not faded out of public view: on the contrary, they demand a place at the table. Furthermore, it is by now clear (if it was ever in doubt) that framing the issue in terms of churches and states ignores a great deal of the action. Churches cannot be assumed to be homogeneous, and states do not represent all there is to say about politics.

Silvert's general understanding of the social role of religion, and his views on the uses and kinds of rationality, rely heavily on the work of Max Weber. Weber's sociology of religion centers attention on the underlying rationale of religious authority and organization (traditional, charismatic, bureaucratic) and made a point of distinguishing rationalities that focused exclusively on ends from those which also took account of the consequences of the means chosen and adjusted for them. Weber also warned against seeking the salvation of one's soul through politics: politics works through force, and the dynamic of force can take over, leading to the loss of souls as well as likely political failure. Although Weber is a prime source on these matters, more Tocqueville and less Weber would have enriched Silvert's view of the matter. What Tocqueville (1990) saw in the United States in the 1840s was that separation of church and state can free both. This has been a condition of the extraordinary and continuing vitality of religion in this presumably very modern nation. The insights Tocqueville still provides suggest that alternative understandings of secularization are available, which underscore arrangements for coexistence and point to the conjunction of secularization with religious growth and diversity (Levine 2012; Stepan 2003).

The general models that frame Silvert's view of religion and secularization take insufficient account of important moments in history where religious groups and supposedly "otherworldly" views energized and legitimized political struggles aimed at opening (not closing) communities. Prominent examples would include the roles of Puritans in the English Revolution, liberation theology in Latin America, or African American churches in the civil rights movement. In any case it is surprising that someone so knowledgeable about Latin America could have been so inattentive to the momentous changes that were reshaping the social and political role of the Catholic Church in the last decade of Silvert's life. Liberation theology articulated a new stance for religion, elements in the churches challenged authoritarian regimes in the name of human rights and democracy, and the ground was laid for the spectacular growth of Pentecostal Protestantism that has done so much to reshape the religious and cultural landscape of the region.

In Silvert's view of things, religion was a prime source of resistance to modernity and a drag on modernization, but it was not alone. Latin America in particular faced other obstacles, especially those derived from what he called "Romance politics," another term for elements of Iberian tradition with corporatist overtones, authoritarian efforts to contain the diversity that modernization brings. This is folded into a broader phenomenon of cultural failure and elite betrayal, which in the final analysis rest on resistance to the extension of full membership in the nation (or to xenophobic reversals, as in Nazi Germany). "The failure to find adequate means for the complete extension of the rights and duties of national life is a major problem in all those older, independent states which have not achieved self sustaining economic structures of a solution to the harshest effects of class difference" (EP, p. 29). The Iberian cultural heritage weighs heavily in Latin America. "For long it has been a common saying," he wrote, "that Europe stops at the Pyrenees. The Iberian Peninsula and its offshoots, Western though they may be, are the only part of the European cultural community so consistently lagging in integrating any effective degree of modernism. Underdeveloped, undefined, and understudied, they have gone their way, the subject either of neglect or of a beneficent Pan Americanism of a rather sticky hands across the border variety" (EP, p. 371). This analysis attributes determining cultural influence to an Iberian tradition (Veliz 1980). But a moment's reflection on Iberian history suggests some problematic ele-

ments. The persistence of tradition cannot be assumed: ideological hegemony commonly entails physical coercion, and in the case of Spain,
wars have been fought, most recently the devastating civil war of the
late 1930s. One side won and imposed decades of dictatorship; one side
lost. Were the losers less modern, or is this as much a question of power
and force as of values and community?

Methods

The contributions to *Expectant Peoples* and *Churches and States* offer
little in the way of methodological guidelines or discussions. With rare
exceptions, individual chapters are conventional narratives cast in historical terms. They are united by the general concerns of each volume,
but do not share a set of specific methods or hypotheses. Silvert's contributions to these volumes is mostly programmatic and typological and
often hortatory. *Expectant Peoples* does have a lengthy appendix of
propositions and hypotheses, but these are more descriptive and typological than methodological.

The only full statement of research design, methods, and reasoning
that we have is in *Education, Class and Nation*, the fruit of a long-term
collaboration with Reissman, and the last book either published before
their respective deaths. This is the most ambitious theoretical and empirical work Silvert ever undertook. Working out of the tradition of
Cassirer and Weber, the research effort is grounded in recognition of the
significance of values for all human action. "The infusion of events with
meaning is what converts a mere occurrence into an event of social significance, a concept basic to our vision of reality" (ECN, p. 13). The
core question they address is how values are inculcated and how they
change; the central mechanism for this process is the educational system. Education, modernization, rationality, and freedom go together for
the authors. Education generates the greater openness and tolerance that
is central to their vision of modernization, which in turn is closely
linked to choice, rationality, and freedom.

The authors advance a theory about the relation between education
and changing identities. They pay particular attention to the content of
emerging identities in Chile and Venezuela, link these to the content and
level of education, and argue that education brings greater identity with
the nation, moving individuals and groups from tradition to modernity.
In their view, public secular education (at all levels) is the prime institution preparing people for autonomous participation in diverse, relativis-

tic, and secular societies. This effect works because greater education detaches individuals from the weight of connections of family, region, or religion, and opens them to broader identities. This holds within all the areas of interest, although the pull of family and religion remains strong. "Even the most modern views of family and religion are more traditional than the least modern view of education and the economy" (ECN, p. 30).

The basic line of change runs from tradition to modernity. Silvert and Reissman acknowledge that "fashion has decreed that the words 'modern' and 'traditional' should be weeded from our thoughts. Political and intellectual current have combined to judge those concepts as being in bad taste, a slur against countries of the Third World, and of doubtful intellectual worth" (ECN, p. 17). But they insist on the value of these concepts and regularly contrast the modern and rational and autonomous with the theological, irrational, and class-bound. Thus, a modern person "is defined, by us, in part as someone who accepts rationality as a reason for acting, as distinct from the traditionalist, who will tend to justify his acts on the basis of ritual. Appositely, a rationalist should also be a relativist" (ECN, p. 19), who, they continue, "is expected to 'see' across class boundaries and to identify in a real working sense with the total complex of his national culture; demonstrating his 'loyalty' by his willingness to accept interim, eclectic solution to problems without imposing absolute mores" (ECN, p. 22). The more modern person sees him- or herself as autonomous and identifies differences as relative and as subject to adjustment within a commonly accepted frame of rules. Individuals of this kind have the cognitive tools and capacity for empathy required to build an inclusive national community of self-adjusting and mutually respecting individuals and spheres of life in which the limitations of ascribed belief and status yield to inclusion and fluidity.

Attitudes and values are not well understood as some kind of free-floating mental stuff. They are formed, communicated, and reinforced in real social circumstances, in close relation to institutions and patterns of action. Capturing this reality requires a particular kind of research design. *Education, Class and Nation* is a model of how to conceive and carry out such research in complex and difficult circumstances.[8] The authors built multiple dimensions of comparison into the study: two countries, rural and urban regions within each country, and multiple levels and groups within the field of education, including teachers, students, and parents. They conducted massive surveys (with more than 10,000 respondents in all) at these levels, and combined the results with intensive historical analysis of the evolution and guiding values of educational institutions in each country. The result is a rich set of data that sheds light on what it means to say that values are inculcated in institutions, how this works, and with what possible effects.

The organization and presentation of the data is complex. The questionnaire covered five distinct areas: family, religion, education, economy, and the polity. These were combined with attention to expressed motivations for behavior and the relative degree of autonomy respondents perceived for themselves and others within a broad community. All these are mapped on the basic dichotomy of tradition and modernity to produce eight distinct types of behavior and orientation, distinguished on grounds of more or less autonomy and ritualistic or rationalistic thinking. The proliferation of issues, dimensions, and types can be confusing, but the bottom line is clear. More education is associated with a greater sense of personal autonomy, enhanced ability to make relativistic judgments, and a capacity to discriminate among social spheres, making relativistic, not absolute judgments.

A puzzling aspect of this book is that despite the authors' vigorous dismissal of functionalist theories in sociology (too oriented to coherence built on consensus), they occasionally forget the general stress on culture as unity in diversity (not just unity) to insist on cultural coherence. Thus they write, "Venezuela still lacks a coherent national culture which is its greatest educational deficit, far transcending in importance the realities of its school system" (ECN, p. 172). It is difficult to know what this statement means, or what the authors mean here by culture or coherence. Venezuela then and now is bitterly polarized (as Chile was during the time of their research), but culture is not properly limited only to politics or values about the nation. If we think about culture in ways that account for a wider range of behaviors and practices (music, sports, food, linguistic usages, styles of interpersonal relations, norms about gender relations, and attitudes to class and race), then it is difficult to see how Venezuela (or just about any other country) can be described as not coherent. In fact it has what we can see as a recognizably Caribbean culture, with strong North American influences (baseball, among others). Is it highly polarized? Yes. Is it an imperfect society? Of course it is; aren't they all?

Conclusion

When I was in graduate school, I remember a very prominent political scientist urged on us all the need for peoples to unite in the struggle for development. I raised my hand and asked, "If it is a struggle, why should they be united?" The professor was not amused, and I dropped the class. Once I left graduate school and hit the ground in Latin America, I had to unlearn a lot of what I had been taught about "development." Having been Silvert's student helped me sort out the realities I was encountering, even if the answers I found were not what he or I expected. Silvert's vision of the unity central to development was different from the one that inspired my graduate school professor. It was much more nuanced and centered on the development of a social coherence that could be self-sustaining precisely because it rested on the capacity of individuals and groups to see beyond themselves and recognize others as part of a larger shared community. Although he was aware of setbacks and conflicts, Silvert's perspective was relentlessly optimistic.

Although he went out of his way to reject rigid stages, much of Silvert's work in fact depends on a notion of transitions and stages. He rejected a static functionalism, but value coherence of a sort was central to his understanding of development, and thus he characterized some cultures as not coherent. Perhaps the most notable failure of theory and prediction lies in an excessive or misplaced faith in a particular kind of rationality. This comes out most clearly in his views on religion and its relation to development. He saw no possibility for change within religion as part of a more general change. He accepted a conventional model of religion as separate from the surrounding world and destined to decline in the long run. Given his interest in ideas and institutions, this is a surprising blind spot, but perhaps it was understandable given the times in which he lived, was educated, and worked. It is uncomfortable to evaluate Silvert's work from the perspective of today, almost forty years after his death. He died at the peak of his productivity and intellectual development. If he had more time, there's no telling where he would have ended up intellectually.

Some of his core ideas have not weathered well, and many of the empirical predictions simply did not work out. His insistence on nationalism as the central vehicle for modernization did not catch on. But the general injunctions to consider ideas in context, to look at ideas as social products in real historical and institutional contexts, to work at what C. Wright Mills (1959) called the intersect of biography and history, all continue to hold up. Silvert was never one to insist on disciples. He looked forward to a good debate, and he respected coherent argument and evidence. Many of his students, including those who do not work on Latin America, have chosen topics and come to conclusions that he might have disputed or disagreed with. What we all learned most from Kalman Silvert is a sense of how to think about issues, identify important topics, and decide where and how to study them. He is best remembered by continuing the search for relations between ideas, actions, and institutions in real contexts and by sharing his bias for openness and freedom.

Notes

I am grateful to Bruce J. Berman and Patrice A. Fletcher for comments and observations.

1. I discuss my own experience of Silvert as teacher and mentor in Levine (2014, 2016).

2. "Silvert's pattern of scholarly performance is not the sort that we routinely associate with the major, internationally recognized academic he was. His publishing career did not feature a groundbreaking empirical finding that reorients the research of many other investigators, nor a transformational reinterpretation of existing data. Instead, as a scholar he was a profound generalist—a relatively rare variety of researcher but one that may have uncommon impact if the historical and disciplinary moment is opportune." Christopher Mitchell, chapter 2 in this volume.

3. Silvert's understanding of the foundations of modernity have much in common with what many scholars now call "social capital," but with a greater focus on values as latency and less concern with the acquisition of specific skills and connections.

4. The preface to *Churches and States* was written by Charles Gallagher, who also contributed the chapter on Iran, and specifically locates this book as a direct extension of the line of thought first articulated in *Expectant Peoples*.

5. The expansion of citizenship is addressed in, among others, López (1997), Yashar (2005), and in a different vein, Van Cott (2008).

6. In the appendix to *Expectant Peoples*, Hypotheses K, L, and M specify in great detail "what we should find" in, respectively, "early phases of transition," "intermediate stages of transition," and "the last stages of transition" (EP, pp. 442–44).

7. Religious traditions that do not easily approximate models of "church" (Hinduism and Buddhism) are excluded from the *Churches and States* volume "because these cases present special theoretical problems which would have broken the continuity of the problem area here treated" (CS, p. 10). These special theoretical problems are not specified.

8. Fieldwork for the study was affected by the Project Camelot scandal, which led to significant problems with universities and university students in the two countries.

4

Silvert and Democratic Theory

Joel Jutkowitz

Kalman H. Silvert was a man of many facets. One was his role as a theorist of democracy, who built his theory block by block out of empirical investigation. This chapter examines the steps he took to reach his understanding of democratic theory and applies that understanding to current situations. In carrying out this task, I underscore that Silvert's commitment to democratic theory was more than an intellectual exercise; it was the very essence of how he viewed his role in the political process. As he commented in his last book, *The Reason for Democracy*,[1] his work had both a scientific and a political dimension, the latter arising from his role as citizen, a condition of his existence he always took into account.

Throughout his career, Silvert was concerned with several grand phenomena and the related issues they raised for democratic development. He focused on the growth of nation-states and within them of nationalism as a social value, defined as the acceptance of the nation-state as the ultimate arbiter of secular affairs.[2] He understood that this acceptance laid the groundwork for an inclusive democratic order that could overcome class, ethnic, religious, and racial differences while at the same time making possible the most extreme authoritarianism. He was concerned with creating freedom, which he understood as the ability of citizens in a nation-state to make rational and effective choices about secular affairs.

In developing his theoretical constructs, Silvert's principal building blocks were a careful understanding of the context of political behavior; a concern with the relationship between nation and class; a categorization of the values of all participants in a political process; an examination of the role of institutions; and, finally, a vision of the types of behavior that actually took place. In all of this, he was concerned with the likelihood and characteristics of conflict and the key role that compromise played in a truly democratic process.

Understanding Context

From the outset of his professional career, Silvert focused on the historical, linguistic, and cultural context of the countries where he worked. This focus is reflected in his early published work, such as *A Study in Government: Guatemala* (1954) and *Conflict Society: Reaction and Revolution in Latin America* (1968) and was carried through to one of his last works, *Essays in Understanding Latin America* (1977).[3] In direct opposition to the prevailing wisdom regarding comparative politics, he did not follow the belief that all politics could be understood as a single system, such as that proposed by Gabriel Almond (Almond and Coleman 1960). He believed that assuming all political systems from an Eskimo village to the United States (Almond's thesis) could be analyzed using the same variables made that analysis so banal as to not to be of any real use in comprehending the character and predicting the likely trajectory of a given polity. He argued instead for grouping polities by their levels of development into appropriate clusters or universes of similar occurrences. This ensured that analysis of these polities and predictions of likely outcomes would be based on realistic and achievable possibilities.

Nation and Class

Silvert's concern with context led him to explore the processes of political and economic development in each universe of similar occurrences from the perspective of the differential ways the conflicts played out between the nation as an expression of the public interest and class as an expression of private interests. For him, the nation as a concept defines the political community in terms of who may participate and how they may do so. Such a definition is given form through the operation of the state. The conception of the nation should infuse the state with purpose. The state should provide the organizational support for the maintenance of the social consequences of the prevailing definition of the nation. Writing in the mid-1970s, Silvert saw Cuba and Chile as extreme cases. Cuba had reached the point of full nationhood—incorporating all citizens within its organizational framework. The Chilean junta under Augusto Pinochet had attempted to "break the Chilean nation," to turn the clock back to the eighteenth century and "repeal the French Revolution" (Silvert 1977, pp. 10, 152). Class interests overrode and in effect substituted for any notion of the public interest. Focusing on these issues today, Silvert would have likely been concerned by the lack of progress in Cuba in responding to dissent and generating what may become a hereditary elite, while looking benevolently on the efforts of the post-Pinochet Chilean political order to rectify many (but not all) of the defects generated by Chile's authoritarian interlude.

Values and Institutions

From his first years in the field, Silvert was struck by the role that values played in shaping political behavior. His analysis of the relationships between indigenous populations and the Guatemalan nation centered on the degree to which the indigenous peoples he looked at understood the Guatemalan nation as another, distant village (Silvert 1968, pp. 35, 45). They identified themselves as outside that Guatemalan national village and for many years since, that perception reflected a reality. Only in the most recent decades have indigenous people seen themselves and been perceived by other Guatemalans as part of the effective Guatemalan nation.

Silvert focused his research in the 1960s and 1970s on several studies that explored the links between values, class, institutions, and political behavior that he had seen in his earlier fieldwork. The first of these studies[4] (referred to below as the 1961 study) dealt with samples in four countries: Mexico, Brazil, Chile, and Argentina. While looking at similar variables, the 1961 study drew its respondents from different universes in each country, students and teachers in Argentina and Chile; businesspeople, workers, and favela residents in Brazil; and members of Congress in Mexico.[5] As Silvert summed it up, one of the study's major findings was that "'modern men' had the ability to see society as open and accessible and to empathize broadly across class lines" (Silvert and Reissman 1976, p. 9).

Drawing from what was learned in the 1961 study, Silvert, working with a longtime colleague Leonard Reissman, carried out an exploration of the relationship between the educational institution, class, and national politics. This study was undertaken in Chile and Venezuela using a survey whose universe consisted of primary and secondary school students, their teachers, and parents. The sampling approach that followed was a stratified sample that ensured sufficient cases in the four locales where the survey was undertaken in each of the following categories: students in public, private, and Catholic primary and secondary schools at three grade levels: upper, middle, and lower.[6]

The study examined the role of the educational process in shaping the underlying values that help people frame their behavior. For purposes of analyzing these tendencies, he generated typologies of beliefs based on two ideal types drawn in part from the two major intellectual streams of Latin American thought. One stream was the Mediterranean organic view of society, based in large measure on traditional Catholic thought, where each person knew his or her place and the ideal political system was a corporate social model made up of "separate and parallel institutions" "laced together by their leaders, who form a pluralist oligarchy" (Silvert and Reissman 1976, p. 9). The other was the liberal tradition, based on notions of education as an instrument of change, along with other liberal notions regarding the free play of goods and ideas within a democratically governed pluralist society. Drawing on these contending world views, Silvert felt that labeling one ideal type as "traditional" and the other as "modern" fit the polar ideological alternatives that had historically been represented in most of the countries in the region over the course of their histories. As we shall see, his aim in using these polar types was to develop a far more nuanced vision of the values of the groups studied.

The study examined the views of those sampled regarding the five grand institutions of society—the family, religion, education, the economy, and the polity. Using closed questions, the instrument elicited responses for these institutions at three levels of values: the person's motivations, the standards for that person's behavior, and his or her attitude toward change. For each concern, the instrument looked not only at what a person believed should be the case but what it actually was to gain insight into a person's perceptions of their beliefs and their behavior. The set of questions regarding family illustrate the form the instrument took. Although the actual instrument varied the response, for purposes of illustration, the first response to each question represents the traditional response and the second, the modern response, in the parlance used by Silvert.

Should you seek to realize your aspirations in life, principally for:
• The benefit of your family
• Your own benefit

In your opinion, is the basic social unit:
• Families
• Individuals

Do you think that a child's education should be determined according to the advice of parents?
• Yes
• No

The family:
• Is basically the same in all societies
• Varies according to the society

As time passes, do you expect that your relations with your family:
• Will remain more or less the same
• Will change greatly

What do you think is the principal duty of a good parent?
• To maintain the continuity and stability of the family
• To stimulate his children to realize themselves

Similar questions were asked for the other four institutions (Silvert and Reissman 1976, pp. 192–202).

Looking at the results in Chile and Venezuela, we see that respondents showed a common pattern regarding the five institutions. Family and religion were seen in a far more traditional way than were the economy and education. Family and religion were seen as expressive institutions, as ends in and of themselves; economy and education were instrumental, a means to an end. The polity sat between these clusters; for some it is an instrument of change and for others a fortress to protect the status quo. As I note when referring to levels of conflict, the role of the polity and its institutional framework for resolving conflicts and generating compromises are key elements in the maintenance of an orderly and democratic process of social change.

The resulting set of responses became the basis for developing a typology of the thought processes of the groups studied. The aim of the typology was to describe how three dimensions of thinking about institutions provides a key element in describing likely political outcomes. Those three dimensions were how much autonomy people felt they had in making decisions (also referred to as the distinction between ritualism and rationalism), the amount of autonomy that the respondents believed others had, and the degree of differentiation and openness of the institutional order. Using these three dimensions, Silvert described eight per-

Table 4.1 Typology of World Views

Self-Autonomy	High Autonomy for Others		Low Autonomy for Others	
Ritualism	Type 1 Organicist	Type 2 Conservative Individualist	Type 5 Corporate Pluralist	Type 6 Liberal Abstainer
Rationalism	Type 3 Anarchic Conservative	Type 4 Corporatist Technocrat	Type 7 Modernist Cynic	Type 8 Autonomist

sonality types ranging from what he labeled an organicist to an autonomist (Table 4.1).

Silvert characterized each type in the following manner (Silvert and Reissman 1976, pp. 45–47).

Type 1—The Organicist had low recognition of institutional differentiation, seeing everything from family to politics in the same light; low in recognizing others' individuality and ritualistic in his or her motivations for behavior. In short, a completely traditional person.

Type 2—The Conservative Individualist had a ritualistic approach to behavior and was blind like the organicist to differences between institutions, although he did judge other people on their merits.

Type 3—The Anarchic Conservative was pragmatic in his or her own behavior, but not with respect to others or the institutional framework of society. This is a very tenuous position, difficult to sustain. In his study, Silvert found so few cases that he dropped the category from his analysis.

Type 4—The Corporatist Technocrat was rational regarding his own behavior and an individualist in judging others but unable to separate institutional spheres, assuming for example that religious and political influences should affect education. These were the sorts of people that provided technical support without qualms to Pinochet's authoritarian regime and other similar regimes.

Type 5—The Corporate Pluralist understood institutional pluralism, but acted ritualistically and judged others in the same fashion. These were the types that fit well with the values operating in Franco's Spain. He or she accepted the process of industrialization and urbanization but did not want the changes that come with a more open and less hierarchical society.

Type 6—The Liberal Abstainer was a person who can judge others as individuals and see institutional differentiation but cannot break out of ritualistic patterns of thinking. These people clung to traditional ways in their personal behavior, but were open to understanding the nature of living in a pluralistic society.

Type 7—The Modernist Cynic saw him- or herself as pragmatic and understood institutional differentiation, but saw others as rigid and set in traditional ways. This highly dissonant view also was held in Silvert's study by only a very few and therefore dropped from his analysis.

Type 8—The Autonomist was rational in his or her behavior, secular in his or her view of institutions, recognizing institutional differentiation and viewed others as open-minded. The widespread presence of such individuals "in an appropriate institutional structure" would be the support for a modern and open society, in Silvert's terms.

Silvert believed that describing the distribution of these values was an empirical task, requiring examination of the distribution in each country. He believed that these values were latent in the sense that they represented predispositions for behavior, not absolute determinants. Here he returned to the importance he assigned to context and the history that formed that context. As he repeatedly noted, behavior took place within institutional frameworks. Understanding the strength or weakness of institutions as operating arenas for the management of political conflict was critical to determining how values influenced behavior.

This mapping of the values of students, teachers, and parents in Chile and Venezuela led to the following broad conclusions:

> Politics in national societies integrates the institutional order. Formal education in national societies is the institution fundamental to preparing persons for autonomous participation in secular and relativistic politics. This effect of education makes possible individual democratic activity in national societies. In incompletely national societies, discord develops around the ability of some individuals and groups to live democratically, and the inability of others to act in effectively democratic ways. In such societies, formal education is a crucial element in creating both the grounds of conflict and the ability to perceive it. In developing capitalistic societies, the principal brake to continued development has been a stress between the opposing pulls of class and nation. The intellectuality promoted by prolonged participation in formal education, however, tends to lead educated persons to value universal national over particular class interests. Therefore, while education as an institution makes possible partially democratic as well as dictatorial national integration, through time it is inherently

in contradiction with class-supportive authoritarianism. (Silvert and Reissman 1976, p. 1)

Silvert viewed with optimism the role that education could play in shaping democracy. But he also recognized that the split between family and religion on one hand and economics and education on the other could wreak havoc with the political process. This concern was reflected in his analysis of the types and consequences of conflict, framed within the character of the relationship between individuals and institutions.

Typology of Conflict

Silvert focused on conflict because he believed it provided a means of approaching the limited possibility of a causal explanation of social change.[7] He operated on the principle that notions of causality in the social sciences have a different connotation than notions of causality in the natural sciences. Whereas in the natural sciences references to causality are empirically comfortable (except in such sciences as particle physics), exact enough in their relationship to observable events so as to admit their use, in the social sciences such references push well beyond the limits of the data. It is more reasonable in dealing with the social sciences to consider events or circumstances as "making possible" other events or circumstances than to refer to causes. The difference, as Silvert saw it, was not merely semantic but a recognition of the possibility of autonomous reactions that limit the sufficiency of a given set of circumstances. As long as we recognize that human choice is a variable in a relationship, we need to think in terms of a separation between what is necessary and what is sufficient to explain an outcome.

Silvert defined conflict as "any overt clash involving all or some of a political institution, motivated by perceived interests among the parties with some power to act" (Silvert 1970, p. 58). In that definition "perceived interest" is recognition of the role played by values and ideologies—that is, it involves asking the question as to whether individuals or groups consider that something is worth fighting for.

To understand the nature of conflict, he developed a typology based on the depth of conflict and the strength of the political institutional arrangements for its containment. Conflicts can be classified in the following manner, ranging from most to least significant.

Value conflict is the most general form, including all other forms of conflict. As a consequence, value conflict admits no possibility of compromise—in other words, value conflict represents a zero-sum game. One cannot compromise one's values without in effect adopting others. As Silvert comments:

> Value conflict, then, in generating differing social realities, involves all other areas of human experience and calls into question total modes of life. It is the kind of conflict most to be avoided if the protagonists want to maintain their social system, and it is also the kind of conflict that must be real and understandable for total revolution. Since it is likely that every society contains individuals and groups who hold very different basic values, it is clear that societies must have systems that prevent value-conflict from emerging if there is to be change without social breakdown. (Silvert 1970, p. 65)

Community conflict concerns the dimensions of the society—"who inhabits the effective community." The questions at this analytical level are which groups will participate and in what manners will they participate. The extension of the community may be merely agglutinative— expanding the number of participants within the context of existing institutions—or it may be revolutionary, involving a redistribution of power. Presumably democratic societies are characterized by the possession of ideological and institutional mechanisms that permit the expansion of community in accordance with the ability of claimant groups to fulfill certain membership conditions, understanding the necessary adjustment of institutions within the effective community.

Ideological conflict draws from the distinction that can be made between values and ideologies. Ideological conflicts involve disputes referring to articulated and politically relevant polemical thought. These disputes may be a part of broader value conflicts when, for instance, protagonists deny their opponents the quality of being part of the same nation (as was the case with McCarthyism in the United States), or they may be used to limit debate to a level below fundamental beliefs, for instance, when liberals and conservatives argue over policy issues but do not question the right of each to participate in the body politic.

Interinstitutional conflicts arise out of the values that individuals place on the importance of specific institutions. As Silvert's research demonstrated, in different groups within a given society, different institutions were more important. This led him to postulate that "people's persistence in holding on to their individual views of institutions produces a hierarchy of intensities and attitudes concerning them" (Silvert 1970, p. 75). In a country such as the United States, Silvert assumed that the institution of politics is the focus for disagreements concerning the ordering of institutions. Recent history suggests the validity of that hypothesis: there is a whole order of dispute regarding health care delivery that centers on the relationship between religious beliefs and the desire to ensure universal health insurance coverage. Interinstitutional conflicts can easily escalate to involve definitions of community and values, but they can also focus entirely at the level of the relations between institutions, for example, the role of the government in subsidizing or stimulating the economy.

Intrainstitutional conflicts are the most frequently observed and the lowest in the hierarchy of conflicts. These relate to the dispute between interests within the context of a given institution. Although it is the lowest level of conflict, the cumulative effect of intrainstitutional conflict may be as significant as that of higher levels. The history of settlement of these disputes suggests whether change is possible within the scope of existing institutions or whether it must be imposed from the outside. A major premise of Silvert's discussion is that as the level of conflict steps outside institutional bounds, the likelihood of societal disintegration increases. Conflicts expand to include definitions of the role of institutions; the extent of the national community all the way up to conflicts over fundamental values. The aim of democratic politics ought to be to look to resolve conflicts within the bounds of existing institutions.

A key part of the resolution of intrainstitutional conflict is the ability to compromise, an ability not available in all situations, resulting as a consequence of the possibility of escalating the level of conflict. We can see that close at home. Observers of current politics in the United States repeatedly comment on the loss of the ability to compromise that has affected our legislative process and the consequent inability of the Congress to act on major issues.

A Framework for Prediction

The framework for analysis and prediction that Silvert developed is extremely useful in examining current political change. We can see its value by looking at current events and by examining the trajectory of political development in the specific case of Chile. In recent years, we have witnessed many of the kinds of breakdowns that Silvert postulated when he put together his typology. When politics takes on the form of street demonstrations and confrontations with authorities, it is a certain sign that the institutional framework for the resolution of conflicts no longer works effectively. This is the point at which Silvert would have suggested that conflict was moving toward broader levels. We can start with the Arab Spring, which in its manifestations in Tunisia and Egypt demonstrated that if state institutions are not responsive to basic demands of a nation, the institutions may need to bend if not break to accommodate those demands. In the case of Tunisia, after a certain degree of delay and prevarication on the part of the leadership, there has been movement toward reestablishing a political process that accedes to the desire of the population while establishing an institutional framework for a more open participatory polity. In other words, there has been the resolution of what amounted to a community conflict (who gets to participate) that was resolved by reforming national institutions to ensure greater openness and participation.

In the case of Egypt, the opening provided by the demonstrations that centered in Cairo's Tahrir Square (January–February 2011) created the impetus for the end of the military-backed Hosni Mubarak regime, which had used the trappings of democracy to legitimize itself but was in fact an authoritarian regime. The key players in this overthrow were the participants in the demonstration and, more important, the military, which ended its backing of Mubarak. What had begun as a dispute over service delivery rapidly escalated to becoming a demand for system change—in effect moving rapidly up the conflict scale to become one of values and community. The result was the first set of free and fair elections in Egyptian history with the winner the Muslim Brotherhood, an Islamist political party that had as part of its platform increasing the role of Islam in Egypt's institutions.

However, the Muslim Brotherhood government did not recognize the limits of its mandate and was seen as imposing a sectarian regime, losing a portion of its public support and undermining its ability to control the one major institution outside the established institutional framework: the military. In effect, although the Muslim Brotherhood was legitimized through the political process, it moved beyond the protection afforded by that legitimation by promoting what amounted to community and value-level conflicts. With the takeover of the political process by the military (July 2013), there has been a rapid descent into an authoritarian regime, cloaked again with the trappings of democracy but little of its substance. For the Muslim Brotherhood, there is a clear value conflict with the new regime from its outset. With the secular forces supporting democracy that played a key role in Mubarak's ouster, there is an emerging value conflict with the new regime as it reveals its antidemocratic character. Value conflicts cannot easily be healed. They are rooted in beliefs that center on expressive institutions such as religion and are particularly intransigent because they reach so far into a person's self-definition. It is safe to say that this conflict model suggests long and difficult struggles, barring effective but unlikely international intervention, to move once again toward a working democratic government, one that would need to focus on binding Egyptians together in a political order that reduces the saliency of value differences.

Repairing Value Conflicts

Value conflicts are difficult to repair. They can remain even if they are latent. As Silvert and Reissman's empirical study of Chile and Venezuela demonstrates, there is a likelihood in any country of widespread distribution of values among its citizens. The essence of the approach to take is to reduce their saliency in political discourse and political action by containing the level of conflict within the norms of effective political institutions. Some examples suggest this is possible. One such example is Chile, which has demonstrated success as an economic power and in developing a pragmatic political process. However, the road to achieving that success has been long and difficult.

In 1973 Chile was clearly in the throes of a value conflict. The Popular Unity government led by Salvador Allende,[8] elected democratically in 1970, had sought to increase economic participation by the working classes through nationalization and land reform, which followed and expanded on earlier attempts by predecessor governments. It met with a fierce opposition, which believed that the democratic process was invalid because it had produced a result that it deemed unacceptable: victory for the left. The opposition grew as the Allende regime was not able to deliver the short-term benefits it had hoped would be possible. The opposition fostered a value conflict with supporters of Popular Unity that in turn legitimized the military intervention that took place in September 1973. The violence of the military repression of political parties and government officials associated with the Allende regime demonstrated the intensity of that conflict—the military dehumanized their opponents, categorizing them, as one coup leader declared, as a cancer to be extirpated from the body politic. Thousands were killed, and thousands more driven into exile or imprisoned. The divide within

Chilean society after the coup looked to be irreparable. But to anticipate the story's conclusions, the value conflict that was patently obvious in 1973 is no longer salient in 2016. That is not to say that there are not value differences among Chileans, but those differences are no longer the stuff of everyday political discourse, and the disputes that arise are dealt with within the framework of the existing and increasingly more democratic institutions.[9]

The basis for the transformation can be found in the efforts to rebuild a democratic consensus, especially the efforts that centered on the opportunity afforded to the opposition by the plebiscite of 1988. The military dictatorship and above all its leader, General Pinochet, felt secure in their control of the country in 1988 and decided (as they had written into their constitution) to hold a referendum that would ratify Pinochet's mandate as president or alternatively end their control of the government. (A "yes" vote ratified the continuance of Pinochet in office as president, whereas a "no" vote ended his term in 1990.) Pinochet and his supporters were certain they dominated the media and the electoral mechanism. And they believed they faced an opposition divided by ideologies and a history of internal confrontation. As Ricardo Lagos, then a leader of the opposition and afterward president of Chile, expressed it:

> By 1988, the junta was no longer murdering dissidents. It didn't have to. To live in Chile at that time was to live in fear—not abject terror, but the low lying, constant stress of peril that puts a person always on edge. If you were a young man in Santiago, you could be grabbed by the military at any time and asked to prove that you were loyal to the regime. As a businessman or an intellectual, your work could be monitored, and strangers seem to know a bit too much about you for comfort. There were rumors of cameras in the voting booths, watching to see which box you ticked. What was true or not about the regime's presence in Chileans' lives was almost irrelevant; fear made everyone a believer. (Lagos 2012, p. 2)

Despite that atmosphere, the leadership of the opposition from across the political spectrum came together to conduct a campaign designed to (1) register as many Chileans who had not previously been on the voter lists as possible, and (2) use the limited access they were accorded to the media to convince their fellow countrymen to vote against acceptance of a continuation of the authoritarian regime. This "Campaign for No"[10] succeeded despite the obstacles it faced. Out of the effort to win the plebiscite and control of government afterward, the opposition formed a coalition of political parties, which, like all coalitions, represented a series of compromises regarding program and strategy, compromises that were embodied in the political alliance that took the name of the Concertación.[11] Formation of the Concertación required overcoming decades of infighting among the political parties that involved significant ideological and even value differences. The recognition of the political opportunity at hand (peaceful transition out of a dictatorship) coupled with the long history of enduring a dictatorship was a powerful tool in building a coalition.

After 1991 when it took control of the government in the first free election after the end of the Pinochet regime, the Concertación was able to win the presidency four times in a row. But the Chilean democratic process has permitted a viable opposition. In a significant demonstration of the openness of the democratic process, the opposition to the Concertación won the fifth election since the end of the dictatorship, and then lost to the successor to the Concertación in the 2013 presidential election. The value conflict that was so evident in 1973 is not the focus of the current political process. The political dialogue remains within the bounds of the appropriate institutions. There are indications of institutional weakness in the form of student demonstrations over the past several years, but these are certainly not threatening to the underpinning of the political process. In short, the breach that undermined the political process more than thirty years ago has mainly been healed by a concerted effort to maintain a democratic political dialogue in spite of political differences and in recognition of the danger that political extremism can represent to that democratic process. Chile is not without political strife, but its democracy is no longer threatened with destruction.

The Future of Democratic Politics

Silvert's overriding concern in his academic work was to provide the keys to building more democratic polities. He sought to define the forces that promoted democracy and understand the forces that threatened and destroyed it. He had found reasons for optimism as a result of his research through the power of education to shape rational values, but he also identified forces that limited that optimism. These included the widespread existence of values that undermined democratic practices and the institutional working of many governments, including limited access to opportunities for the less advantaged. His many insights into the forces sustaining those that supported democracy and those threatening it remain valid today.

As his research demonstrated, education—above all the passage through secondary education—builds the value set most supportive of democracy. The content of that education appears to be far less important than the fact of education itself. Expansion of educational opportunities, which is taking place throughout the world, bodes well for the future of democratic development. But to be effective in promoting democracy, that expansion needs to overcome the class and ethnic barriers that limit access to secondary education. Secondary education is the principal site, as Silvert's empirical research demonstrated, where values move toward those supportive of democracy.

In developing the concept of nationalism as a social value referred to early in this chapter, Silvert made an in-depth analysis of the meaning and analytical value of nationalism. That analysis assists us today in understanding the forces at work in various parts of the world. In Russia, one sees the growth of the kind of xenophobia that Silvert identified as associated with the use of nationalism as an ideology. He predicted that nationalism of the sort currently being exhibited by Russia in its relationships with Ukraine, and earlier Georgia, restricts the freedom of others to build their own national power and identity just as it enhances the likelihood of authoritarian rule in a country bound up in such xenophobia. Nationalism in effect becomes a reason for the sort of irredentism that Russia displays toward its neighbors, coloring its external relations. At the same time, although it does play the role of a populist unifying force for ethnic Russians, this rabid nationalism serves to justify the limitations that are placed on minorities within the country (e.g., the Chechens) and as a means of justifying limitations in freedom of expression for all Russians.

The democratic political process remains at risk where value and ideological conflict overcomes institutional arrangements for political decisionmaking. There are too many cases where intractable conflicts appear over religion, over the definition of community, and over the rights of one group against another. Defining the community by a person's religion or by his or her ethnicity, gender, sexual preference, and other arbitrary criteria or excluding people because their beliefs do not fit with yours constitute threats to democratic development. The broad repugnance toward the actions of the Islamic State in the Levant is in large measure a reaction to a political group that takes its religious beliefs to the extreme—demonstrating total intolerance of other religions and even of adherents to somewhat different versions of their own faith, denying all others the right to their beliefs.

Stated in Silvert's terms, the active involvement of certain personality types such as those he labeled organicists in the political process of a country makes the possibility of democracy far less likely if not impossible. Looking at today's political scene, he would have likely predicted that an Afghanistan torn by cleavages based on value and community conflicts and populated by organicists of the sort that make up the Taliban, of ethnic groups that historically have demonstrated only limited tolerance of others, and of a weak nation-state that never effectively integrated its citizens into a national society was unlikely to produce a stable democracy. Silvert also pointed out the need for building the institutional and ideational basis for compromise as a tool for maintaining conflicts within manageable limits. Recent events point to an attempt to build a power-sharing arrangement in Afghanistan that crosses community lines at the highest level—the resolution of the presidential race between a Pashtun and a Tajik leader. It remains to be seen whether this remedy—one that did not directly address issues of value and community conflict—can preserve the democratic content of Afghanistan's political order.

Generating Compromise out of Conflict

Silvert believed that Lincoln's rhetoric was wrong. A nation can live as half free and half slave if slavery meant poverty and lack of government services. A clear example of this can be seen in the case of Colombia. A quick overview of that nation's history points to significant contradictions in its political order. Colombia has a long record, stretching back to 1958, of uninterrupted formal democratic representative government. It has a strong executive and a Congress that is one of the more effective ones in Latin America. Its most recent constitution, written in 1991, calls for a degree of citizen participation and reinforces a process of decentralization that is considered one of the better examples in the continent. Colombia is a nation of significant urban centers, several of which (such as Bogotá, the capital, and Medellín) can be considered quite modern. Bogotá, for example, is connected to the broader global society.

At the same time, Colombia remains caught in a protracted conflict that has lasted almost four decades, a conflict that has been generated by guerrilla movements and spawned vigilante groups (referred to as *paras* or *auto-defensa*) that have controlled large stretches of rural areas and even reached to the outskirts of its major cities. Over the past decade, Colombia has been the principal cultivator of coca and opium poppies and the largest producer of cocaine and heroin in the Americas. Drug production and trafficking has fueled the conflict in recent years, providing the financial resources required by both guerrilla groups and paras to maintain their respective military forces.

The background to all analysis of Colombia's politics needs to be the continuing internal conflict that has divided the country into different "universes of occurrence." The principal problem facing Colombia is that politics there operates in two distinct such universes. One universe, which we can call *institutionalized Colombia*, is characterized by a representative democracy, with relatively well-functioning institutions (although not without their problems), possessed of liberty of expression, a general respect for human rights, a high degree of democratic competition, state presence, and social investment. This universe, largely urban, has a high degree of socioeconomic polarization but within a framework of a set of operating institutions. The other universe, *Colombia in conflict*, possesses little if any space for democratic process; rather, it is dominated by a continuing conflict, by the imposition of governance by force, and by the lack of freedom of expression. There is little state presence, little in the way of democratic competition. In fact, the force exercised by armed bands (guerrillas, auto-defense forces), which do not recognize the rules of democratic governance, stifles competition.

The current president, Juan Manuel Santos, backed by a popular mandate, is seeking to end the overt conflict between state and guerrilla movements while also expanding efforts by the state to extend its effective presence into all parts of the country. The key to ending the conflict has been a willingness to reach an agreement first with the principal guerrilla movement, the Fuerzas Armadas Revolucionarias de Colombia (Revolutionary Forces of Colombia) and then with the Ejército de Liberación Nacional (National Liberation Army). The essence of those negotiations is the willingness to compromise on the part of the government and the guerrillas. Defining that compromise has been a long and difficult process, but it is slowly being achieved. The underlying assumption is that it is time to make peace, to build a more complete nation. With that assumption comes an effort on the part of the government to build new institutional relationships that include central government reform, processes of more effective decentralization, and greater transparency in governance.[12] In short, this is the sort of nation-building effort that Silvert would have both admired and supported.

Silvert believed that if people are to live in a democratic polity, there is an imperative to build the possibility of compromise even in the most difficult of situations. As he stated in the conclusion to his last book, referring to the United States but certainly with implications elsewhere:

> If democracy is our choice, then the only direction is toward it and the only way is freely—building organized power through new and established institutions, and making a conscious attempt to think our way through the situation. We probably need less of the power component of democracy than we do of the knowledge factor, for we are still in many ways a free society, an exciting and open one. What we lack, by and large, is the habit of thinking about action in a democratic manner. (Silvert 1977, p. 131)

Over and over again, we have seen people in settings as disparate as Eastern Europe, the Middle East, and Hong Kong risk their freedom and their lives for the right to think and behave democratically. If building democracy is our goal, we need to encourage these efforts to broaden citizen participation and assist in building the institutional supports that enhance rationality and promote compromise. Building the institutional framework for democracy, as Silvert suggests, is about educating a broad section of the population to think rationally and accord that privilege to others. It is a long and at times difficult process, but the rewards make it a worthwhile endeavor—a more democratic future for all who desire it.

Notes

1. Silvert (1977). Silvert saw this book as a polemic that argued for the value of reason, thoughtfulness, and courtesy in promoting democracy.
2. Silvert, "The Strategy of the Study of Nationalism," in Silvert (1963), pp. 3–38. This chapter lays out his analysis of the various concepts of nationalism in the literature.
3. Silvert (1954, 1961, 1977). The first is a monograph on the nature of the government in Guatemala and the other two are collections of writings drawn from his extensive observations of politics and society in Latin America, in part a product of his years spent working and reporting in almost all of the countries of the region.
4. This study was originally undertaken in collaboration with Frank Bonilla, who subsequently withdrew from the authorship of the final report.
5. The sample and its diversity are described in Silvert and Bonilla (1961), pp. 1–29.
6. In Chile, the four locales were Santiago (the capital) Antofagasta, Chillan, and La Molina. In Venezuela, the four locales were Caracas,

Barquisimeto, Maracaibo, and Ocumare del Tuy. For a discussion of the sampling approach see Silvert and Reissman (1976), pp. 188–89.

7. For a fuller discussion see Chapter 1, "Elements of Politics," in Silvert (1970).

8. Unidad Popular in Spanish. The government included socialists, communists, radicals (representing the Chilean political center), and parties drawn from the left and youth wings of the Christian Democratic tendency (MAPU and Christian Left).

9. Since 1989, Chileans have eliminated many of the antidemocratic features of the constitution they received from the military. They have also begun to experiment with alternative approaches to participation, including automatic registration of all eligible voters and an end to compulsory voting.

10. There is a considerable body of literature about this campaign, including the techniques used to get the public to understand the meaning of a positive negative.

11. The name can be translated as "coalition," but in truth it represents the notion of compromise, which was the underlying premise of the political alliance.

12. The blueprint for that effort is contained in part in a recent OECD report to the government of Colombia. See OECD, 2013.

5

Mentoring a Generation

Martin Weinstein

Perhaps Kalman Silvert's most important contribution and legacy are the many students and colleagues in the United States and throughout Latin America whose lives and work he touched in ways that exemplify the highest standards of teaching and mentoring. He imbued these students and mentees with values and standards that guided them as they followed their own successful careers. This chapter discusses what Silvert's gifts looked and felt like for those he mentored.

In the post–World War II period, the trajectory of US–Latin American relations and the study of Latin America in the United States intersected over such issues as democracy, human rights, the Cold War, and the independence and integrity of social science research about (and in) the region. Because of his intellectual prowess and institutional positions within and outside academia, Silvert was in a unique position to affect both the people who would study and teach about Latin America and the direction of policy and institution-building throughout the Americas. This chapter looks at his role as teacher and mentor in this process.

Silvert's teaching and mentoring were strikingly successful, even when his own writing did not always resonate strongly in the fields of political science or Latin American studies. He was certainly inspirational in the classroom, as is well documented in Peter Cleaves's interviews with Dartmouth graduates and my conversations with some of his graduate students at NYU, including Morris Blachman, Ronald Hellman, Joel Jutkowitz, and Tommie Sue Montgomery. Perhaps great teaching really comes down to great mentoring. In this arena, Silvert had a profound and enduring influence on students and colleagues. The chapter by Peter Cleaves and Dick Dye on his role in the Ford Foundation clearly demonstrates this in a nonacademic setting, one that was crucial to Silvert's ability to sponsor individuals and institutions that expanded and reinforced his role as teacher and mentor.

Silvert's greatest legacy as a teacher was to instill in his students the idea that competent research could not be conducted without empathy—the ability to put oneself in others' shoes or see the world from their point of view. For him, empathy was a lifelong guide for responsible professionalism by the researcher, especially when in the host country. One should constantly remind oneself to avoid distorting the reality of the individuals or the society being studied. David Brooks (2014) in a *New York Times* column captured the concept beautifully when he spoke of "the sea of empathy in which you swim, which is the medium necessary for understanding others, one's self and survival." Silvert taught that concept to his students to an extraordinary degree.

Along with empathy, Silvert stressed the need for competence. He felt that without competence, the scholar/intellectual could not be relevant. Competence was a combination of methodological training, voluminous reading, astute synthesizing of the materials and data, and of course, sufficient language skills.

Honesty and ethics were the glue that held all of this together. Honesty meant being aware of your own biases and respecting the data you found or were presented with. It also meant simply not lying about your work, which includes complete transparency concerning your funding sources and institutional affiliations. This last point was particularly sensitive in view of Project Camelot, a US Army–funded research project in Latin America that sought to uncover the dynamics of peasant rebellion. The revelations about the project in Chile led to an intellectual and political firestorm. Silvert correctly felt that Project Camelot had done serious harm to the ability of US scholars to carry out research in Latin America by putting a huge cloud over their funding sources and motivation. He devoted two full class lectures to the subject, and his preoccupation with its implications was apparent in his letters of introduction, written on my behalf to Uruguayan scholars including Carlos Rama and Aldo Solari, where he pointedly said: "No hay nada de Camelot en este hombre."

Once you got to know him outside the classroom, you saw another side of Silvert. You began to grasp just how much he did not just talk the talk but also walked the walk. He made it clear in class just where he stood on the political issues of the day and did not hide his feelings about fellow social scientists, but it was over coffee or at the apartment—salon or no salon—that you appreciated all that he was grappling with personally and professionally. What you took away was the sense that nothing should slow you down in the pursuit of your professional goals and nothing should prevent you from taking a position on public policy issues. You should never engage in self-censorship in your academic work or when acting as a public citizen. You should also admit when you got it wrong. Silvert had been naive in his assessment of US involvement in the coup in Chile. He felt that Chileans had managed to screw it up so badly and that the situation under Salvador Allende had become so polarized that US intervention was superfluous. When the facts demonstrated otherwise, he made a public apology at a large forum on Chile at New York University (NYU).

When I read the set of interviews conducted by Peter Cleaves (2013) with Silvert's students at Dartmouth, I was struck by how fondly they spoke about Kal's influence on them. Their comments on a man who had been their undergraduate teacher in the early and mid-1960s and who died in 1976, nearly forty years before the interviews, are a testament to Silvert's influence and continued impact on their intellectual growth, career paths, and the fascination with Latin America that he instilled in them.

What accounts for the remarkable endurance of his teaching and mentoring? There is no simple answer to this question. On an intellectual level, it was encyclopedic knowledge that impressed. Silvert combined that with a passion for his subject. Passion was good, but it needed to be tempered by reason and ethics. He called for ethical behavior on the part of citizen, government, and especially the researcher—thus his preoccupation with the ramifications of Project Camelot.

Silvert's "messages" were wrapped in a cocoon of music, food, anecdote, and most important, humor. His personality drew you into his world, and the legion of academics he trained and influenced frequently made Latin America their vocation and avocation. Silvert used music to emphasize the need to pay attention to details. Good musicianship was based not on how the note was started, but on how it was finished. He had his students read *Philosophy in a New Key* by Suzanne Langer (3rd ed., 1996), a volume that argued that music was the greatest symbolic abstraction of human communication. As Richard Morse put it in a reminiscence: "Dozens of young men and women throughout the hemisphere owe not simply a field of interest, but an intellectual calling to that avuncular pied piper of Tulane, Dartmouth, NYU, and the University of Buenos Aires" (1977, p. 507).

Silvert's mentoring was usually subtle and effective, but at times direct. He never dictated a choice to students. Instead, he counseled that the path they chose should be the one that led to more choices. After a suggested familiarization trip to the region in anticipation of my comprehensive exams and dissertation proposal at NYU, I returned to say that I had eight pages of a proposal on Chile, but something was happening in Uruguay that no one was writing or talking about: the rise of the Tupamaro guerrillas, social unrest, and economic decline in the supposed "Switzerland of Latin America." His response was quick and decisive: "Everyone and their mother is trying to get to Chile—go to Uruguay. Write up your impressions and a new proposal and get it to me."

The Cleaves interviews are replete with other examples of Silvert's teaching and mentoring. Walton Smith observed that Silvert's course on methodology was the only course notes he had saved from Dartmouth and commented on how Silvert taught his students how to read a book. For example, students often omitted the dedication, acknowledgments, and table of contents from their reading of a volume—to the detriment of their understanding of the work. Peter T. Knight became a Latin Americanist despite a huge investment in the Middle East. As he put it, "Kal had planted a seed in my head that was ready to blossom" (Cleaves 2013, p. 48).

Silvert mentored students in terms of career paths, life direction, and research. He was in a position through his post at the Ford Foundation to sponsor them indirectly by funding of their institutions or more directly through fellowship programs. These included the Foreign Area Fellowship Program and the Social Science Research Council, which received significant funding from the Ford Foundation.

Silvert also mentored by example. As Chris Mitchell has noted, Silvert was upset and professionally offended by NYU's arbitrary decisionmaking, especially on personnel matters, during its financial crisis in the 1970s. He refused to rubber stamp the draconian personnel decisions the administration was forcing on the Politics Department. He resigned from the Planning and Personnel Committee of the Politics Department in protest over the cuts being required by the NYU administration in light of the university's fiscal crisis. He also indicated that he would no longer vote in the department meetings since policy was dictated from above (Mitchell 2013).

When the rumors started spreading that the Marxist political scientist Bertell Ollman might be denied tenure because of his role in the anti–Vietnam War demonstrations on campus, Silvert told his graduate classes that he would leave NYU if Ollman were denied tenure. He felt that Ollman's book, *Alienation: Marxist Concept of Man in Capitalist*

Society (1961), was as good as anything that had ever been written on this subject and was the primary reason the Politics Department had recommended his tenure.

In the relatively short time Silvert spent at NYU, he salvaged the academic career of two individuals by admitting them to the Ph.D. program in politics after their unhappy and unsuccessful experiences elsewhere. They both went on to earn their doctorates, one of them with distinction. Silvert was more a European social theorist than a US-style social scientist. He was a Weberian in the European sense, as opposed to the interpretation of Weber he felt had been incorrectly fostered by Talcott Parson's translation.

He was a Weberian through and through, especially in terms of his approach to class as the amalgam of economic, social, and political position. Silvert taught in a Socratic style, that is, training the student to open up the question rather than providing the answer. He left it to students to interpret the facts. He gave them a platform on which they could go off on their own and learn, engage in research, and make their way in the world. He taught his students to think in new ways about social science. Thus, one did not look at an institution as a reified object, for example, the State Department or Congress, but as a "routinized behavior pattern." He taught the theoretical context guiding empirical analysis by skillful use of narrative—great stories punctuated with his terrific sense of humor. But Silvert could be intimidating in the classroom; he did not suffer fools gladly. This was equally true in the context of the university or the Ford Foundation.

The European-style salons that Silvert made part of his teaching and mentoring took place in Buenos Aires, Vermont, and New York. These encounters were indelibly inked in the minds of his students at Dartmouth, at NYU, and in Latin America as amply demonstrated in this volume. I met Enrique Iglesias, Fernando Henrique Cardoso, Guillermo O'Donnell, and Julio Cotler, among others, at Kal and Frieda's NYU apartment. These cocktails/dinners or late night sessions would sometimes end at Café Dante in the wee hours of the morning. Silvert would also occasionally have a make-up class at the apartment, where he would pull the books right off the shelves as he made reference to them or read directly from them.

Good teaching often involves performance. The class needs to be entertained, and this requires humor and storytelling. Silvert was a master at using vignettes to construct a larger narrative, which was frequently attached to difficult theoretical constructs or a discussion of seminal literature in the field. His sense of humor was keen and witty.

Gifted teaching and mentoring are acts that influence a student or colleague in an indelible manner. Silvert meets this test with flying colors. His encyclopedic knowledge, moral compass, and public citizenship helped make him a role model who infused the personal and professional lives of those he touched. One reason he proved to be such an effective bridge builder was his enthusiasm, perseverance, and moral commitment to Latin America. As Richard Morse trenchantly captured it, "The prima donnas of American academe are too self involved for the years of *convivencia* needed to cultivate cultural and human reciprocity with Latin Americans" (Morse 1977).

Silvert's institution building and mentoring extended to other institutions in which he was directly involved. His letters for the American Universities Field Staff (AUFS, a consortium of universities that put professors in the field to write country reports and share resources upon their return) are a delight to read. An edited version of some of his reports made up many of the chapters in *The Conflict Society* (Silvert 1961). When he became Director of Studies at AUFS, he was instrumental in changing the institution's environment—professionalizing the staff, suggesting themes to be researched, and recruiting the right people to do the work. Examples of these efforts include the volumes *Discussion at Bellagio* (1964) and *Expectant Peoples* (1963).

In a report dated May 1, 1958, Kal talks about his less than friendly reception at the University of the Republic in Montevideo, Uruguay: "Welcome to the Fold, Mr. Nixon, or, Ariel and the Dilemma of the Intellectual." In a brilliant analysis of the Uruguayan left's anti-imperialist and hence anti-US stance, Silvert tells the vice president to relax after his unfriendly reception in Montevideo. "Tchah, Mr. Nixon, don't be upset. It happens to all of us in Uruguay." He points out that "no man's competence, integrity, or motive are taken for granted if he is in Uruguay on an American passport." He ends the letter with this observation: "There is little doubt that Uruguay has national attitudes in ample measure but playing against it is its smallness, its over-readiness to ingest European ideas, and its physical isolation from the mainstream . . . the frustration of the anti-imperialistic intellectual here is a sorry thing to behold and his brusqueness must be understood in terms of this frustration" (Silvert 1958, pp. 1, 18). Here Silvert insightfully captures the rise of the Tupamaros and the Uruguayan society I later found myself studying for my dissertation research in 1969–1970.

After a sad trip to Uruguay in June 1974, just one year after the start of the dictatorship there, I returned to New York and had a long conversation with Kal. I told him the stories about the arrests, torture, and political firings. I told him that the situation was in some ways worse than Chile because Uruguay was so small and had only one university. My academic friends had all lost their jobs and were in deep trouble financially. He told me I was too close to the situation and too emotionally involved to be objective. He literally kicked me out of his apartment with these words, "I can't save everybody."

Silvert made a trip to Uruguay the following year and when he returned, he told me that I was right and that the situation there was as bad as or worse than in Chile. A few months after he died, I had a conversation with Jeff Puryear, who had been a program officer for the Ford Foundation in Chile. He asked me how my friends were doing in Uruguay, and when I expressed surprise by the question, Puryear told me that Silvert had funded them. Silvert was hired full-time by the Ford Foundation in 1967, and was consulting for them as early as late 1959 when he coauthored a report on Argentina with Alfred Wolf and Reynold Carlson titled "Ford Foundation Mission to Argentina, August–September 1959." In June 1960 he submitted a book-length report on Mexico titled "A Survey of Mexico." This document reads like a not very illuminating undergraduate text, but it contains some gems: "We may as well concede from the beginning that the intertwined subjects of social class and social mobility are contained within a stone wall of factual ignorance in turn surrounded by a moat full of the fungus of amorphous theory. In any rigorous sense we do not know what we are talking about, not only in Mexico but in most other parts of the world" (Silvert 1960, p. 89).

Silvert found the best response to the shortcomings in the insightful work of Max Weber. Whether in *Politics as a Vocation* (1966) or *The Methodology of the Social Sciences* (1949) or the other Weber classics that he made mandatory reading for all his students, he imbued his students with a definition of class as "the intergenerational carriage of power," while never ceasing to remind us that proper class analysis, à la Weber, required an analysis of the economic, social, and political position of the individual or group in question. The mentoring of colleagues at the Ford Foundation, including his insightful memos, led to a greater sensitivity to issues concerning human rights, academic freedom, and a deeper understanding of democratic theory and practice. Ford's significant and timely response to Pinochet's coup, including the placement of fired and exiled academics in US, Canadian, and European institutions and the protection of students and faculty that chose to stay in-country, was clearly influenced by the intellectual groundwork and increased sensitivities that Silvert nurtured at the Ford Foundation.

Silvert's lectures, like his memos at Ford, shared one thing in common: you had no doubt where he stood. He was unvarnished, as Lou Goodman observed, and this may have rankled some colleagues and some students. His demands for transparency by government, researcher, and citizen and his valorization of democracy as a process, not a product, left an indelible mark on the individuals and institutions he touched.

Silvert died shortly before he was due to testify before Congress on the political and human rights situation in Latin America. The coup in Argentina took place on March 26, 1976. Silvert died less than three months later, on June 16. After the 1973 coups in Uruguay and Chile, the pressure on him personally and professionally to aid the academic community in the Southern Cone built constantly, and this became psychologically crushing to him with the brutal collapse of democracy in his beloved Argentina.

In his tribute to Silvert at the memorial service held at NYU, Irving Louis Horowitz said: "Egotism was the enemy of intellect for him, and that made him a very special person: the target of wrath as well as admiration." He added: "It is no exaggeration to say that he was one of the few people I have known who knew as much about the societies he went to as that from which he emanated" (Horowitz 1976, pp. 10, 12).

Silvert studied and knew history, but he was always looking to the future: the future of his students; the future of Ford grants and the impact on their recipients; the future of the social sciences; and most important, the future of democracy. His focus on education was driven by his attempt to understand the relationship between the social sciences and the development process. He saw education as the key to development and as a necessary but not sufficient ingredient to ensure democracy.

Kalman Silvert was an unforgettable teacher and mentor who was as comfortable in Buenos Aires or Mexico City as he was in New York. His influence on Latin American Studies and US–Latin American relations through his roles as professor, foundation executive, researcher, friend, and public citizen were all enhanced by his keen intellect, humor, high moral and ethical standards, and deep commitment to the democratic way of life. It was a privilege to be his student, colleague, and friend.

6

Nurturing a Transnational Scholarly Community

Jorge Balán

This chapter deals with Kalman H. Silvert as a bridge-builder between academic and policy cultures across nations. I focus on his ability to communicate and act across different cultures to build a sense of community among social scientists and policymakers concerned with Latin America.

For Seymour Sarason, sense of community is "the perception of similarity to others, an acknowledged interdependence with others, a willingness to maintain this interdependence by giving to or doing for others what one expects from them, and the feeling that one is part of a larger dependable and stable structure" (1974, p. 157). For this sense to emerge across different cultures, there is a need for bridge-builders, people in a position of influence who have exceptional personal skills, including fluency in different languages and the ability to communicate clearly across scholarly and bureaucratic lexicons, seeking common understandings within diverse national, disciplinary, and organizational settings. Another such skill is the ability to generate trust—the capacity to be seen by others as an honest, fair, and reliable broker. Trust develops over time, through extended face-to-face interaction within informal settings, reinforced by public presentations and publications; it tends to grow as the messages become consistent over time.

Silvert became trustworthy to many key actors in the United States and Latin America within diverse academic, policy, and philanthropic circles. He was able to build a sense of community essential for the success of new organizations and networks in the field.

The period from the 1950s to Silvert's death in 1976 was very much in need of brokers and bridge-builders. The dividing forces were many and strong, yet new paths for collaboration across cultures were emerging in the social sciences. The overall climate of suspicion, tinted by the Cold War and the hegemonic position of the United States as a military, economic, scientific, and cultural Western power—only to be challenged by the several "miraculous" recoveries of its close allies in Western Europe and Japan—created shifting oppositions and new opportunities. Recent studies on internal politics within organizations such as UNESCO (Rangil 2013) and on the professional and institutional growth of the social sciences in Latin America highlight those cleavages.

The wave of democratization initiated in Latin America by the end of World War II achieved its peak in the early 1960s but then was reversed by a series of military interventions establishing authoritarian regimes in the following decade. Faith in economic development and the consolidation of democracy became seriously eroded while armed confrontations between governments and radicalized youth groups, often inspired by the Cuban revolution, occupied a central position in the political scenario. The social sciences gained visibility and professional status in the region throughout this period, within higher education and in government agencies, while social scientists became more vocal as analysts and actors within the national political scene of the major countries. Last but not least, social scientists participated very actively in the growing network of governmental and nongovernmental regional organizations within Latin America that strengthened regional identity and culture.

Silvert first visited Latin America as an undergraduate student at Penn. He went to Mexico for the 1940 elections. In 1942—soon after graduating from Penn and marrying Frieda—he was drafted for military service, spending the next three years with the Air Transport Command's intelligence unit in Africa. Sometime after his return, he considered becoming an anthropologist, following the steps of his mentor, Heinrich Albert Wieschhoff, a German refugee with considerable experience in Africa. But Wieschhoff left Penn to work for the United Nations, and Kal chose political science instead, earning a fellowship for travel to Chile to work on his doctoral dissertation. In the introduction to his 1948 PhD thesis, he acknowledged help from more than twenty Chileans in New York and Santiago, carefully indicating in each case title and position. He conducted extensive fieldwork in Spanish with little help from US scholars, clearly understood Chilean academic and political cultures, and built a local network that served him well a decade later when he returned to Chile.

In between, he took his first academic position at Tulane in the fall of 1948. After spending the summer of 1951 in Quetzaltenango, he returned to Guatemala for a full year in 1952–1953. The so-called democratic spring initiated there in 1944 was quickly coming to an end when Silvert completed the first draft of his book, *A Study in Government: Guatemala* (1954). This was the first opportunity to demonstrate his skills as a bridge-builder in the foundation of an organization with long-lasting importance in that country, the Seminario de Integración Social Guatemalteca. According to Oswaldo Hernández (2014), who directed the Seminario from 1963 to 1985:

> The Seminario was founded in 1954 under the presidency of Castillo Armas. It was born thanks to the initiative of Kalman Silvert, a gringo who had done research on the revolutionary government, the national congress's composition, and the democratic spring. While conducting his research project he found there were no academic publications dealing with Guatemala, so he started to compile documentation about the country and translated it into Spanish. We should be reminded that there was no academic community in Guatemala at that time. An additional problem was the government under Castillo Armas, an ignorant and mediocre military man. How could a project such as this go through without being suspected as communist? Silvert very shrewdly suggested the search for a respected member of the Guatemalan elite who would be trusted by the government. Jorge Skinner-Klee, a very conservative but well-educated person, was found to be a candidate, selling the idea that a documentary archive would enhance the regime's international standing. (translation mine)

From 1955 through 1962, Silvert worked under an arrangement between Tulane and the American Universities Field Staff (AUFS) that allowed him extensive travel in Latin America alternating with frequent lectures hosted by universities within the AUFS network. As Richard Adams (1976) indicates, this combination was particularly useful for Silvert to explore a variety of topics and countries of interest while becoming better known in the United States. Silvert aimed to sensitize the US intellectual environment about both the importance and potential of Latin America—at that time the relatively more developed of the "developing countries"—the study of which was at the bottom of the prestige ranking within the emerging field of "area studies."

Richard Morse's (1977) reminiscence is telling:

> When I was at Columbia in the mid-1950s someone began circulating to me the AUFS Latin American reports. In those days as in these, on-

the-scene reporting from the southern lands was not conspicuous for blazing illuminations. It was startling, then, to discover the fresh and authoritative letters of one "K.H. Silvert," identified as a political scientist who had begun his career at age nineteen by observing the 1940 elections in Mexico. The voice was fresh because it had its own language, rendered things directly, sliced through to issues.

I first met Silvert in Buenos Aires in 1960 while he was a visiting professor in the sociology department directed by Gino Germani. Silvert, who had been teaching sporadically in Argentina since 1957, offered a seminar on comparative politics. He had gained the respect of the first cohorts of mature students and young faculty who made up the core of the department's intellectual life. His teaching continued beyond the classroom in the many informal meetings at his home in Palermo (Buenos Aires), where students, faculty, family, and occasional visitors mingled (with considerable amounts of food and wine) to discuss political events during the troubled administration of President Arturo Frondizi, an intellectual politician fully identified with "development," the international challenges confronting President John F. Kennedy in the United States, and the hopes and concerns raised in the region during the early days of Castro's Cuba.

Silvert was a close and respected advisor of Gino Germani, the leading Argentine sociologist, and his staff vis-à-vis relations with US academia and philanthropy. The Ford Foundation from 1957 on had indicated an interest in initiating programs in Latin America, comparable to its work in Asia and Africa. In 1959 it sponsored the work of a visiting committee to the region that included three top-notch, Harvard-trained international economists with considerable academic reputation and experience with the US government.

Silvert, the fourth and most junior member of the committee, was a political scientist with extensive academic contacts in the region but low visibility in the United States. He was the only one who had not served the US government in any capacity, and he did not become, like the others, a US ambassador or high-ranking political advisor. The visit to Buenos Aires included extended conversations with Germani, the first foundation grantee in Argentina.

Silvert's reporting to AUFS during this period often focused on the university and intellectual life in the Southern Cone. *The Conflict Society*, first published in 1961, incorporated many essays that stand out as fresh and eloquent comments on higher education traditions and modernizing reforms in Uruguay, Argentina, and Chile in the 1950s.

Rereading them today, I am particularly moved by his candid

remarks about the drag of Argentine academic culture and the quality of his students in Buenos Aires. He writes: "There are few better ways of finding out about a country than to learn from one's students. And the ones I had were quite a treat: uninformed, badly disciplined, and mightily opinionated; but intelligent, eager, willing, faithful, and in some cases, no less than admirable human beings" (Silvert 1961, p. 174). Also, Silvert noticed caustically the biased perceptions of Argentine university faculty and students about their own institutions and academic life in neighboring countries or in the developed world. Clearly he pulled no punches, yet his writing showed empathy with reformers, a keen understanding of university politics, and considerable distance from the paternalistic attitude held by many other foreign observers.

In 1962 Silvert moved north to Dartmouth College and became research director of AUFS, thus extending his commitments in the United States while remaining involved with Latin America. The region was shaken at the time by a series of events: the Bay of Pigs failed invasion of Cuba (1961), the Cuban missile crisis (1962), Kennedy's assassination, the military coups in Brazil (1964) and Argentina (1962 and 1966), and the US invasion of the Dominican Republic (1965).

The boiling cauldron of political tensions within the social sciences concerning the role of US government agencies and philanthropic funding erupted in 1965 around Project Camelot. Social scientists in Chile invited to participate in the project—a rather grandiose set of studies supported by the US Department of the Army and designed to measure, predict, and control social conflicts that might lead to revolts and upheavals—declined to do so, all of them quite rapidly, thus raising serious doubts about the project's feasibility. Nevertheless, Project Camelot became a cause célèbre when the leftist press made it public and denounced the whole idea as political espionage by the US government. Soon thereafter, the Chilean government and Congress set up special committees to investigate the affair.

A careful review of the documents available reveals that thanks to this publicity, public opinion in Chile and elsewhere in the region became convinced that all US support for social sciences research in Latin America was meant to produce political information as part of the Cold War. Furthermore, it supported the idea that external support made any research subordinate to the interests of funding agencies that would impose research goals and methods to the supported parties whatever their nationality (Navarro 2011).

Silvert was in Chile at that time. He personally knew most of the key actors on the scene and thus could follow the events closely. It did not take long for him to write a scathing piece addressed to US readers in the social sciences community and in government. His perspective was that of a "participant observer," since he was conducting a study involving surveys that had to be interrupted like all other fieldwork touching on current issues. He wrote as an "engaged scholar," concerned with what was going on in Chile and in the United States, where open participation of US forces and undercover activities in Vietnam had become hot political issues that would frame the reading of US involvement in the developing world until the end of the Cold War.

"American social science is in a crisis of ethics," wrote Silvert, but "American social science is not broadly aware of any particular problem." Area studies, in Latin America and elsewhere, posed issues that may have seemed marginal to mainstream social scientists in the United States, since the broader ethical issues regarding the candid disclosure of sources of support, governmental or otherwise, were not typically subject to open review in American academia. There was no agency, such as the National Science Foundation in the natural sciences, performing a brokerage function between government and social scientists regarding these issues, and there were no consistent public debates on academic objectivity and public policy, as was the case in physics. The result, argued Silvert, is that social scientists had crossed the lines separating academia from policymaking subject only to their personally held standards of conduct. Things were made more complicated working abroad, not just because of nationalism and local sensitivities but also because academic competence was at stake: area studies were a recent and relatively weak segment within the social sciences with poor or nonexistent representation in the more prestigious academic departments, as Silvert documented for political scientists with a Latin American expertise.

The lessons of Project Camelot guided much of Silvert's agenda in the following years, at the crossroads between research involvement in the region and the promotion of area studies by philanthropy, and public engagement with American higher education and the social sciences. In Latin America, he was already a well-known, respected, and trusted US scholar whose political views—clearly identified with liberal democracy—were consistently and repeatedly stated even if not necessarily very popular in the region. Julio Cotler, the noted Peruvian political sociologist, recently provided his own recollection of his interactions with Silvert during those years:

> My relationship with Kalman Silvert was built upon sporadic, infrequent meetings. Yet, we were able to establish trust, leading to a most

valuable intellectual exchange that contributed to guiding my academic life and, more importantly, to strengthening my democratic commitments. . . . During our encounters in different places we shared our concerns about the problems in the region, in particular the impact of the cold war upon the development of anti-democratic ideas and behavior. Kal's strenuous defense of liberal democracy threatened by these ideas in different contexts was the occasion for many harsh attacks by leftist Latin American intellectuals who claimed that the defense of those bourgeois values run against the possibilities for building true, direct democracy (Years later the military dictatorships would lead many of them to change their views). (Cotler 2012, translation mine)

In 1967 Silvert moved from Dartmouth to New York, becoming closer to the center of academic circles concerned with Latin America and US political life, as a senior professor in politics at New York University and director of the graduate program in Latin American studies, while doubling as social science advisor for international programs with the Ford Foundation. My own career brought me close to him again between 1968 and 1971, when I was appointed as an assistant professor of sociology at New York University—becoming interim director of the Latin American program when Silvert took a one-year sabbatical—and then as a project specialist with the Ford Foundation in Brazil between 1971 and 1973. In New York we also became neighbors and friends, living in the same NYU building. This proved to be more important and influential in my own biography than the formal relations at NYU or later on at the Ford Foundation.

I conclude with a word about the more informal environment at the Silverts' home, where I learned much about the world and also on coping with boundaries between the personal, professional, intellectual, and political realms. Kal and Frieda occupied a rather large apartment (by New York standards) in the Village. Space was essential because both worked often from home with their colleagues and students. Frieda was teaching sociology at City College and was often engaged in conversations with her German colleague, Marlis Krueger, leading to what became their book on radicalization of the student movement in the city's public university, *Dissent Denied* (1975). Kal often met after office hours with his students and recent graduates to discuss their work and other matters, since all were involved in the city's social movements as well as the politics of higher education. The Silverts' living room hosted a variety of organizing efforts in academic struggles, such as planning meetings in a forthcoming conference, and in antiwar demonstrations in the city streets, which drew extensively from the ranks of college campuses.

All sorts of visitors showed up for informal conversation around good food and drink in the evenings, not unlike what I had witnessed a decade earlier in Buenos Aires. Most noticeable for me was the presence of Latin American writers and social scientists who happened to be in New York. I got to meet personally more of them at that time than ever before. The usual conversation topics dealt with politics, society, and culture and easily moved between topics and across cities, countries, and continents.

The Silverts made no attempt to establish rigid boundaries between personal, professional, political, and intellectual concerns. Children and family would move in and out easily from these conversations. *Man's Power*, Silvert's book published in 1970, illustrates this perfectly. It is dedicated to his parents, "for teaching me that there can be no love without courage, and that there is no freedom without love." In his preface, as many authors might have done, he acknowledged the contribution of Frieda, who "has a professional and emotional hand in everything I do." He also thanked his mother-in-law, for "valuable suggestions concerning content as well as tone," and ended stating his belief that "families can be the scenes of intellectual as well as affective and emotional creation." Last, but certainly not least for me, the copy I'm using here bears a hand-written message saying "con afecto vecinal, de Kalman y Frieda."

7

Striving to Improve
US–Latin American Relations

Abraham F. Lowenthal

One of Kalman H. Silvert's primary goals was to help improve relations between the United States and its diverse Latin American and Caribbean neighbors. He was devoted to the national civic creed of the United States and inspired by the American dream, as Louis Goodman emphasizes (see Chapter 10). But he was also drawn to Latin America and Latin Americans, and he studied and respected the histories and cultures of the region. He emphasized that North America and Latin America had very different colonial experiences, demographic compositions, religious and political traditions, as well as institutions, and he underscored the asymmetry of various kinds of power between North and Latin America.

Silvert was not ignorant or naive about the power of vested interests—economic and others—and of bureaucratic turf protection, whether by civilian, military, or religious institutions; nor did he ignore racism and prejudice as factors shaping inter-American relationships. But he believed that the best interests, properly conceived and over time, of the United States and of the countries of Latin America were, or at least should be, fundamentally compatible. At its best, he argued, the United States is committed to human freedom. He contended that Latin American countries, as they modernized, generally shared this ethos and would generate larger numbers of citizens with attitudes and interests open to cooperation with the United States on common goals.

In the face of repeated examples of conflict between US policies and Latin American preferences, Silvert argued that the legitimate core interests of Americans, north and south, could and should be reconciled, and he tried to show how this could be done. He called for much greater efforts in the United States to disaggregate Latin America; focus on its many subregions; understand their different social structures, levels of national integration and of economic and institutional development; take note of their diverse relationships with the United States, and respect their sovereignty and independence. He urged Latin Americans to understand the plural and complex nature of US society and politics and to appreciate its political institutions, energy, and capacity for absorption and innovation.

At times, Silvert's faith in the fundamental compatibility of US and Latin American interests was sorely tested, but in his last years, he remained cautiously optimistic, and he tried to persuade others to reexamine their approaches to make cooperation possible. This was particularly evident in the role he took in the last two years of his life as a member of the Commission on United States–Latin American Relations (the Linowitz Commission) and by his spirited defense of that commission's report.

Silvert sought consistently to overcome ignorance, prejudice, resentment, fear, paternalism, immaturity, imposition, dependence (especially when self-imposed), dogmatism, confusion, and incoherence in US–Latin American relations. He saw examples of and reasons for these flaws on all sides and was not afraid to point them out frankly and often vividly to his compatriots and to Latin Americans. He advocated and exemplified competence, knowledge, and respect, as well as serious commitments to dialogue, political freedom, and above all empathy. Silvert's underlying political philosophy, normative compass, and analytic framework were guided by support for individual human rights, the right and responsibility of political self-determination, and the right to develop one's own abilities fully. His profound rejection of totalitarianism and "hypernationalist" movements that trampled on individual rights, from the right or the left, was central to his scholarship and his actions. It was also important for Silvert's evaluation and critique of US policies, particularly his advocacy of consistent US support for the protection of fundamental human rights, without unilateral imposition of US preferences.

Silvert's approach to comparative politics focused on nations and institutions, and therefore on governments and their policies. As an analyst and critic, he sought to understand why governments acted as they did and to lay down principles for more appropriate government actions and public policies that would better serve the interests of people throughout the Americas. He analyzed the roles of actors beyond governments: political leaders and followers, corporations and trade unions, soldiers and priests, students, and especially scholars and intellectuals. His own activities enhanced the influence of nongovernmental organizations, civil society institutions, philanthropic foundations, professional associations, leadership forums, study groups, and commissions. In his expanding work in these sectors, Silvert went well beyond his role as scholar, but he always remained true to the values and procedures of academia.

Silvert became an influential actor in Western Hemisphere relations, respected in Latin America and in the United States by fellow scholars, politicians, government officials, public intellectuals, and opinion shapers and by the foreign policy establishment of the United States. From the late 1950s until his sudden death in June 1976, he was widely recognized both as an academic authority on Latin America and increasingly during his final decade as a player in US–Latin American relations. Silvert's multiple professional activities in the last years of his life—in New York, Washington, US academia, and throughout Latin America—made him a central figure, whose great contributions were abruptly cut short by his fatal heart attack.

Early Scholarship on Latin American Politics and US–Latin American Relations (1948–1959)

After completing his PhD dissertation on the Chilean Development Corporation, a significant institutional effort at modernization undertaken after Chile's 1939 earthquake, Silvert in 1951 began a research project on Guatemala and its 1944 reformist government. He aimed to write a detailed treatise, grounded in extensive fieldwork, on how that country's political system functioned. His approach was guided by comparing Guatemala's experience with that in other countries then undergoing "Westernization"—as he and several others at the time termed what others were calling "modernization"—and in particular the emergence of nationalism as a force for social coherence and strengthening the role of the state as a builder of community.

A Study in Government: Guatemala (1954) distinguished itself from other monographs of that period by going beyond formal institutions, as Christopher Mitchell points out in Chapter 2. Silvert analyzed the intent and decisions of relevant actors on the basis of such empirical data as legislative debates; personal interviews with drafters of the constitution; quantitative demographic, economic, and social data; and insights from budgetary analysis and anthropological research. He looked beyond national institutions to study society and politics at the local and departmental levels. Importantly, he situated Guatemala's 1944 "revolution" squarely in the context of that country's history as well as that of the whole Central American region, rather than approaching it through the lens of US geopolitical concerns.

Silvert's 1954 monograph was insightful, well argued, and rich in relevant data. But, as Mitchell notes, it underestimated the continuing power of conservative elites in Guatemala, who ultimately played a role in bringing about the covert US intervention against the reformist government of Jacobo Árbenz, leading to his overthrow very soon after Silvert's study was completed. In a subsequent *Foreign Affairs* essay (Gillen and Silvert 1956), coauthored with anthropologist John Gillen and drawing on further visits to Guatemala in 1955 and 1956, Silvert portrayed the overthrow of Árbenz and the first years of the subsequent Castillo Armas regime as rife with ambiguities. The authors refrained from drawing any firm conclusion about the role and motives of the United States in the ouster of Árbenz, but noted that Latin Americans generally and vociferously attributed the coup and its aftermath to the United States, regardless of the actual extent and impact of its involvement.

In a subsequent essay, "Guatemala after Revolution," authored by Silvert alone in 1961, he observed that Latin Americans generally did believe the US government had intervened to eliminate the Árbenz administration, and he implied that the evidence to support this view was persuasive. He conceded that his own hopes immediately after the coup—that the overthrow of Árbenz might actually lead to further social reforms—had been dashed. In impressive detail, Silvert demonstrated a knowledge of Guatemalan society and politics that vastly exceeded that of the US officials who had made the decision to intervene in Guatemala to counter what some of them saw as communist inroads. By the same token, Silvert suggested that Latin Americans generally had shown no greater interest in understanding Guatemalan realities than had US interventionists, but they roundly condemned the US role nevertheless, and that "probably few of us in this country recognize the wave of resentment which swept [Latin America] with the overthrow of Árbenz."[1]

In concluding his report, Silvert suggests that "to win the propaganda victory, it is incumbent upon [US] policymakers...to demonstrate that it is really Communism to which we are opposed, and not liberal nationalistic development of what seems the inevitable and inexorable kind we are witnessing in almost all underdeveloped areas" (1968, p. 82). He understood and anticipated that US foreign policy elites would feel threatened by movements like those led by Arévalo and Árbenz in Guatemala. From an early stage, he argued repeatedly that the United States should carefully distinguish such nationalist and developmentalist movements from the ideologically rigid and hostile clients and followers of Soviet communism. Over the years, he was often disturbed by Washington's failure to do so.

From 1955 through 1963, Silvert broadened and deepened his understanding of Latin America by residing in and writing mainly about the Southern Cone countries—first Chile, then Argentina, and Uruguay. As a Tulane University professor and a faculty affiliate of the American Universities Field Staff (AUFS), Silvert took full advantage of the AUFS personal letter/report format to unleash his curiosity and powers of observation, his analytic capacity, and his expository skill on a wide variety of topics. These reports, more than thirty in all, helped him develop and demonstrate an extraordinarily well-informed and sophisticated understanding of social, economic, and political changes in Latin America; even six decades later, these sparkling essays make rewarding reading. They also developed and strengthened his conviction that to improve US–Latin American relations it would be critical to US policymakers to achieve greater understanding, respect, and empathy for Latin Americans, and to comprehend how and why Latin Americans regarded the United States as they did.

During this period Silvert also succeeded in getting to know and exchange ideas with numerous Latin American social scientists, as well as political, business, labor, and cultural figures. He began to build a significant network of friends, colleagues, and acquaintances that became part of his distinct professional assets and his social world, and helped shaped his outlook and his influence.

The Changing Context for Silvert's Work

Silvert's extensive subsequent writings and his evolving role in US–Latin American relations beyond scholarship were greatly influenced by the changing context in which his career developed. He began his professional work in the 1940s and 1950s, during a period both of anticolonial ferment and emerging nationalist movements around the world: in Africa, Asia, and in a somewhat different way in Latin America. His initial work on Chile and Guatemala focused on just such nationalist and developmentalist movements; he studied how aspects of Westernization took on particular characteristics in Latin America, owing to different kinds and degrees of economic and social change, varying social and class structures, and diverse political institutions and practices.

This was also a period, however, of growing mutual suspicion and hostility and deepening Cold War tensions between the United States and the Soviet Union. This rivalry took shape in Europe, Asia, and Africa. In Europe, nations liberated from Nazi occupation by Soviet troops confronted anticommunist states in Western Europe. Fierce competition emerged for the futures of Italy, France, Greece, Turkey, and Spain and for defining their international alignments. In Asia, communist forces took control of China and part of Korea, and gained strength in Vietnam and elsewhere, while India sought nonaligned status. In Africa, communist groups linked in different ways with many of the struggles for national independence.

By the end of the 1950s, pro-Soviet movements were also gaining some leverage in several Latin American countries, particularly in South America. Then, in 1959, Fidel Castro's 26th of July Movement took power in Havana and quickly began to assert Cuba's national autonomy. Cuba soon developed significant ties with the Soviet Union, at least in part in defensive response to US pressures, and won considerable sympathy in Latin America. The Soviet Union meanwhile was gradually moving toward a policy of material support for "wars of national liberation" around the world, a policy announced by Soviet Premier Nikita Khrushchev in January 1961. These tendencies, reinforced by dubious analogies and simplistic analysis in the US foreign policy community and by spinning worst-case scenarios in the US intelligence community, pushed Washington into an approach to Latin America by the late 1950s that focused sharply on countering supposed communist movements rather than supporting the nationalist and state-building tendencies that had captured Silvert's interest.

Silvert argued that the US policy establishment was ignoring important ways that Latin America differed from other regions. Among these were that most Latin American nations had much longer experience and identification with national independence than did Asian and African countries. Only a few Latin American countries had social structures that could provide many likely followers for socialist or national populist movements. Many Latin American nations were closely tied to the United States, compared with emerging nations in other regions. He pointed out these realities to those in Washington who were suddenly focused on Latin America's perceived relevance in the Cold War and to the new "experts" who were rushing in to fill the national near vacuum of expertise on Latin America (Silvert 1968, pp. 11, 34).

As a scholar who had already accumulated considerable in-depth experience in Meso-America and the countries of the Southern Cone, Silvert was flabbergasted by the poor quality of work on Latin America that passed for expertise as Washington's attention began to turn south. In commenting on Project Camelot, a study commissioned by the US Department of Defense to analyze the conditions leading to internal revolt and what could be done to contain or channel revolutionary movements in Latin America, he wrote bitterly about a "decade of amateurism in Latin America," prompted by the sudden US focus on the region. He skewered the

> increasing flow of Fulbright scholars as well as other highly trained and mature specialists [on other regions now] flooding into Latin America. . . . Some have never learned a requisite language; barely anyone has studied the cultures in depth. . . . Now the entire world knows that their technical shortcomings have an effect beyond their articles and books. They prevent other articles and books from being written; they bring disrepute to American academic life in general, and they mislead policymakers, thirsty for reliable information and imaginative analysis. The most pathetic result, however, is political. Many sympathetic Latin Americans who have been distinguishing between United States policy and other sectors of American life are now becoming convinced that they were wrong. (Silvert 1968, p. 155)

Silvert clearly understood that his own relations with Latin American colleagues could be adversely affected by the obsessive US turn to anticommunism; by the low quality, out-of-focus, and instrumental approaches of the new US analysts coming to Latin America; and by the growing appeal in Latin American university and professional circles of the Cuban revolution. His own dedication to Latin America and the motives of other US actors, including the Ford Foundation, were being challenged in the region because of the US response to Castro and because of the disclosures about Project Camelot and the exaggeration and distortion of that project by Latin American leftists (Silvert 1968, pp. 146–154).

Silvert's consistent emphasis on academic ethics, on collegial rather than hierarchical or exploitative relations with Latin American intellectuals, and the integrity of his own work, helped him navigate this period and indeed retain and expand his relationships and influence in the region. (See chapters by Balán, Cotler, and Lagos in this volume.) His own reputation and the quality and integrity of the Ford Foundation's programs and staff in Latin America, helped Silvert and the foundation build relationships that later became very important for preserving Latin

American social scientists and their work and helped make possible their contributions to democratic politics and the pursuit of greater social equity in Latin America.

Silvert criticized both the amateurism of the professors and journalists who were entering the field and the educational institutions that were training (or failing to train) them. He emphasized that little high-quality attention was being paid to Latin America by the best educational institutions in the United States, especially in the field of political science. He pointed out that none of the top-ranked US political science departments had a tenured professor of Latin American politics in the mid-1950s, and only two did so in the early 1960s. He lamented that the first response to this lack was to "retool" young professors who had studied other areas and issues, rather than develop a new generation of students and scholars well grounded in Latin American realities (Silvert 1968, pp. 155–162).

From this time on, Silvert devoted a considerable part of his immense energy to help strengthen academic expertise on and improve elite and public understanding of Latin America in the United States. He did this through his own writing and teaching, through supporting and advising institutional efforts to build centers for Latin American studies, through encouraging inter-American academic cooperation and exchange, and by numerous activities to enhance the quality of attention devoted to Latin America in a variety of existing institutions and newly established ones.

By the end of the 1950s, Silvert was already beginning to be recognized in the United States as one of the most insightful observers of Latin America. Fortuitously, this recognition came just at the time when US policy circles were becoming more interested in the region, mainly in response to the success of Castro's movement. This was the context in which Silvert first connected with the Ford Foundation, when he was invited to serve as a junior member of a study mission the foundation organized in 1959 to explore the prospects for and begin to develop a Latin American program at the foundation.[2]

Silvert's growing reputation also led him to be invited to provide a background paper on "Political Change in Latin America," analyzing the multiple implications of that change for the United States as well as the dangers posed by misperceptions or faulty understanding. The paper was commissioned for discussion at the American Assembly, a prestigious leadership forum affiliated with Columbia University. He joined Frank Tannenbaum, the venerable Columbia University professor; Herbert Matthews of the *New York Times*, best known then for his exclusive interviews with Fidel Castro in the Sierra Maestra; and Reynold Carlson of Vanderbilt University, a distinguished economist who later became the US ambassador to Colombia. Silvert worked with these experts and others to help shape the American Assembly report on Latin America of December 1959. The assembly report contributed to Washington's new thinking about Latin America, to the US government's acquiescence in 1960 to establishing the Inter-American Development Bank, and to the planning that produced the Alliance for Progress, initiated by the new administration of President John F. Kennedy in 1961.

Silvert's own contribution to the American Assembly's volume, focused on US responses to the "newly synthesizing societies of Latin America gaining the power to force themselves on world attention." He emphasized the diverse histories of these countries and their different trajectories, concentrating attention on social class and social structures, various levels of nationalism, and differing views of democracy. He made astute distinctions among the multiple ways force is used in Latin American politics; lucidly discussed the role of the armed forces in different Latin American countries, as well as the roles of parties, pressure groups, and ideologies; and knowledgeably considered the role of the Roman Catholic Church and how and why it varied in distinct countries and time periods.

He emphasized that

> The wide variation in the political development of the Latin American republics precludes the application of overly narrow rules to the processes of interpretive analysis and policymaking. . . . The modernizing elements in Latin America in general want revolutionary changes, whether with violence or without. The United States is modern in its views and skeptical of wrenching change. Latin American countries are in the early, romantic stages of nationalism. The United States is emerging into a cautious but firm commitment to internationalism. . . . The United States has often demonstrated itself insensitive to the currents of internal Latin American politics, as well as to the variety of solutions possible to these countries. Too often have we defined private ownership as equal to capitalism without taking into account the importance to the maintenance of our system of competition and countervailing powers; we have viewed expropriation as equal to socialism and nationalism as the same as supernationalism; the government authority of dictators has been treated as an honorable equivalent of legitimacy, and rote anti-Communism as full partnership in the community of free nations. . . . This . . . cannot be understood by narrow ideologists thinking in bromides. (Silvert 1968, pp. 33–34)

This was vintage Silvert: acute, conceptual, nuanced, vigorous, and committed to improving understanding in the Americas in both directions, south to north and north to south. His was a voice for inter-American cooperation, based on shared values and grounded in enhancing awareness of how the United States and Latin America were changing.

Silvert as a Public Intellectual, Philanthropic Executive, Profession Builder, and Establishment Figure (1960–1976)

Silvert became increasingly engaged over the next fifteen years in several of the networks in the northeastern United States where influential foreign policy discussions took place: at the Council on Foreign Relations, where he was elected a life member in 1966; the Brookings Institution; the Center for Inter-American Relations; and the Social Science Research Council. He began to take a leading role, working with senior colleagues in prestigious universities and at the Library of Congress, to develop a proposal to establish a professional organization for Latin Americanists; in 1966 this gave rise to the formation of the Latin American Studies Association (LASA), with Silvert as its first president. The founders' emphasis on building LASA as an organization of individual members rather than a consortium of universities and institutes reflected Silvert's focus on individual participation and expression.

Silvert's participation and visibility in these important networks as well as his professional influence through former students and mentees were facilitated by his move from Tulane to Dartmouth College in 1962, and then by his migration in 1967 from Dartmouth to New York City to become senior program advisor to the Office for Latin America and the Caribbean at the Ford Foundation and concurrently a full professor of politics at New York University.

During the last decade of his life, Silvert's influence and impact on US–Latin American relations came mainly from his roles as a public intellectual, a participant in the US foreign policy establishment, an interlocutor for leading Latin American social scientists, and especially an influential figure at and through the Ford Foundation, rather than from his scholarship. He continued to write and publish on inter-American relations and broader issues of democratic theory and practice, spurred by his growing concern about Latin America's turn to authoritarianism and his increasing anxiety about both the domestic politics and the foreign policies of the United States. (See Chapters 2,

3, 4, and 11.) Silvert's dismay at the US invasion of the Dominican Republic in 1965 and the Lyndon B. Johnson administration's deceitful justifications of that action; the covert intervention against Salvador Allende and Unidad Popular in Chile (disclosed by the US Senate Intelligence Committee's investigation in 1975); and the dubious assumptions underlying the Vietnam War galvanized his redoubled policy-focused efforts.[3]

Many of these diverse contributions beyond scholarship are discussed in other chapters of this book: his role as builder of transnational scholarly community (Chapter 6), as a philanthropic official (Chapter 8), as a valued interlocutor for Latin American intellectuals (Chapters 6 and 9), as a strategist and practitioner in helping build social science institutes and rescuing Latin American social scientists who later helped build transitions from oppressive authoritarian rule toward democracy (Chapters 8, 9); and as a public intellectual (Chapter 11).

Two other particularly important aspects of Silvert's contributions to improving US–Latin American relations during the final decade of his life deserve special mention. First, he played a vitally important role in the Ford Foundation's work to develop and strengthen Latin American studies in major university centers throughout the United States and in Europe. The celebration of LASA's fiftieth anniversary in 2016 is an appropriate opportunity to recognize his role and that of Latin American, North American, and European colleagues in developing Latin American studies as a significant multidisciplinary undertaking. Silvert's impact on Latin American studies in a variety of institutions during these formative years is evident in many universities, even where it is no longer remembered.

The second major area of Silvert's continuing influence is his impact, directly and indirectly, through his students and mentees and the institutions he helped strengthen on improving understanding of Latin America by policymakers and broader publics in the United States and on enhancing inter-American communication, cooperation, and exchange. He played these key roles through his contributions to the Joint Committee on Latin American Studies of the American Council on Learning Societies (ACLS) and the Social Science Research Council (SSRC); his increased activity at the Council on Foreign Relations, where he conducted study groups and nominated new council members, including this author; his role in the emergence and programs of the Center for Inter-American Relations, where he was an active board member; and his support for Larry Birns's initiative to establish the Council on Hemispheric Affairs (COHA), created in 1975 "to encourage the formulation of rational and constructive US policies toward Latin America"; Silvert also served as a COHA board member.

Perhaps the most influential of Silvert's efforts in this regard was his active role in the Commission on United States–Latin American Relations, established under the auspices of the Center for Inter-American Relations and convened in 1974 by Sol M. Linowitz, a senior Washington lawyer, who had been board chairman of Xerox and had later served as US ambassador to the Organization of American States in the Johnson administration. The Linowitz Commission, as it became known, was a nongovernmental undertaking involving twenty-three individuals convened in their personal capacities at the initiative of Linowitz as an independent, bipartisan group of private citizens. The commission's membership was blue-ribbon, including four university presidents, nine top business leaders, four prominent lawyers, the former president of the Rockefeller Foundation, the president of the Guggenheim Museum, and four prestigious university professors, including Silvert.[4] Several of the commission's members had extensive prior experience at high levels of the US government, and a number had major experience in Latin American and inter-American affairs. The quality, visibility, and personal influence of the commission's members were no doubt higher than those of any group, before or since, convened to address issues in US–Latin American relations.

The commission directed its findings and recommendations to the US government and the broad US public. The timing of its deliberations and public report were significantly affected by the knowledge that Linowitz shared with its members that a parallel high-level policy review was already under way within the US government at the instruction of Secretary of State Henry Kissinger, and that those involved in the governmental process were eager to receive the knowledgeable and independent analysis and recommendations of this highly qualified group. Silvert and others recognized that this initiative, its auspices, and timing presented a major opportunity to influence the thinking of US government officials at senior levels in the executive branch and Congress and broader concentric circles of policy influentials.

Silvert's aim was congruent with that of Linowitz: to bring Washington's understanding of the realities and stakes of US–Latin American relations up to date and into focus.[5] He invested significantly in the commission's work: he attended five of the six formal meetings of the commission, wrote a background paper and various informal memoranda, participated in subgroups, provided drafts for particular sections of the report, and reviewed and commented extensively on drafts of the entire report. He also participated in several programs to stimulate discussion of the commission's report and its recommendations and published a strong defense of the report, responding to a critique by Arthur M. Schlesinger Jr.

The exchange between Schlesinger and Silvert in the pages of the *New Republic* provides a fascinating window into the debate about the scope for and limits to liberal interventionism. Schlesinger criticized the Linowitz Report for insufficient attention to democratic values and to the Alliance for Progress as a defense of those values. Silvert strongly affirmed those values and the commission's devotion to them, but he defined the essence of the Linowitz Report's message as "a move from paternalism to fraternalism" in inter-American relations, and emphasized the commission's effort to create a policy that would

> oppose meddlesomeness, let alone interventionism, and that would yet be consistent with democratic aspirations in Latin America. . . . The commission thought it beyond the capacity or will of the United States to dictate what kinds of nations the Latins should build for themselves. We thought it enough to state that it was time to stop trying to hinder the building of national communities — in other words, to get out of Latin America's way, letting those countries find their own path to wherever they may be going. . . . If we can provide expert help, some money, and meaningful good will, then fine. But in no case should we employ covert or overt force of a military or economic nature to enter directly into the internal play of Latin American politics. We thought this prescription good for both the United States and Latin America, and therefore it could be the basis for a foreign policy of mutual self-interest."[6]

Although I was too involved in the Linowitz Commission to be objective, there is considerable evidence that the commission and its two reports—*The Americas in a Changing World* (October 1974) and *The Americas in a Changing World: Next Steps* (November 1976)—made significant contributions to public understanding, elite opinion, and policy formation on US–Latin American relations. The reports received significant attention in government and nongovernmental organizations, the media, and the academic community. They were widely credited—and blamed by others—for helping to bring about the changes in US policy toward Latin America undertaken by the administration of President Jimmy Carter, including its strong commitment to negotiating a new treaty relationship with Panama, recognizing that country's sovereignty in the Canal Zone; moving toward the normalization of US–Cuban relations; and strongly emphasizing the protection of human rights in the Americas.

The substance and tone of the 1974 Linowitz Report reflect Kalman Silvert's outlook and influence from its first sentence—"The United States should change its basic approach to Latin America and the Caribbean"—to its final paragraphs:

> The time is ripe for a new US approach to inter-American relations. Neither old rhetoric nor new slogans will suffice. A fundamental shift in the premises underlying US policy is required.
>
> We must base our actions in the future on the recognition that the countries of Latin America and the Caribbean are not our "sphere of influence," to be insulated from extra-hemispheric relationships. Nor are they marginal to international politics. Rather, they are increasingly active participants on the world scene, nations whose friendship and cooperation are of increasing value as we confront the realities of global integration.
>
> We must also recognize that the nations of the region are not homogeneous. They are diverse, with varying goals and characteristics, at different levels of development. They are not, and need not be, replicas of our country, nor do they require our tutelage. They are sovereign nations, able and willing to act independently, but whose interests in forging constructive solutions to regional problems will often coincide with ours. . . .
>
> The approach we suggest is based on the proposition that the United States cannot neglect, exploit or patronize its hemispheric neighbors. It is based, too, on the proposition that justice and decency, not disparities of power and wealth, should be the guiding forces in hemispheric relations. Both self-interest and our fundamental values require that we nurture our common interests and historic ties in the Americas, and that we cooperate in helping to build a more equitable and mutually beneficial structure of international relations. (Commission on United States–Latin American Relations, 1974, pp. 1, 53)

Concluding on a personal note, my own efforts to build the Latin American Program at the Woodrow Wilson International Center for Scholars and then to work with Sol Linowitz to establish the Inter-American Dialogue were rooted both in the Linowitz Commission experience and networks and in the formative teaching and example of Kalman Silvert. Like other contributors to this volume, I was inspired and energized by Silvert. His work continues.

Notes

1. See Silvert, "Guatemala after Revolution," republished in Silvert (1968), p. 80.

2. See Chapter 8. As Silvert pointed out, the Ford Foundation turned to Latin America only after starting its programs in Africa and Asia, just as *Foreign Affairs* added a section on Latin America to its quarterly book reviews only after covering all other major world regions.

3. See also Silvert, "Coming Home: The US through the Eyes of a Latin Americanist," in Silvert (1977, pp. 3–14).

4. Members of the commission, besides Linowitz, included presidents Alexander Heard of Vanderbilt, Rev. Theodore M. Hesburgh of Notre Dame, Arturo Morales-Carrión of the University of Puerto Rico, and Clifton R. Wharton Jr. of Michigan State; W. Michael Blumenthal, chairman of Bendix; G. A. Costanza, vice chairman of First National City Bank; Henry J. Heinz II, chairman of H. J. Heinz Company; Andrew Heiskell, chairman of *Time*; Lee Hills, chairman of Knight Newspapers; Nicholas Katzenbach, corporate vice president and general counsel of IBM; Charles Meyer, vice president of Sears, Roebuck; Peter G. Peterson, chairman of Lehman Brothers; Nathaniel Samuels, partner in Kuhn, Loeb; the president emeritus of the Rockefeller Foundation, George Harrar; the director of the Guggenheim Museum, Thomas Messer; attorneys Rita Hauser of New York and Elliot Richardson and William D. Rogers of Washington, DC; and professors Harrison Brown of Cal Tech; Albert Fishlow of the University of California, Berkeley; Samuel P. Huntington of Harvard; and Silvert.

5. Their aim also coincided with the goal of this author, who served as the commission's special consultant and drafted many sections of the report. In my research for this chapter, I found a five-page single-spaced memorandum dated April 15, 1974, that I prepared for the executive director, Arnold Nachmanoff, in advance of the commission's first meeting, suggesting specific topics and possible recommendations the commission might consider, with some twenty-five or thirty handwritten comments and suggestions on this memorandum by Silvert. Silvert had a major influence on the Linowitz Report, not only through his role in the commission's discussions and in the drafting process, but also because of his formative impact on my own thinking.

6. Silvert, "Turning Ideals into Reality: Democracy in Latin America," published in the *New Republic,* March 22, 1975, and republished in Silvert's posthumous volume, *Essays in Understanding Latin America* (1977).

8

Bringing Vision, Mission, and Values to Philanthropy

Peter S. Cleaves and Richard W. Dye

From 1967 to 1976, Kalman H. Silvert was the Ford Foundation's Senior Social Science Program Advisor for Latin America. This chapter covers this major portion of his career. It describes how his values, knowledge, and operating style influenced the Ford Foundation, promoted social sciences development, and contributed to democratic processes in the region. While Silvert was still in his thirties, the foundation asked him to consult on designing its approach for Latin America, which differed significantly from their "development assistance" in Asia and Africa. He eventually led the foundation's efforts to support local social sciences research and training centers. Fundamental to this effort was a modification of the relationship between Latin Americans and the foundation from clients to partners.

Silvert was a prominent member of the foundation's crisis teams responding to the Latin American military coups of 1973 and 1976. His outgoing personality and well-reasoned arguments helped maintain collegial relations with colleagues, even when they disagreed on policy. The chapter concludes with ways Silvert's history in the Ford Foundation provides lessons for other philanthropy professionals. His effectiveness was based on ethics, competence, intercultural empathy, focus in pursuit of excellence, and an ingrained idealism tempered by realistic expectations. The whole of his professional activities was consistent with an implicit theory of change.

The Ford Foundation in Latin America:
The Early Years (1959–1967)

From Asia and Africa to Latin America

Silvert's first association with the Ford Foundation was before its international activities included offices in Latin America. Understanding the foundation's orientation at that time is important for evaluating Silvert's later impact.

The foundation's Overseas Development Program began in the early 1950s in India, Pakistan, Indonesia, Burma, and the Middle East; the Nairobi office opened in 1962.[1] The foundation chose the term "representative" for the heads of these overseas offices and relied heavily on them to propose country- or region-specific programs. Support focused on assisting recently decolonized countries to cope with nation-building needs. This objective remained the case when the foundation added programs in Africa in the late 1950s and early 1960s. Operationally, the offices made extensive use of US and European technical specialists to work with and train local counterparts. Program priorities typically included higher education in economics and management, development planning advice, public administration, agriculture, and population. Areas of concentration were strengthening institutions and building human capacity. Regular back and forth occurred between the foundation's field offices and its New York headquarters; the foundation's upper management generally supported the initiatives proposed by local representatives. This decentralized structure later also characterized the Latin American program.

Launched in 1959, the Office for Latin America and the Caribbean (OLAC) faced two major challenges. First was the need to cope with a steep learning curve. Latin America and the Caribbean were significantly different from other world regions in their long histories of independence, their ethnic composition (indigenous, European, and African origins), and their complex and ambivalent attitudes toward the United States. This diversity required the presence of foundation staff who were broadly versed in the region and proficient in Spanish or Portuguese, as well as having the required technical competences. The reality, however, was that the foundation did not have these kinds of staff capabilities, nor were they readily available in US academic and professional circles.

Second, the program began at a time when Cold War competition was becoming increasingly significant in the region. While the foundation had approved grants in Latin America as early as 1957, subsequent to the 1959 Cuban Revolution, it was natural from a US perspective for a major national institution like the Ford Foundation to increase its regional involvement.

Program Management

In 1959, Ford Foundation staff located in New York managed the program. The early directors came from careers in US academia, banking, and Asia and Africa but without Latin America experience. They based initial grants on the recommendations of visiting missions, the first of which, in 1959 to Argentina, included Silvert. By 1964 the foundation had created a network of field offices in Argentina, Brazil, Colombia, and Mexico, with the later addition of Peru. Of the new representatives, only Reynold Carlson in Brazil had significant Latin American knowledge.[2] Harry Wilhelm, after several years in the Asia Program, was appointed representative in Buenos Aires. Though not a specialist on the region, he later played a key role in molding the Latin America program joined by Silvert.

The early program emphasis was on higher education at local universities and science and technology councils that funded research and graduate fellowships.[3] Economic planning headed the list of fields of study, followed by public and private management, population, and urban studies. Agriculture was prominent, particularly in Mexico and Colombia, where the Rockefeller and Ford Foundations established international agricultural research centers.[4] In Argentina and Brazil, graduate training stressed agricultural economics. The social science disciplines of sociology, anthropology, and political science received comparatively less attention (See Manitzas 1971; Bonilla 1971; Manitzas and Fagen 1973). One grant that concentrated uniquely on social sciences was to Santiago's FLACSO (Facultad Latinoamericana de Ciencias Sociales), principally supported by the Ford Foundation and UNESCO.[5] Another was a short-lived program of support for departments of sociology, economics, and public administration at the University of Buenos Aires. Such was the general program environment when Silvert joined the foundation in 1967.

Political Environment

The 1959 Cuban Revolution contributed to a rise in leftist ideology and activism throughout the region, primarily based in the public universities. Conservative regimes and military establishments pushed back strongly and received US support via the Alliance for Progress and military training and equipment programs.

These developments affected the Ford Foundation in ways that persisted throughout Silvert's tenure as Senior Social Science Advisor. First, the universities most affected by ideological struggles and often virulent anti-Americanism were among the ones where the foundation had begun its Latin America program. The *dependencia* (dependency) theories arguing for independent economic, social, and foreign policies in Latin America (and other developing countries) challenged US development models. In this context, the foundation was forced to conclude that especially in the social sciences, it was impossible to continue working with several of the most affected institutions, notably the University of Buenos Aires, the National University of Colombia, the Autonomous National University in Mexico, and San Marcos University in Peru. The foundation redirected resources and attention toward private universities and research and policy institutions, like the Torcuato Di Tella Institute in Argentina. Silvert much regretted the foundation's inability to work effectively in the large and influential public universities.

The second major impact on the Ford Foundation, one that plagued its work well into the 1970s, were suspicions in leftist circles that the foundation was not the wholly independent, private, nonprofit actor that it claimed to be. The view that Ford was an institution with close ties to the US government and the country's establishment elite raised questions about its role and motives. Silvert along with other foundation staff chafed at broad-brush allegations from the far left that they were tools of capitalism and the "dominant class."

A third major impact was the series of military coups that occurred in the 1960s and early 1970s, which in varying degrees affected the foundation's work. Military coups occurred in Brazil, Argentina, Chile, Uruguay, Peru, Ecuador, Bolivia, Guatemala, and Honduras. The effects were significant. Particularly in Brazil, Chile, and Argentina, academics were arrested, expelled from their jobs, or driven to emigrate. Others who chose to remain found their academic freedoms limited, requiring them to self-censor or collaborate to survive. As a firm believer in democracy, Silvert was deeply troubled by this trend and joined with others inside and outside the foundation in seeking ways to respond. Indeed, much of the history of the foundation in the region during his tenure, as detailed later, involved adapting its program approaches to confront these circumstances.

Promoting Competence in the Social Sciences

In 1959, Silvert was in Argentina on leave from Tulane University under the auspices of the American Universities Field Staff (AUFS). His AUFS reports were already widely read and admired.[6] The Ford Foundation took early advantage of Silvert's knowledge by including him in the initial 1959 mission to Argentina. Over a six-week period, he joined with Vanderbilt University economist Reynold Carlson and New York University nuclear chemist Alfred Wolf to review the foundation's programs. While concentrating on one country, the consultancy report contained the seeds of Silvert's assessment of developmental needs in Latin America and the basic concepts of institution-building and discipline-building that characterized his future foundation work. The section most reflective of Silvert's political thinking noted that the recently toppled Peronist government raised questions about the strength of the country's commitment to democracy.[7] He maintained a relationship with the foundation with a consultancy report on Mexican higher education. A measure of his prominence in this period is his major role in the 1966 establishment of the Latin American Studies Association (LASA), of which he became the first president.[8]

In 1965, Harry Wilhelm became OLAC director and subsequently made the decision to recruit well-regarded academics as Regional Program Advisors to coordinate the office's work in priority fields. The first such appointment was Lowell Hardin from Purdue University to oversee the agriculture sector. Other PhD-level appointees headed the Education and Population programs. Wilhelm recruited Silvert as Latin America Social Science Advisor. In that position, Silvert obtained a firm base to operationalize concepts he had developed earlier and promote his principles within the foundation and more generally.

Values Underlying Foundation Programs

From the beginning of his foundation tenure, sometimes stated and always implicit, Silvert's core values included democracy, empathy, equality, reason, and knowledge. These values guided his work with the foundation and appeared frequently in his recommendations, discussion papers, and analyses of the region and the foundation's role in it. Silvert believed that the foundation's first responsibility was to assist Latin American scholars in conducting research that illuminated the social sphere from which institutional actors could draw to formulate solutions to pereeived problems. More generally, he supported the view that a foreign entity like the Ford Foundation should dedicate itself to assisting the long-term development of Latin American societies by Latin Americans themselves. Both concepts became central to the Latin American program's work.

Silvert's academic prestige, intelligence, relationships with several leading intellectuals, and affection for the region were of great value in gaining acceptance of the foundation despite continuing suspicions in leftist quarters of Ford's capitalistic origins and North American provenance. His efforts helped build up programs in sociology, anthropology, and economics departments at more than twenty major Latin American universities, support doctoral studies for promising young academics, and finance Latin American studies in US universities and research entities.[9] He strove to introduce social science research into Ford's traditional population and agricultural grants, recommended funding consortia like the Social Science Research Council (SSRC) to provide graduate training and research, urged the SSRC to include leading Latin American scholars on its selection panels, and approved the staffing of foundation field offices with senior and some junior social scientists to support this mission.

His philosophic approach was groundbreaking, at least within the foundation. In his words, "social science research and the employment of research findings by policy-makers…is at the heart of our own development activities." But he warned that an academic who develops a policy proposal, defends it in the classroom, and then joins government to help implement it, diminishes greatly his or her claim to academic relevance.

> All social science inquiry is irrelevant if incompetently accomplished; all social commitment denying the particularity of the scientific enterprise in itself invites the incompetence that guarantees essential irrelevance; all politically motivated research that damages the autonomy and freedom of the professional task is also destructive of competence, and thus assures irrelevance.[10]

He argued that academics promoting their policy prescriptions distanced themselves from critical and independent examination of the same policy, stating that

> In our applied work, we must seek always to have our project officers stop short either of making specific policy recommendations, or sometimes even accepting administrative responsibilities for the policies they advocate. That is, our role should be that of helping Latin

> Americans learn how to amend legal systems toward development, plan the shape of their cities or their national economies, or how to employ modern management techniques—but not determine the ends for which these tools will be employed. (Silvert, "Draft of Policy Guidelines," 1969, p. 15f)

In sum, for Silvert, a "relevant social science...necessarily must be an *academic* one based on a *primary commitment to* the intellectual part of the task"—rather than policy promotion and execution. Stated differently, "concrete problems of development can be defined only within a theoretical system, and ultimately imply selections stemming from value commitments" (Silvert, "An Essay on Interdisciplinary and International Collaboration in Social Science Research in Latin America," 1968, p. 15; emphasis original).

Influencing Ford Foundation Policy

During Silvert's foundation tenure, his formal role was to advise the OLAC head, first Harry Wilhelm and then William Carmichael, of the orientation, content, and results of grants in the social sciences. Most of his written reports analyzed and offered suggestions on developing academic staff resources, budget allocations, and institutional and political relations. At the same time, he promoted a vision of social science research, publications, and training enriching a society's ability to continuously confront challenges, evolve, and advance. He believed that democracy was furthered when a society had an institutionalized ability to continuously make new choices.

These principles were summarized in the white paper "Draft of Policy Guidelines for Social Sciences in Latin America," (1969) and subsequently consistently drawn on in memoranda, evaluations, one-on-one conversations, and internal reviews. In 1972, Carmichael asked him to comment on the program strategies submitted by the three Latin American field offices for grants in their territories. While "sympathetic" to what the offices "thought" they were accomplishing, Silvert was frank in challenging whether they were operating with sufficient conceptual and operational rigor (Silvert, "Field Office Budget Proposals," 1972). To wit,

• "All the documents want to help Latin Americans solve problems. Not one defined what a problem is. ...We will be engaged in hollow verbalizing unless we decide what...we mean by 'problem-solving, problem- relevant,' and such other catchy words."

• "Many of the documents talk (about) helping the underprivileged. Not one defines the term, or resolves the conflict between the creation of elites...and help to the underprivileged."

• "Many mentions are made of the relative degree of maturity of at least some individual social scientists....But...no word appears about economic structuralism, dependency, the meaning of 'Marxist social science,' marginality, the evolution of the 'Chicago school' of economists. Are there specialist opportunities...for making something more out of dependency 'theory' than what it is?"

• "No paper asks whether what is going on generally in Latin American social science might be useful outside the region."

• "There is no mention at all of the quality of the social science program advisors we should have....The more expert the Latin Americans become, the more we will have to worry about this kind of question in our hiring."[11]

• "In sum, we are long on form and procedure, short on quality and substance."

Aside from upgrading the social science disciplines in Latin America, Silvert endeavored to infuse broader social science approaches into other foundation program areas, specifically population and agriculture.[12] In much of his writing and in frequent interventions at in-house conferences, he urged his New York colleagues to consider the wider dimensions of their initiatives in these fields.[13] To the degree he persuaded others to add a social science approach to their programs, he was able to state, "We regard our work in the social sciences as a critically important underpinning for our endeavors in all other rubrics, and we would expect to retain a major commitment to basic capacity-building efforts in that field well into the 1980s" (Silvert, "Budget Cuts Revisited," 1974, p. 8).

For Silvert, "population" issues called for interventions that went far beyond family planning programs and access to contraceptives. "It is illogical to seek to understand relative overpopulation by analyses that vary population size and hold constant such other factors as distribution and employment patterns, social classes, political systems...and normative predispositions" (Silvert, "'Population' as a Social Science 'Problem,'" 1972, p. 5). With congenial but persistent prodding, he encouraged his New York colleagues to consider these issues as appropriate for the foundation's Population Program in Asia and Africa.[14] For Ford's Latin American field office staff, interacting with Silvert, it became apparent that supporting Latin American scholars doing demographic studies encompassing structural causes of migration, gender studies, and family psychology were essential complements to family planning and population policy initiatives.

The Ford Foundation's Agricultural Program in collaboration with the Rockefeller Foundation found considerable success in scientific improvements for the yield of wheat varieties at Mexico's CIMMYT. These breakthroughs led to what was labeled the Green Revolution and an eventual Nobel Peace Prize for Norman Borlaug. Silvert acknowledged these gains but was concerned about the social consequences implied by changes in land tenure, employment relations, and access to finance for economically poor rural populations. OLAC launched a program in rural development to increase understanding of rural realities that would inform public policies to help subsistence farmers improve their livelihood. Silvert wrote "social scientists can readily describe and explain many facts of rural life critical for the professional work of the production specialist and the more subtle judgmental endeavors of the policy maker."[15] Advocates of the "agricultural" and the "rural sociology" positions sustained a dialogue inside OLAC without coming to a resolution on how to merge their approaches.[16]

The Crisis Years: Challenge and Response

Silvert was profoundly troubled by the overthrow of elected Latin American governments and by the crimes and abuses of the military dictatorships. When these regimes became authoritarian, Silvert was an active and effective contributor to programmatic solutions consistent with his deeply held values.

While politics in Latin America are rarely routine, Latin American governing systems at the beginning of Silvert's tenure at the Ford Foundation were relatively conventional. Elected governments were in office in Mexico, Chile, Colombia, Venezuela, and Peru.[17] While the Brazilian and Argentine generals had carried out coups in 1964 and 1966, respectively, the interventions were mildly repressive compared to later brutalities, and civilian rule returned to Argentina in 1970.

A more extreme situation presented itself in Brazil, however, with the promulgation of Institutional Act No. 5 (AI-5) of December 13, 1968, which sharply increased the regime's authoritarian control. AI-5 led to a brutal campaign against known or suspected opponents of all stripes, including scholars with ties to and enjoying the confidence of the foundation. After their expulsion by the military regime from the

University of São Paulo, Fernando Henrique Cardoso (the future Brazilian president) and colleagues approached the foundation with a proposal to create an independent center, which took the name CEBRAP (Center for Analysis and Research). The Brazil office approval was eventually confirmed by New York, but not without some internal opposition and reportedly also some resistance from the US embassy in Brazil. The CEBRAP grant in Brazil and the earlier grants to the Di Tella Institute in Argentina were groundbreaking in that the foundation, perhaps for the first time anywhere, was assisting and protecting groups that were known to be critical of the governments in question. In both countries, other aspects of the foundation's programs continued normally.[18]

In 1970, the Cold War spotlight shifted to Chile with the election of Salvador Allende, leader of the Socialist Party, and a government openly committed to "socialism through democracy." Allende's election caused great excitement among the left in Latin America together with concern in Washington. Following the Allende victory, the foundation retooled its office and staff in Santiago, under the leadership of Peter Bell, and added to its sizable program base. For the next three years, in the face of a steadily deteriorating political environment, the Santiago office worked in the social sciences predominantly through the University of Chile and the Catholic University, with projects in economics, sociology, education, and law. Silvert had a long history of involvement in Chile and close personal relationships with academics and intellectuals particularly within the Christian Democratic camp; he was an active participant in decisionmaking on social science matters and was supportive of the overall program.

In 1973, the situation changed abruptly, with virtually simultaneous political upheavals in Uruguay, Chile, and Argentina, which significantly altered the foundation's working environment for the remainder of Silvert's life.[19]

The demise of Uruguayan democracy, which was crumbling under the onslaught of the Tupamaros, a Marxist urban guerrilla movement, occurred on June 27, 1973, when the elected president, Juan María Bordaberry, abolished the legislature and transferred the bulk of power to a military junta. This de facto coup created a civil-military dictatorship, dominated by the latter, until June 1976 when the "civil" part was eliminated.

On September 11, 1973, the Chilean military under General Augusto Pinochet overthrew the elected government of Allende. The regime quickly became infamous for its extreme brutality and for the thoroughness of its assumption of supreme power in every aspect of society, including economic policy and education.[20] The result, in the opinions of Ford Foundation staff in Santiago and New York, emphatically including Silvert, was a movement toward creating a totalitarian state (Silvert, "Chile," 1974, p. 4).

In 1973, Juan Perón returned from exile and a new Peronist government in Argentina was formed under his leadership. When he died a year later, his wife, then Vice President María Estela (alias Isabel), became president and began a reign notable for its harshness, intolerance, and incompetence, aggravated by a plummeting economy and generalized chaos, including the rise of an insurgent group, the Montoneros, an Argentine version of the Tupamaros.[21] In 1967 this disastrous government was overthrown by the armed forces under the leadership of General Jorge Videla, whose government pursued repressive policies against the Montoneros and later extended them to any perceived opponent in the academic, political, journalistic and labor sectors of society, in a campaign known as the "dirty war."

The combination of these Southern Cone developments obliged the foundation to decide whether to remain or pull out of the afflicted countries and provoked a considerable amount of soul-searching in which Silvert was an active participant. Referring to the foundation's programs in Asia as well as Latin America, he set out parameters for a decision about whether to remain in a country ruled by a highly authoritarian regime.

> On the one hand we may find . . . inhuman treatment of political prisoners and a cowed group of intellectuals; on the other, we may find an expanding industry, major public work programs, experimental agricultural stations, and great hospitality to "apolitical" technical assistance [that] provide[s] employment and increase[s] the tax base. . . . Closing our eyes to evil elements on the grounds that we are helping governments only to do their focused good is a very dangerous practice. . . . If we cannot make a very strong case for distinguishing our activities from the support of politically repressive behavior in the host country, then we should withdraw. If, however, we see our programs in a given host country as contributing to the preservation of some pluralism that may come to flourish even in an undefined future . . . then we should remain.[22]

Adopting a course of action consistent with Silvert's concepts, the foundation ultimately chose to remain in the Southern Cone and responded to the coups with a combination of emergency and long-term program actions.

The emergency phase addressed the severe disruption the coup caused for the foundation's existing grantees, as well as the urgent need for rescue and refugee programs to assist academics and intellectuals to leave the country who were imprisoned or physically threatened.[23] Two large and sustained rescue programs for threatened academics, students, and intellectuals were initiated soon after the coup. One was a Latin American initiative by the Latin American Council for the Social Sciences (CLACSO), led by its president, Enrique Oteiza. The beneficiaries were relocated throughout the region. The other was a LASA initiative, the Emergency Committee for Aid to Latin American Scholars (ECALAS), led by Richard Fagen of Stanford University and Riordan Roett at the School of Advanced International Studies (SAIS) of Johns Hopkins University. The resulting program turned out to be more than LASA could handle, and ultimately it was relocated to New York University under the leadership of Bryce Wood of the SSRC.

Silvert's leadership at NYU and close relationship with SSRC were essential to the funding and success of the LASA and CLACSO programs. He also led efforts to involve British and Canadian support for the refugee program under World University Services (WUS) sponsorship. He collaborated with the Rev. William Wipfler of the World Council of Churches and engaged with Swedes and Germans to relocate academics abroad. Program beneficiaries were of all ages and political views, from multiple fields of endeavor, and required different kinds of assistance. Some needed jobs and others needed fellowships. Some were political prisoners whom the authorities, under a variety of pressures from abroad and also locally influential bodies such as the Catholic church, were persuaded to release from prison as long as they had jobs waiting for them.[24] Some student recipients of assistance were abroad at the time of the coup, and, because of their backgrounds, they had lost government fellowships and needed help to continue their studies.

Silvert played a key role in the conceptualization and support of the refugee programs, and was personally active, often behind the scenes, in identifying and channeling information on numerous people in need to the various sources of assistance.[25] He was also prescient in organizing seminars to bring key refugees, with a range of perspectives, together to discuss the future in the region and their individual countries. Ricardo Lagos, who later became Chile's president, was a notable beneficiary. Accepting a professorship at the University of North Carolina, Lagos was one of a select group of refugees who participated in a regular series of seminars that Silvert convened in New York to discuss and develop strategies for pushback against the Pinochet regime and for democratic transitions, when the opportunity should arise.

Data on the beneficiaries of the refugee programs are scattered but sufficient to provide a sense of magnitude. The CLACSO program, for example, by 1975 had benefited 650 refugees. ECALAS beneficiaries the same year included approximately 600 names (see Ford Foundation n.d.). WUS Canada and WUS UK assisted approximately 100 additional scholars each, making for a total of around 1,500. They do not include Argentine refugees following the 1976 military coup or funding to assist refugees who returned to Chile when circumstances permitted in the early 1980s. Like the change in the Ford Foundation's in-country program strategies, the scholar rescue programs had a significant, positive effect on the foundation's image in the region and in US and European higher education.

The long-term strategy consisted of three main components.[26] The first was to work with academic leaders and groups who had been expelled from the universities but who sought to establish independent, nonprofit centers of research and teaching in their home countries.[27] A corollary was to support other institutions, such as FLACSO and CEDES, that were hard-pressed to survive.[28] The goal was to sustain, to the extent possible, streams of free academic research and assist leading scholars in monitoring and documenting the crises through which they were passing and to contribute to debates over the future.

The second component was a large graduate fellowship program open to applicants from throughout the Southern Cone (see Dun 1979). The goal was to help develop a corps of young professionals ready to serve in the government, universities, and civil society when democracy was restored. Prospective fellowship candidates included junior staff and trainees at the centers who wished to remain in the country but were excluded from access to higher education at local universities, and those who were outstanding candidates for graduate training abroad. Some beneficiaries were students already abroad whose fellowships had been abruptly canceled by the military government. Under this component, the Ford Foundation office in Santiago in 1974 funded graduate fellowships for some seventy-five young Chileans, and similar numbers of fellowships were funded annually for the next several years.

The third component, limited to Chile, were small grants to the Catholic Church's Academia de Humanismo Cristiano to support research and publications by its members, many with Christian Democratic Party backgrounds, and to the Vicaría de la Solidaridad, which was assisting families of political prisoners and disappeared people both materially and in their legal efforts to gain redress from the regime. In sum, the overall strategy prioritized human rights and democracy building with development objectives.[29]

The strategy was developed and proposed to New York by the field-based team, in line with the long-standing Ford Foundation tradition of delegating responsibility and leadership to the representatives and their professional staffs.[30] The New York office, for its part, was receptive and supportive, even though the foundation at the time was facing serious financial constraints. Silvert's role in the development of the strategy was critical in conceptual formulations; confirming its legitimacy; intermediating with US, Canadian, Swedish, and German partners; and convincing the foundation to provide funding.[31]

Kalman Silvert as Professional Colleague

Personal Recollections

Decades after his passing, former Ford Foundation colleagues had clear memories of Kalman Silvert. Their assessments speak to his breadth of knowledge, powers of persuasion, humanistic ethos, love for Latin America, commitment to free expression, and the complexity of his personality.[32]

- "Conversations with Kal were always engaging, often wide-ranging and concerned with broad development issues and the social sciences in the United States as well as in Latin America" (James Himes).
- "Whether in New York or Lima, my impression was—What a powerfully strong articulator of situations and relationships and of sensible ways to go about the Foundation's funding...and all expressed with humility and warmth" (James Trowbridge).
- "He was always someone who thought differently and, when he spoke, was worth listening to....Personally, he was above all a workaholic, a man of tremendous energy on a mission" (Lowell Hardin).
- "Kal conveyed to me his love and passion for [Latin America]. How very at home he felt there....He exuded that passion in a winning and active way" (Abraham Lowenthal).
- "Kal asked the right questions. He was a superb consultant with immense and perhaps unmatched background for the issues" (William Carmichael).
- "I saw Kal as a complex person" (Peter Bell).

These testimonials help explain how his relationships inside the foundation allowed him to influence programs, which offer lessons for others in similar situations.

Ways to Influence Programs

Silvert was officially an advisor outside the foundation's management chain of command. The two heads of the Latin America office to whom he reported were supportive of the emphasis on social science development (although their own superiors were not necessarily so inclined). Part of Silvert's agenda was to convince program heads in more technical fields like economics, population, and agriculture to examine more closely the assumptions of their interventions and the social implications of resulting policies. This ambition created some tensions in the hierarchy. Silvert buttressed his position by insisting on high-quality analysis, encouraging the appointment of established academics (and promising junior staff) to field office social science positions, and a tireless work ethic—complemented by a warm and congenial personality.

Silvert had an advisory role in OLAC and did not control resources. His influence depended on his intellectual prowess and negotiating style. His approach included using workshops to promote his vision, extensive memo writing, trips to the field when he met with Latin American grantees and contacts, support of young colleagues, and communicating and forging alliances with professional and managerial peers. For the young, he was charismatic. For Latin Americans, his stature generated trust and respect for the Ford Foundation. For some of his foundation colleagues, relations could be strained but gentlemanly within bounds. He had the advantage of promoting an approach that corresponded closely with the views of his direct reports, Wilhelm and Carmichael, and a number of allies in the foundation's professional staff.

Like Wilhelm and Carmichael, Silvert felt that periodic Ford Foundation staff meetings were essential to review country programs, the status of leading grantees, and political and operating challenges in different country situations and most of all to achieve consistency in the foundation's mission. His custom at staff conferences was to present thought pieces that tended to be philosophical. His papers made references to sociologists like Talcott Parsons, thinkers like Immanuel Kant, and democratic theorists like Charles-Louis de Montesquieu and Alexis de Tocqueville. Staff members read these papers with considerable interest even when sentence structure was sometimes obtuse, the vocabulary exotic, and the references unfamiliar.[33] In his practical comments, by contrast, Silvert expressed his views on staffing needs, budgetary allocations, assisting grants in trouble, and dealing with authoritarian regimes.

> He was always someone who thought differently and was worth listening to....In the Ford context, he was a bit more the professor. Overall, he was always a presence. (Hardin, interview, July 17, 2013)

> Kal's blessing on projects—even if only oral—was important. I can imagine [Foundation President McGeorge] Bundy saying "Kal's had a good look at this," and that would carry the day. (Himes, interview, August 27, 2013)

The combined approach resulted in a great deal of admiration for his intellectual breadth and a receptive audience for his recommendations on day-to-day decisions. Besides educating younger persons and influencing colleagues, Silvert engaged in "managing upward."

> I have a clear recollection of Kal speaking with me about [sensitive] issues. Not in the form "This is what we must do," but more as a tutor. He asked the right questions. He was a superb consultant with immense and perhaps unmatched background for the issues. We had our hands full...particularly after Pinochet. I learned a lot from him. I felt his was the best style of consultant cum full-time staff member relationship. (William Carmichael)

Field staff looked forward to Silvert's trips to their regions. His attitude was consistently positive toward the office's grant portfolio. Staff could detect his true level of satisfaction, however, between strong affinity for grants that fit with his program priorities and a statement that the initiative was "unobjectionable." The latter descriptor was sufficient for locally based staff to try to improve on performance. Most stimulating, however, were the meetings accompanying Silvert with leading social scientists. Partially due to his presence in the Ford Foundation (and the foundation's own track record in the region), the offices had access to virtually all top Latin American social scientists.[34] Silvert's visits provided opportunities for stimulating discussions with accomplished researchers and world-class intellectuals who helped mold political and cultural expectations in their societies. The meetings were valuable learning experiences for the foundation's younger staff.

Constructive Disagreement

Relations among senior foundation professionals in the Latin American office were respectful, collegial, and friendly. At the same time, each of them had an ego nurtured by their stature and accomplishments. Silvert was known for objecting to "technical" solutions for perceived social problems. "In terms of social science development, he was pushing back against the prevailing trends, such as Walt Rostow's modernization or development based on agriculture, economics, and population control" (James Himes). Elliptical criticisms in his writing and sometimes direct disagreements in meetings could ruffle feathers. One contemporary noted that "he came down pretty hard sometimes and this might have miffed some people" (Lowell Hardin), but apparently this behavior did not create much animosity toward him. Former colleagues note

> I was not in the social science area—but in agricultural economics....I respected Kal a lot....He was strong willed and had very firm opinions in the social science area....[But he] did not try to push an agenda on to me....He did not bother me nor did I bother him. (Norman Collins, interview, August 12, 2014)[35]

> I recall a humanist/technocratic difference between Kal and other program areas. Not in a pontifical or academic way, but with humility and warmth. He engendered positive feelings even when he was correcting a person's view....This was not an abrasive confrontation...Kal clarified and put into perspective the innovations and transformations going on. (James Trowbridge, interview, August 17, 2013)

> As for Kal's style of persuasion, I do not remember any heated controversies....He was not confrontational in the slightest—but a sensitive [advocate]. He knew what he wanted to happen, but he never took a belligerent stance or got on a high horse. Nor do I remember anyone saying that he did. (William Carmichael)

A key to Silvert's effectiveness was forging allies and followers within the foundation. Allies were senior professionals who shared his vision and ethics, beginning with Wilhelm and Carmichael. It continued with Richard Dye in the New York office and Peter Bell in Chile in the formulation and execution of the foundation's initial strategy after the Chilean coup and with Dye and others in carrying out the new long-term strategy for Chile and Argentina. The relations were reciprocal and mutually reinforcing. The appointments of senior and junior social science program staff in the field offices strengthened the contingent of like-minded individuals to carry out the program. They spoke the same language and shared the same respect for their Latin American counter-parts—who in essence *were* the foundation program. This combination of factors, which Silvert helped build and take advantage of, helped create the conditions for the long-term impact that was in evidence more than four decades after his death.

In short, Silvert contributed to a dynamic tension in the Latin American programs that assured that different approaches were vetted.[36] At the same time, he succeeded in moving the overall Latin American program toward an analytical approach to development issues relying on the tools of social scientists, a deep ethical belief in freedom and democracy, and in association with others a humanitarian concern for the persecuted.

Impact, Legacy, and Lessons

In the four decades since his death, Silvert's impact was observable in several facets of the Ford Foundation's work. The emphasis on strengthening academic institutions and disciplines continued through social science grants throughout the region. The protection of academics under threat became a foundation operating principle. The new program focus supporting civil society organizations was consistent with Silvert's concept of Tocquevillian democracy. The former head of the Latin America office came to lead the International Division. In that role, William Carmichael made social analysis and human rights a program priority for the foundation's offices in Asia and Africa. The maintenance of working social scientists in independent centers allowed for critical analysis, progressive policy recommendations, and continued training of younger social scientists during the dark days of military dictatorships. With the return of democratic governance to Latin America, many in the generation of individuals supported and protected by the foundation became national leaders—heading departments, universities, and government ministries and even occupying presidential palaces. The younger colleagues they had trained and nurtured filled positions down the line.

Silvert's legacy is partly personal and partly shared by others who worked with him in the foundation.[37] His impact on the Ford Foundation was major and enduring, but with the passage of time, his contributions are regrettably less fully recognized. His position at the foundation also helped him further key objectives of his own in the development of the social sciences in Latin America, Latin American studies in the United States, and US policy toward the region.

In the Ford Foundation

Silvert brought to OLAC a remarkable knowledge of Latin American society, matched only by the breadth and depth of his personal relationships with the pioneers of modern social sciences in the region. Their students in turn formed part of a new generation of leaders and actors to cope with the crises ahead in their respective countries. Though he was not the first in the foundation to appreciate the importance of the social sciences, he brought passion and deep understanding to the task, which over time gradually spread to other sectors and regions. He also sought to challenge persistent assumptions that US and European models were sufficient to guide Latin American development. He was one of the first to recognize the potential value of Latin experience and scholarship to understanding and resolving problems in the "developed world," and at every opportunity pressed the value and importance of US–Latin American partnership in both the academic and policy areas.

> There was a mythic quality to Kal, one that the Ford Foundation never tried to shake off. I don't recall anything ever said bad about him. . . . After his death, what we did . . . was a "building on"—through fellowships and . . . social sciences in many universities. Rather than thinking of modernization theory to act on society, we needed to build capacity through research and knowledge about society. (Shepard Forman, interview, August 29, 2013)

Silvert had a major impact on the foundation's response to the Southern Cone crises in the 1970s. First was his role with others in influencing the foundation's decision to remain in Chile and Argentina and pursue a fundamentally human rights and democracy agenda.[38] Second was his close involvement with the scholar refugee programs, which saved lives and preserved human talents across the political spectrum. When these individuals eventually were able to return home, they were important in the transitions to democracy and helped staff the new governments. That agenda not only helped create the institutional and human civil society resources that were critical to the democratic transition process but also over time obliterated prior doubts and permanently cemented understanding and appreciation of the foundation's independence.

From the 1950s to the time he joined the foundation in 1967, Silvert was a determined advocate for development of the social sciences in Latin America, increasing and institutionalizing US knowledge of the region and advocating for better-informed and balanced US foreign policies toward the region. He focused on these objectives as a leader of the AUFS, as he did during his Tulane University and Dartmouth College years. Involvement in the establishment of LASA and his service as its first president, which brought Latin American, US, and other scholars into a greater and more equal relationship, was also of great importance. While Silvert was busily bringing the same objectives and accompanying values to the Ford Foundation, he actively promoted them in other settings in ways described elsewhere in this volume.

Democratic Transitions

The contributions of Kalman Silvert and the Ford Foundation are traceable in the democratic transitions in Chile, Argentina, and Brazil.[39] In all three countries, civil society institutions and people that the foundation had assisted played instrumental roles, such as CEBRAP, CEDES, CIEPLAN, FLACSO, and the Church. During the military periods, they produced knowledge and models for application for the eventual political opening. They were reservoirs of leadership and skills to staff future democratic governments. When displaced socialist leaders returned to Chile after formative experiences abroad, like Ricardo Lagos and Sergio Bitar, or continued their academic work in the midst of military regimes, like Fernando Henrique Cardoso and Alexander Foxley, they played critical roles in restoring democracy and setting their countries on a resurgent socioeconomic path.[40]

Latin American Social Sciences

Silvert and the Ford Foundation in the 1960s and early 1970s were instrumental in supporting a new generation of Latin American scholars both in the region and the United States. By the early 1980s, it had become possible, after the heavy investment in overseas graduate fellowship that took place in the 1970s, to talk about the emergence of a second generation that was to play important roles in the new democracies that emerged. It is likely that these individuals, whose careers matured during the crises, had some sense of Ford's and Silvert's contributions, but there is little evidence of this memory in subsequent generations.

Drawing on Silvert's decade of foundation work, contemporary philanthropists and administrators can find valuable lessons in his adherence to a consistent set of humanistic and democratic values, insistence on professional competence, energetic pursuit of focused programmatic goals, promotion of desired outcomes without the advantage of bureaucratic line authority, assessing risks and opportunities in challenging political environments, and adoption of a cogent theory of change.

Years after his death, the impact of Silvert in the Ford Foundation is still evident. By this longevity measure alone, his contributions were important and his tenure successful. What were the ingredients of his approach that account for this result? Are there characteristics of Silvert's makeup that other aspiring foundation or philanthropic professionals could appreciate and emulate to enhance their own contributions?

A set of values defined Silvert's moral code and lay behind virtually all his actions. These values included democracy, freedom of inquiry, respect for individuals no matter their station in life, and an abhorrence of dogmatism, inequity, and political repression. A close observer of his behavior in the public sphere could always discern the link between his behavior and these values.[41] They were the platform from which he viewed the world and determined his role within it. His firm support with others of the scholarly rescue program was fully consistent with his ethical core. The fact that these values were laudable garnered the respect of others, even when they differed with him on policy, personnel, or procedural matters.

The relevant questions for philanthropic executives just starting out or creating their own foundations are: What are my values? Do they govern all my actions? When acting on my values places me at institutional or physical risk, do I have the courage to remain steadfast? Under what circumstances would I compromise my core beliefs, if at all? Should I think more about what my values really are?

Silvert had a clear purpose, consistently pursued, and he saw that promoting high-quality social science was an effective way for the Ford Foundation to have a lasting and positive impact on Latin America. He maintained a vision of a desirable future state—namely, a complex of academic institutions throughout Latin America (particularly in the largest countries) engaged in research, training, and public debate that generated empirical analysis within a logical framework for their own citizens to make rational choices. Although Silvert loved art and played the violin, and the Ford Foundation was a major supporter of the arts in the United States, he did not encourage the foundation to expand in those directions in Latin America.[42] Because of his appreciation of Tocqueville, Silvert might have urged the foundation to support civil society organizations in Latin America. He could have reduced his frustration level with bureaucracy had he aspired to and obtained managerial positions controlling budgets. But this shift would have distracted him from applying his full energy and skill to the social sciences. He remained disciplined and focused on using his talent to promote his main goal.

The implicit questions for professionals with leading roles in foundations are: How clear is my philanthropic purpose? Am I sufficiently idealistic and dedicated to persevere even when faced with discouraging odds? Is my focus sufficiently concentrated to maximize the allocation of available resources to reach the goal? By becoming too stretched in my activities, am I diminishing the chances of achieving my philanthropic purpose?

In his writing and oral presentations, Silvert stressed the importance of professional competence. He joined the Ford Foundation when it was transitioning from a senior staff with "traditional backgrounds—business, banking, journalists, historians, *bons vivants*...to ratchet itself up to become a more rigorous and effective decision- making group" (Peter Bell, interview, August 1, 2013). Silvert tended to co-identify competence with Ph.D. degrees and helped hire and mentor younger persons with doctorates.[43] Most of the individuals he helped hire proceeded to impressive careers after leaving the foundation. Silvert also appreciated the abilities of those who were talented managers. On the other hand, he was impatient with professional competence that seemed to be ritualistic, parochial, and reactive against change. It was the "right kind" of professional competence that he favored—"rationalistic, relativistic, and anticipatory of change" (Silvert, "Rural Development as a Social Problem," 1975, p. 5). The result was a community of serious, studious, and hard-working professionals associated with OLAC's social science program. One of his talents was to promote his program priorities among senior peers with just enough doggedness and courtesy that they continued to like him personally while gradually diversifying their programs in his direction.

For executives in foundations, implications lie in hiring personnel, choosing funded beneficiaries, and upgrading the professional skills of staff and grantees. In job announcements, a philanthropic manager would ask questions like: Have we defined with sufficient thought the education, experience, and motivation requirements for new staff? What steps are we taking for our staff and grantees to become widely admired as leaders in their communities? How do we ensure that when they leave our grant portfolio or our employment, they will have broadened their options for successful careers?

Silvert loved Latin America.[44] He felt perfectly at home in the major capitals, speaking Spanish and interacting with intellectuals.[45] He extolled good governance.[46] While making few forays into rural areas, he expressed sincere compassion for the farming families who did not gain much from being members of their national society. His affection for the region dominated his life, including his academic writing, teaching, work with professional associations like LASA and SSRC, and in inter-American affairs, the commitments described in other chapters of this book. Latin America engaged him to the extreme that some might attribute his premature death to overexertion and overenthusiasm for the region.[47] Even so, this affection helped make him a consummate expert on the region—its history, culture, diversity, idiosyncrasies, and those aspects to praise or criticize. Silvert's dedication to Latin America imbued him with enormous authority which often (but not always) would carry the day in discussions on how to proceed programmatically or operationally.

The lesson for foundation executives is to ensure that their staff have a deep understanding of and mainly sympathetic appreciation for the geographic region where they work. Social change interventions rarely succeed when devised in and imported intact from other "more advanced" regions. In a practice followed later by Ford, a foundation can count on local knowledge by appointing citizens of the country to leadership posts.

Silvert articulated a theory of change that was elegant by having only a few components and connections to the ultimate purpose. The goal was to equip a society with a knowledge capability, allowing it to continuously develop policy solutions for economic growth, social and political equality, national integration, and responsible international citizenship. The institutional sources of this knowledge were universities and research centers. The foundation's role was to support the institutions, train expertise, promote avenues for communication, and in the last analysis, protect the assemblage when under attack.

The first task for philanthropic leaders is to ask simple questions about their theory of change: What do we want to accomplish? What is the strategy to do so? How reliable are the causal connections between components of the plan? How should our resources be best deployed? How do we measure success? Do we have the right people to implement the strategy and make adjustments over time? Will the results be sustainable even after our programs end?

Although the questions are straightforward, the process of answering them is an enterprise in itself. In the case of the Ford Foundation's Latin American program, its theory of change appears to have stood the test of time. Silvert contributed importantly to that result.

Notes

The authors are grateful to the Rockefeller Archive Center, Pocantico Hills, New York, which holds the archives of the Ford Foundation, for their invaluable assistance in accessing internal foundation documents referenced in this chapter. We also express our appreciation to former foundation staff and Latin American colleagues who provided personal interviews and written testimonies.

1. Among the books written by former staff on the Foundation's Asia programs are Bresnan (2006), Staples (1992), and Sutton (1961).

2. Carlson had been director of Vanderbilt University's Brazil Institute and later became US ambassador to Colombia. For a first-person report on the initial years of the Latin America program, see Atwater and Walsh (2011), pp. 135–53.

3. Major donations in the late 1960s were the ten-year $10 million University of Chile–University of California program and endowments to the Colegio de México and Argentina's Di Tella Institute. Each included financing for the social sciences, as well as other academic fields like public administration. See Bell (1967).

4. The Latin America-based agricultural research centers were CIMMYT, the Centro Internacional de Mejoramiento de Maíz y Trigo in Mexico and CIAT, the Centro Internacional de Agricultura Tropical in Colombia.

5. See Carmichael (1964), FLACSO survived its early leadership problems and the impact of the 1973 Chilean coup and eventually grew to include operations in thirteen countries.

6. "When I was at Columbia in the mid-1950s someone began circulating to me the AUFS Latin American reports. In those days as in these, on-the-scene reporting from the southern lands was not conspicuous for blazing illuminations. It was startling, then, to discover the fresh and authoritative letters of one 'K. H. Silvert,' identified as a political scientist who had begun his career at age nineteen by observing the 1940 elections in Mexico." Morse (1977).

7. See Wolf, Silvert, and Carlson (1959). The report included the sentence "Argentina is a country in turmoil."

8. In his honor, in 1982 LASA created the Kalman H. Silvert Award "to recognize senior members of the profession who have made distinguished lifetime contributions to the study of Latin America." Awardees mentioned in this chapter are Osvaldo Sunkel (1994), Richard Fagen (1995), Richard Adams (1998), Guillermo O'Donnell (2003), Julio Cotler (2012), and Manuel Antonio Garretón (2015).

9. Silvert was a strong advocate for the foundation's support for area studies in the United States. See his "Area Studies Look Outward" (1969).

10. Silvert, "Social Science Research and Social Relevance," p. 1.

11. Silvert supported the appointment of accomplished senior social scientists to field office staff positions and as consultants to support the strategy. Among them were historian Richard Morse, anthropologist Richard Adams, political scientist Richard Fagen, and Silvert's AUFS colleague sociologist Frank Bonilla.

12. William D. Carmichael recalls, "I identify Kal with a major switch in the focus of the Ford Foundation in stages. Latin America at first was with a more

technical aspect of development—for example agriculture and working with relevant government agencies....We were heavily in agricultural economics, but not political science or social anthropology....Kal had a prejudice but I shared it, against appointing expensive consultants to government....For Harry Wilhelm, Kal was a reason for thinking through a new paradigm for development assistance from the late 1960s." Carmichael, interview, August 13, 2013.

13. "He was critical of excessively technocratic approaches, and thought the Foundation should do more to strengthen capacity in the 'softer' social sciences, dealing with the central issues of politics and identity." Abraham F. Lowenthal, interview, August 25, 2013. Paul Strasburg adds, "Kal was quite a skeptic of what the agricultural program was doing—high-yield rice and wheat. Kal wanted to know more than just yield. He would ask lots of questions. Who is going to benefit? How will this affect the whole social structure? Not (just) how many people would be fed." Paul A. Strasburg, interview, August 30, 2013. Peter Hakim concurs: Silvert had "a big impact on the Ford Foundation programs, by emphasizing social sciences more than the instrumental fields of economic development, education, population and agriculture in which the Foundation had been largely engaged." Interview, July 29, 2013.

14. Barry D. Gaberman recalls, "The Latin American program was very different from Africa and Asia...by being the first to move to grants with private institutions, particularly universities. It moved away from governments earlier than the rest of the Ford Foundation....The Latin America program had an understanding of the 'soft side' of development. The 'hard side' in Asia was in agriculture and economics programs....The soft side was social justice and human rights and some money into the arts and to NGOs, which took longer to move to Asia." Gaberman, interview, September 2, 2013. Robert H. Edwards, former head of the foundation's Middle East and Africa program, writes, "Kal was a major intellectual force in the Latin American program, which was a good deal more sophisticated in the social scientific realm than what, in my time, the Middle East and African beat involved." Correspondence with Peter Cleaves, August 13, 2013.

15. Silvert, "Rural Development as a Social Science Problem" (1975). Lowell Hardin, who was head of the Agricultural Program, comments that "Kal was in the forefront of changes. One was enlightening colleagues and others of the importance of the social sciences in understanding and dealing with underlying issues in the development field." Lowell S. Hardin, interview, July 17, 2013.

16. The debates also took place in the Ford Foundation's Asia program. See Staples (1992).

17. In 1968, however, the Peruvian armed forces overthrew the Belaúnde government and embarked on a reformist and mildly anti-American agenda heavily steeped in dependency theory said to have been derived in part from officers' attendance at FLACSO in Chile. Unlike the Brazilian and Argentine coups of the 1960s and the Chilean and Argentine coups in the early 1970s, the Peruvian coup did not disrupt the foundation's work and, indeed, was accompanied by increased support, particularly in economics and education.

18. There is no evidence of Silvert having been involved in the creation of CEBRAP, but he was firmly in support for it at the time and subsequently.

19. Much of the information in this section is based on coauthor Richard Dye's first-person account as OLAC's coordinator of responses to the Chilean coup and subsequently as representative for the Southern Cone (from 1970) and for the Andean Region and the Southern Cone (from mid-1974 to 1981).

20. Peter D. Bell comments, "After the coup, many Christian Democrats, especially persons on the center right, believed they would be the beneficiaries of the coup and would return to power and authority. The CDs did not understand the coup was not only against leftists; it was also anti-politics....Like many others, Kal was torn apart by the coup." Bell, interview, August 1, 2013.

21. "There was a specific ideological and political shift after Perón's death (July 1974). The authorities in the Ministry of Education and at the University of Buenos Aires changed, and the new ones (very much to the right of the political spectrum) began purges and dismissals, causing many academics to leave the country due to threats and violence." Elizabeth Jelín, correspondence with Richard Dye, March 26, 2014.

22. Silvert, "Distasteful Regimes and Foundation Policies Overseas" (1971), p. 2 (emphasis added). In "Chile" (1974), p. 5, he wrote, "The Foundation must not be subversive of the regimes in which it operates. At the same time, it must not ask of its officials that they suspend their most profoundly decent sentiments and refuse to assist fellow men who are lawlessly persecuted."

23. Sergio Bitar, a minister in the Allende government who after the coup was imprisoned by the Pinochet regime for over a year, reports that he received important support from the Ford Foundation to go to Harvard to research and write. Sergio Bitar, correspondence with Richard Dye, November 3, 2013. After his return to Chile, Bitar became a senator and subsequently served as a minister in the presidential administrations of Ricardo Lagos and Michelle Bachelet.

24. For details, see Ford Foundation (1975).

25. José Joaquín Brunner was supported by the Ford Foundation at Oxford University after being expelled from the University of Chile. Correspondence with Richard Dye, September 28, 2013.

26. Operationally, the foundation kept the Chile and Argentina offices open with New York appointees Nita Manitzas, Jeff Puryear, and Gary Horlick relocated to either Lima or Bogotá. Dick Dye managed the strategy with advice from Silvert in social sciences, Hardin and Norman Collins in agriculture and economics, Gordon Perkin in population, and Richard Krasno in education. The local offices received inquiries from Chilean and Argentine contacts, communicated these to the program staff, and arranged follow-up meetings. The approach included regular visits to monitor the political situation and develop programs. See, for example, Dye's comprehensive evaluation "Report on my Trip to Chile and Argentina" (1974).

27. Alejandro Foxley recounts, "Social scientists were forced out of the universities, and we started independent think tanks....The Ford Foundation was the first institution that allowed us to exist—to survive under the Pinochet dictatorship." Foxley, interview October 9, 2013. He later served two Chilean democratically elected governments as minister of finance and minister of foreign relations.

28. CEDES is the Centro de Estudios de Estado y Sociedad (formerly

Centro de Investigaciones en Administración Pública). Researcher Elizabeth Jelín recalls that after the coup, "CEDES' newness allowed it to operate under the radar for a while and avoid repressive conditions that afflicted some organizations. [But] staff lived with the fear that 'something' could happen." Several CEDES members had "records" and for safety reasons left the country. Correspondence with Richard Dye, January 26, 2014. Silvert had long admired CEDES director Guillermo O'Donnell and the group for their intellectual sophistication and research competence.

29. Manuel Antonio Garretón, at thirty years old already a recognized Chilean intellectual, recalls, "I most remember the dinner [with Silvert very soon after the 1973 military coup]. I retained doubts about the Ford Foundation, even after the Foundation was providing fellowships and institutional support...[A]s a representative of the Ford Foundation, he had close knowledge of the situation. He knew what to support—and what not to support." Garretón, interview, October 11, 2013.

30. Southern Cone staff members Manitzas and Puryear wrote comprehensive summaries of the strategy. See Manitzas (1980) and Puryear (1982).

31. Alejandro Foxley says that the "Ford Foundation's support...was very important to plant the seeds that would later shape democratic government....It provided support for think tanks and research centers to help understand why Chile got into such a conflict and develop ideas of how to get out of the crisis." Foxley, interview, October 9, 2013.

32. Citations for these quotes appear in other endnotes with the speaker's name and the date of the interview.

33. "Were there shortcomings? One would be verbosity. He could talk forever. I didn't understand [everything] of what he was saying. I wish I did." Strasburg, interview, August 30, 2013.

34. The exceptions in the early years were scholars on the far left opposed to and suspicious of the foundation for its US and capitalistic origins. See Plotkin (2015) and chapter 9 in this volume.

35. Another former staff member had a different reaction to Silvert. "He wanted to make me one his boys. He wanted to be my mentor. That sent me full speed in the other direction. I resisted, gently I hope. I did not want to become one of his boys. I did not depend on him...and was already a full professor." Anonymous, interview conducted by Peter Cleaves.

36. "As for the working relations between executives in New York, at times they pushed each other's buttons. There were strong differences in approach— [the 'hard side'] versus the 'soft side,' which (the former) referred to pejoratively....The view was that 'development action' was in Asia and Africa. Latin America was better off economically, their program was a side show, and there was less reason to be working there. Latin America got less and less of the money. And when there was discussion about closing offices, the question came up whether to close Latin America altogether. The Ford Foundation rejected that idea since, to be global, it needed a footprint in Latin America." Gaberman, interview, September 2, 2013.

37. "I think of Kal as an inspiring, passionate person, who attracted attention by the force of his personality and his physical style. He attracted protégés. He was a very fine analyst and observer. He had a real talent for developing

general meaning out of vignettes." Lowenthal, interview, August 25, 2013.

38. See Brunner (1985) for an insider's view of the impact of civil society on the democratic transition.

39. Manuel Antonio Garretón reflects on Silvert and the foundation: "Kalman Silvert [was advising] the Ford Foundation to help develop…an institutional infrastructure for social sciences leading to research on the new configuration of power—military, oligarchy, and civil-military. Of course, it was *our own activities in this mission* that the Ford Foundation was assisting. The foundation was helping us against this historical crime." Garretón, interview, October 11, 2013.

40. Foxley was head of CIEPLAN, the Corporación de Investigaciones Económicas para Latinoamérica (which later changed its name to Corporación de Estudios para América Latina). "If you look at the Concertación governments from 1990—Aylwin, Frei, Lagos, Bachelet—of the five Ministers of Finance, four of them were from CIEPLAN. If you look at the cabinet members of the Aylwin government … you will find a significant number of PhDs and persons from think tanks with previous Foundation support. … If the Foundation had not [supported them], all of us would have migrated to other countries and Chile would not have had this social capital in favor of political receptivity and fresh ideas. We recognized the mistakes made before the military coup. During the period of Foundation support, we accumulated the wisdom not to make the same mistakes again." Foxley, Interview of October 9, 2013.

41. Additionally, Silvert "was troubled by the intellectual obtuseness of the far left, those who said…'I'm not going to listen to you because I know you are wrong.' He was from another generation, ethics and culture. He defended freedom of speech over shouting from the left. He believed in civilized discourse." Himes, interview, August 27, 2013.

42. Already stretched thin, Silvert did not exert much effort to influence a social science concentration in the foundation's Asia and Africa programs, except by way of example. The most influential intervention was from anthropologist Clifford Geertz, who wrote in language reminiscent of Silvert: "For Indonesians to cultivate the social sciences is to join one of the great movements of contemporary thought." See Geertz (1971), p. 30.

43. Political scientist Riordan Roett credits Silvert with "a significant impact on me and others of the limited number of budding new Latin Americanists in the 1960s….His impact on my generation was very important. Professionally, he was highly regarded and known for his openness and his penchant for looking more deeply and broader than most." Riordan Roett, interview, August 26, 2013.

44. "Kal spoke authoritatively and affectionately of his times in Latin America. He referred frequently to checking his theoretical interpretations with Latin American scholars in long and far-reaching debates in Buenos Aires coffee houses." Cleaves (2013), p. 45.

45. Silvert "was much appreciated by grantees in our part of the region. He communicated respect and concern for them and their ideas." Jeffrey M. Puryear, interview, August 15, 2013. Lowenthal adds, "He had relations of *confianza* with Argentine, Brazilian, Chilean, Uruguayan and other Latin American

social scientists, and a reputation for integrity and commitment to democratic values." Interview, August 25, 2014.

46. "One specific conversation with Kal has stuck with me. He had just returned from Costa Rica. Someone arranged a meeting with the Costa Rican president....Kal went down to the lobby and saw a man standing there. He introduced himself 'I'm the president.' They got into a tiny car and went to a little restaurant and spoke until late in the evening. Kal told me the story gleefully...'This is the kind of country that I want to live in. The president who runs the country is so accessible and the country is so safe.'" Strasburg, interview, August 30, 2013.

47. "This constant, high level of effort and the accompanying stress may have contributed to his early death." Hardin, interview, July 17, 2013. Cleaves (2013), p. 45, adds, "He did not take care of himself. He smoked heavily, was overweight, and did not exercise. He admitted in class that he drove automobiles too fast (which could be said to be the way he drove his life)."

9

Combining Ideas and Action

Julio Cotler

Kalman Silvert moved freely between his defense of principled
ideas and opportunities to carry out purposeful actions. He had a major
impact on individuals and institutions during his relatively short professional life, and he is a role model to be studied by the generations who
follow him.

I met Silvert in Caracas in the early 1960s, at a time when Latin
America and particularly the Caribbean were experiencing intense
social and political change. Sharp ideological debates and overt conflict
in the region affected relations between individuals, among social
groups, and between Latin America and the United States. In Venezuela,
the toppling of Marcos Pérez Jiménez in 1958, the consensus-building
Punto Fijo Pact, and the election of Rómulo Betancourt inaugurated a
transition to democracy. Popular support for the Acción Democrática
government provided the background for a series of important institutional, political, and social reforms. Simultaneously the 1959 Cuban
Revolution and its confrontation with the United States galvanized
enthusiastic youth for radical positions throughout Latin America and
particularly in Venezuela.

After the US intervention in Cuba and the negative Latin American
reaction, Washington modified its Latin America policy in a new design
supporting reformist political parties and leaders. The Alliance for
Progress initiative distanced the United States from its classic allies—
the oligarchs and the military. Despite this change in the US posture, the
leaders of the "reformist" political organizations did not abandon their
hostility toward and mistrust of the United States. They remembered,
among other things, the persecution they suffered from dictatorships

supported by the United States and the stigma of being accused of being communists.

In these conditions, a group of Venezuelan politicians and professionals founded CENDES, the Center for Development Studies at the Central University of Venezuela, with the objective of studying Venezuelan and Latin American underdevelopment. The goal was to train professionals to plan, formulate, and implement measures needed to achieve social and economic development within a democratic framework—in an intermediate position between Cuban collectivism and statism on one hand and US-style capitalism on the other.

Jorge Ahumada, the Chilean economist graduate of Harvard University who was undersecretary of CEPAL, agreed to become CENDES director. He organized a two-year training curriculum in economic growth. He contracted leading CEPAL economists to be the trainers, several of whom later joined the Chilean governments of Eduardo Frei and Salvador Allende. The role of sociologists and anthropologists like me was to complement the technical training by concentrating on the "social and cultural obstacles to economic development."

Despite the intention to insulate the institution from political controversy, the highly charged atmosphere eventually arrived at CENDES's door, involving a generalized questioning of its technocratic bias. Ahumada responded by submitting its "rational" and "technocratic" aims to a public debate, with the intention of demonstrating that they had no ideological origin. He invited scholars to engage in a discussion of the problems of underdevelopment in Venezuela and Latin America and the policy formulas to address the challenges. The participants from various disciplines were from Venezuela, Latin America, and the United States, including Kalman Silvert and Frank Bonilla.

In these sessions, the presentations by Silvert and Bonilla were in a category apart from those offered by the economists, psychologists, and political analysts, because their theoretical construct to understand the problems affecting Latin America and the transformations under way generated animated debate. In synthesis, Silvert and Bonilla argued that the existence of growing pressure from the popular sectors in Latin America to democratize social and political relations ran up against the persistence of premodern principles that were the legacy of medieval Catholic concepts consistent with an Iberian heritage. Their argument emphasized the contradiction between social and economic structures with the persistence of anachronistic political and cultural patterns. The underlying problem was that the *process* of modernization was not accompanied by the *values* of modernization.

They put forth these positions while citing a multitude of facts from particular countries and the region in general. They were able to command this wealth of information because their engagement with the American Universities Field Staff (AUFS) had allowed them to reside relatively long periods of time in different Latin American countries, analyzing their problems and reporting on options to resolve them. Their writings distributed among AUFS consortium universities made Silvert and Bonilla well known in the United States as experts on Latin America.

After his research in Guatemala, Silvert resided in Argentina and in Chile. Bonilla, after defending his dissertation at Harvard, lived in Brazil and carried out market studies in various Latin American countries. Both established relations with trade union, political, and intellectual leaders who were promoting change in their countries. As a consequence of these experiences, Silvert wrote *Guatemala: A Study in Government* (1954), and a broader treatment, *The Conflict Society: Reaction and Revolution in Latin America* (1961). He later brought together various works in the edited volume *Expectant Peoples: Nationalism and Development* (1963), in which he raised questions that still resonate: how to consolidate democratic communities with the nation-state being the arbiter and integrator of diverse interests. The book addressed these questions in the chapters by Silvert on dysfunctions in Argentina, Bonilla on nationalist ideology in Brazil, and Richard Patch on the Bolivian Revolution of 1952.

Although the writings of Silvert and Bonilla on Argentina and Brazil attracted attention, their research project *Education and the Meaning of Development: A Preliminary Statement* (1961) aroused special interest in CENDES. At the time, radical political movements were violently challenging the Venezuelan constitutional order. The research proposed to explore first the values and attitudes of strategic social sectors and, second, their willingness to come together to resolve conflict in a peaceful manner.

The CENDES leadership invited Silvert and Bonilla to carry out this research (which they named "Conflict and Consensus") under a contract with the Massachusetts Institute of Technology, with which Bonilla was then affiliated. Silvert acted formally as research coleader until he joined the Ford Foundation as Latin America Social Science Advisor. One might speculate that the Ford Foundation appointed Silvert and MIT recruited Bonilla because of institutional needs to have top-level specialists on Latin America, capable of suggesting measures to improve hemispheric relations and help insulate them from the threats that surrounded them.

After four years in Caracas at CENDES, I transferred to MIT in 1964 to complete the analysis of the surveys and interviews of Venezuelan elites. In Cambridge, Massachusetts, I met several well-regarded professors—ironically even some former Trotskyists and communists—who were advising the US government on security and foreign policy matters. They justified US interventions in Latin America—including the Dominican Republic in 1965—as important to halt the communist advance in the region. They did not believe in changing the anachronistic social and political structures in the region because that would negatively affect US interests and favor the Soviet Union. These people represented the crudest stereotypes prevalent at the time within the US foreign policy establishment, defending positions that contradicted even the timid reformist pretentions of the Alliance for Progress.

After nine years' absence, my family and I decided to return to our home in Peru. I resigned from CENDES, including the research on Venezuelan elites, and turned down an offer at MIT. Soon after returning to Peru, I joined the Institute of Peruvian Studies (IEP) and San Marcos University, about the same time Silvert assumed his new functions in the Ford Foundation. He started to promote Latin American social sciences, in part through graduate fellowships abroad. Paradoxically, the fellowship program was criticized in the countries benefiting from it because it was interpreted to further the general interests of imperialism and specifically the CIA, an accusation strengthened by the revelations around Project Camelot. Likewise, my sense was that the fellowship program raised concerns in the upper reaches of the Ford Foundation because it could generate criticism in Washington.

Nevertheless, Silvert was able to overcome these resistances, broadening the fellowship program, supporting the Latin American Council for the Social Sciences (CLACSO), and the Latin American Social Science Faculty, while helping consolidate the Latin American Studies Association, of which he was a founder and its first president. These Ford Foundation actions caused surprise in some circles because often the beneficiaries had nationalist, "*dependencia*," and even Marxist orientations. These examples of tolerance and pluralism helped alleviate the suspicions that weighed on the foundation and the academic community it was assisting.

In Peru, the Ford Foundation supported scientific training at Lima's Cayetano Heredia University, but the attempt to do the same in the social sciences departments of San Marcos University failed. University authorities and student leaders rejected support for the fellowship program, a specialized library in the social sciences, and temporary appointments of US professors, alleging that these were new ways for the empire to exercise its dominance.

Such was not the case at the Institute of Peruvian Studies (IEP). After the 1968 Peruvian military coup, the IEP was critical of the increasingly authoritarian nature of the "Revolutionary Government of the Armed Forces." The military responded by threatening reprisals against the IEP and its members. Silvert, in a personal meeting, offered IEP the tentative support of the Ford Foundation, with no conditions other than to continue what we were doing while maintaining our independence. Our immediate response was to express legitimate doubts about the offer, given the prevailing political situation. But Silvert convinced us to accept the support, which we never regretted. Over time we counted on the collaboration of Ford Foundation representatives who assisted us discreetly to strengthen IEP and with whom we developed personal relations of trust and friendship. Among these were Abe Lowenthal, Peter Hakim, Richard Dye, Jim Himes, Peter Cleaves, Jeffrey Puryear, Nita Manitzas, and Antonio Muñoz Najar. From the moment of Silvert's meeting at the IEP, we maintained a valued relationship with the Ford Foundation, which remains today.

At the beginning of the 1960s, along with Fernando Henrique Cardoso and Osvaldo Sunkel, I was named to the Joint Committee for Latin America Studies of the Social Science Research Council (SSRC) in New York to select and award prizes to the best research proposals on Latin America. These appointments were a sign of the changes proposed by the Ford Foundation, since previously the joint committee was composed exclusively of North Americans. Our membership coincided with an increase in Ford's financial support and, under the direction of Bryce Wood, Latin Americans became eligible to qualify for grants. Even more important, joint membership contributed to research and conferences with participation from both North and South America, such as the 1972 conference I co-organized with Richard Fagen on interhemispheric political relations. While such collaborative activities today are considered normal, they were not so at the time. The influence of Silvert at the Ford Foundation facilitated the expansion of professional and institutional relations in the social sciences between the United States and Latin America, whose fruits afterward was the development of strong institutionalized disciplines in the region.

The SSRC meetings in New York created opportunities to reunite with Silvert, to meet his collaborator, Joel Jutkowitz; his wife, Frieda; and their children and participate in meetings with his friends and colleagues. In this informal and friendly setting, in which we discussed the new political realities of the region, the conversation often turned to Chile. Silvert was certain that the political trends occurring in Chile during the Allende government could end up badly for that nation and other countries in its wake. He felt that the Popular Unity government should tone down the political positions of its allies. He anticipated that leftist extremism and sectarianism could generate a reaction that would rebound against democracy, as had occurred in Europe before World War II, with tragic consequences. It did not take long for events to prove him right.

The upshot from these encounters for me was to recognize that liberty and democracy were necessary conditions for the construction of a society of equal citizens. This conclusion was reinforced in two ways. The first was when—in an example of arbitrariness—the Peruvian military government expelled me from the country. I had criticized its pretension of "democratizing a society through authoritarianism." The IEP risked being shut down by the military, with the complicity of certain civilian colleagues and former friends linked to the government who thought they were "king's philosophers." The second was the revulsion occasioned by the human rights violations by the governments of Argentina, Bolivia, and Chile and of the Soviet bloc, including Cuba. These experiences induced me to rethink my political positions and reread the liberal classics, following Silvert's advice, while putting aside the Marxist structuralist texts I found unreadable.

At the end of September 1973, I arrived as a deportee in Buenos Aires and met Silvert in the CLACSO offices, where he was worried about the fate of many friends after the Chilean coup. He spoke of plans for the Ford Foundation to assist exiled Chileans who could do postgraduate studies in disciplines and countries they selected, even in the Soviet bloc, because he did not hide his hope that people would reject authoritarian regimes and adopt some form of democracy, which is what eventually occurred, often in dramatic ways.

Over time I had the chance to appreciate Silvert's efforts to support institutions to survive the military dictatorships and establish programs to help displaced and persecuted researchers for their political positions, while seeking the cooperation of other US and European institutions with the same objective. These efforts and backing for organizations defending human rights contributed to the Ford Foundation's earning the credibility and confidence it enjoys today.

The sudden and lamentable death of Kalman Silvert left us without a colleague, friend, and admirable intellectual who did his best to make the world a better place.

10

Silvert and the "American Dream"

Louis W. Goodman

Kalman Silvert was keenly aware of the American Dream. He used it as a template for his lives, both professional and personal. He was deeply committed to the Weberian concept that ideas are the value basis of human action and to Ernst Cassirer's premise that engaged citizens are necessary for a state to "secure its eudaimonia, its real happiness" (Cassirer 1946, p. 76). Thus he presented the American Dream as a frame that motivates human behavior all over the world. He did this both analytically and personally.

In the classroom,[1] Silvert talked about his roots and those of his parents as Jews with Central European heritage. He talked with wonder about the unprecedented opportunities the United States had given people from around the world, including the privileged and the oppressed, to build dignified lives based on their abilities and their hard work. Silvert spoke of the struggles and dreams of his grandparents as penniless migrants from Poland; his parents, Henry and Ida, as hard-working Philadelphia merchants; and himself as the first of his family to receive a college education, let alone a doctorate and then a professorship in Ivy League colleges.[2] He further stated that continuing to provide such opportunities, to his descendants and to other American newcomers, would be a measure of the quality of the future US political system.

The American Dream is the notion that all US citizens can achieve personal goals through determination and hard work without the restrictions of class, ethnic origin, race, or religion. It is an ethos central to US nationalism. It was explicitly codified in 1931 by James Truslow Adams (1931) as "life should be better and richer and fuller for everyone, with opportunity for each according to ability or achievement."

As part of the underpinning of the political system of the United States, the American Dream is based in the eighteenth-century founding documents of the republic. The Declaration of Independence (1776) states that "all men are created equal, that they are endowed by their Creator with certain unalienable Rights, that among these are Life, Liberty and the pursuit of Happiness." The US Constitution, especially its Bill of Rights (1789), provides citizens with protections of basic civil rights that make that pursuit possible. Citizens are guaranteed equality before the law and freedoms of expression, assembly, and religion ensuring that neither the state nor other private citizens can deny them the opportunity to realize that dream. In essence, US citizens are granted the autonomy to create and pursue their own personal dreams.

To be sure, all citizens have not had equal capacity to achieve the American Dream throughout the history of the United States. At the outset that right was reserved for free and propertied men. Over time the laws have been changed to ensure equal opportunity for women as well as men, for people of all races, for people of all religions, and for the poor as well as the rich. When those assurances have been found wanting, additional changes sometimes have been made to national legislation, a process that is expected to continue as US citizens evolve their understandings of this basic concept.

Critical for Silvert was that the American Dream is more than material. The core for him was

> the ability to exercise freedom . . . in (a) societ(y) where the power deriving from the consensual participation of a total citizenry is the product of the reasoned understanding that the maximum personal difference is promoted by raising the level of achievement from which everyone starts off . . . (and by) trying to make us more alike in the growing profundity of our uniqueness . . . build(s) a personal-social body always better able to take care of itself, our world, and the heritage we shall leave for our followers. (1977, p. 104)

When Silvert used his family as exemplars of the importance of the American Dream, he contrasted the dismal prospects for Jews in nineteenth-century Central Europe with those imagined (and realized) for people able to cross the Atlantic and find their way in America.

The American Dream was a promised reality for those who were able to cross the ocean; it was also an ideal to be realized for those who stayed in Europe and elsewhere. That this dream had not been realized for so many was a tragedy to Silvert. Still he saw the American Dream as a worldwide motivating force. During the Cold War era, many underprivileged individuals, especially in developing nations, just "kept their heads down," not daring to take steps to better their lives or those of their children. They feared that success, or even the appearance of striving, would target them as victims for elites guarding privilege. It is tragic that Silvert did not live to see the post–Cold War "global awakening"[3] with citizens from all walks of life in so many countries daring to dream that they too could achieve better lives through their abilities and hard work. Convinced by his empirical research that education is the key to the creation of empathetic, empowered individuals, Silvert would have seen further evidence for this in the spectacular expansion in demand for increased education, especially university education (see, e.g., OECD 2014).

Part of Silvert's American Dream was his vision of the foreign policy of the United States. He thought that the United States could be a force for making the American Dream a reality for humans around the world. As he saw it, his role was to accelerate this process through his work as a social scientist. As a Weberian social scientist, he aimed to create ideas that would clarify options for humans, especially for policymakers who could advocate measures that would advance prospects for the realization of the American Dream worldwide. That Cold War US foreign policy did not always advance these prospects was deeply troubling to him. That it sometimes slowed or reversed such prospects, as he thought he had observed in Guatemala, the site of his PhD dissertation and his first scholarly monograph, was tragic, perhaps even criminal. In *The Reason for Democracy* he was explicit about US policy toward Salvador Allende's Chile and Fidel Castro's Cuba: "Our leaders decreased the chance that Cuba can move from nationalism to democracy, erased the hope in Chile, and endangered democratic institutions at home" (Silvert 1977, p. 68). Had he been alive in the early twenty-first century, his thoughts about US involvement in Afghanistan and Iraq are relatively easy to surmise.

Foreign policy, of course, was not the focus of Silvert's scholarly work. His focus was national development—economic, social, and especially political development—with special attention to national development in Latin America. He examined the histories and contemporary situations of Latin American countries to try to understand how national development took place. He understood that national development had to be contextualized separately for each country. He tried to uncover patterns that transcend individual national situations and could be used to understand the development process more broadly. In the fuzzy parlance of his time he used the term "modernization" to describe the process of political development. Silvert used the term to describe a complex, uneven process of social change, as did economist Albert Hirschman and sociologists Seymour Martin Lipset and Joseph Kahl. He did not use the term "modernization" to describe a teleological and staged process, as was suggested by the scholarly work of economist Walt Rostow and social psychologist Alex Inkeles.

While Silvert viewed Western democracy as desirable because of its guarantees for the rights of individuals to dream their own dreams, he also recognized that political development needs to be described differently for each national situation. Thus he was adamant that nationalism not be viewed as "a negative sentiment, backward looking, exclusivist, anti-foreign and, at times, even insane" (Silvert 1961, p. 16). Rather, with Rupert Emerson, he perceived "nationalism within established political units as a social value elevating loyalty to the state and to the citizenry included therein to a supreme position."[4]

With the great value Silvert placed on the American Dream (and other national dreams) he focused much of his intellectual energy on trying to understand how nations could create economic, social, and political institutions that would make those dreams possible. He viewed nationalism as essential for mobilizing individuals to engage in projects with a wider purview than family or community. He viewed "modern" individuals as essential to the construction of such institutions. For Silvert, "modern" meant, among other attributes, having the capacity for empathy; empathy was essential for "extending the size of the 'We' group, the enlarged social relationships being regulated in the last analysis by the state" (Silvert 1963). For him, then, nationalism and empathy constituted "requirements of the ability to follow a modern style of life" (Silvert 1963). Finally he carried out original research to try to understand how individuals could learn to be empathic. His *Education, Class and Nation* (Silvert and Reissman 1976), based on surveys carried out in Chile and Venezuela, led him to the conclusion that well-framed education is essential for creating empathetic individuals, capable of creating national institutions able to sustain human dreams.

Silvert made this case conceptually in his monograph *Man's Power: A Biased Guide to Political Thought and Action* (1970). In its introduction, he stated, "The prime ethical purpose of (social) order, and its only long term assurance, is the furtherance of human autonomy" (p. xx). Framing this with characteristic neo-Weberian self-awareness, Silvert presented his main "thesis" in the final paragraph of the introduction: "'Good' politics, a politics that widens the areas of effective choice, is desirable in itself, a public interest whose defense is worthwhile intrinsically as well as is essentially identical with private interest" (p. xxiv). In short, US politics that protects the American Dream is a prime individual good and a prime public good; other nations' politics, which protect their national dreams, are similarly prime individual and public goods.

Silvert expressed his fears about the possible erosion of the capacity of the United States to sustain the American Dream for future generations in his posthumously published monograph *The Reason for Democracy* (1977). The book is a self-described "polemic" arguing for "the eminent practicality of democracy" and "the impracticality and inefficiency of tyranny, of unaccountable power" (Silvert 1977, p. xiii). It begins with a description of "the normative and structural changes that have developed since the establishment of the Republic." Featured are descriptions of clashes "between democratic and undemocratic ideals and between private interest and public welfare." It continues to discuss the international behavior of the United States, which Silvert characterizes as operating "under only minimal legal and political constraints." Next, in his discussion of democracy in the United States, he warns, as did President Dwight Eisenhower in his 1961 Farewell Address,[5] that freedom and democracy can be threatened by "pseudo-democratic, technocratic intellectuals." Silvert saw this threat exemplified by Samuel Huntington's arguments that "the troubles of the 1960s were an evidence of a 'democratic distemper'—of too much democracy."[6] He argued that a position like Huntington's would result in elites identifying the public interest with their private interests, thus limiting access to education and opportunity as well as the chance for all citizens to realize the American Dream. He would argue that increasing wealth and income inequality in the United States are signs of the erosion of democracy, and subsequent books like Heather Cox Richardson's *To Make Men Free: A History of the Republican Party* (2014) describe how that process has evolved.

Posing and arguing about[7] such questions made Silvert an inspirational teacher. His style was to argue because he believed that arguing was necessary for each individual to express his or her unique position. Those who understood that his broad-smiling arguing genuinely aimed to achieve fuller understanding of others' positions were profoundly encouraged by his style. Being with Silvert in the classroom, in a professional setting, or in a personal context, tended to be a very animated experience. This liveliness encouraged, as Silvert intended, fullness of expression. The word people chose to describe him in these settings was "mensch"—Yiddish for someone to admire and emulate with a warm and engaging nature. In the 1960s "menschlich" Silvert raised nuanced questions that other scholars were just beginning to pose in their writings and in the classroom. He refused to resort to reductionist answers for key human issues and grappled with the complexities that he encountered in intellectual traditions and, extremely importantly, in the overseas environments he came to know so well.

Silvert spent more than eight years carrying out research in Guatemala, Argentina, and Chile. Early in his scholarly career, he joined the American Universities Field Staff (AUFS). His job was to live overseas (he spent time for AUFS in Central America, Argentina, Uruguay, and Chile) and send reports in the form of letters to the roughly two dozen US universities that sponsored AUFS. AUFS employed seasoned overseas hands to send personal reports about the countries in which they were living to be used by faculty and students in these universities. Silvert began at AUFS in 1955. During his professional career, especially when he lived in Latin America, he built a remarkable set of personal relationships. He built deep and mutually respectful collegial (and often personal) relations with Latin Americans, some of whom were critical of aspects of US society, US foreign and domestic policy, US politics, and the capitalistic basis of the US economy. These relationships changed Silvert's views of the world; they also changed the views of many of the individuals with whom he engaged, often convincing them that the American Dream is a goal that should be pursued irrespective of the momentary policies or characteristics of the United States.

Silvert's combination of sensitivity to local conditions and his conceptual turn of mind resulted in his being named AUFS Director of Studies (in effect, intellectual-in-chief). His reports were so well received in the university world that a number of the AUFS sponsor institutions invited him to join their full-time faculties. In 1962 he agreed to join the Dartmouth College Department of Government with the rank of professor.

In conversations and in the classroom, Silvert's discussions of national development were always salted with stories from his experiences outside the United States. His ability to discuss "great issues" while humanizing discussions was legendary among his students and professional colleagues. His ability to humanize his observations was widely noted and was the subject of an extraordinary obituary by Yale historian Richard Morse (1977) in the *Hispanic American Historical Review*. This capacity made sensitivity to what Silvert called "human autonomy," a core element of the American Dream, infectious for individuals reading, conversing with, or learning from him.

Silvert's humanizing capacities were critical for the formation of the Latin American Studies Association (LASA) in 1966. LASA was incorporated in Washington, DC, as a "non-profit professional body created by scholarly area specialists to meet their particular and growing needs" (Cline 1966). The incorporation of LASA was the culmination of a long process initiated in the 1950s by the Hispanic Foundation of the Library of Congress and ultimately successfully by the American Council of Learned Societies (ACLS) and the Social Science Research Council (SSRC) forming the Joint Committee on Latin American Studies (JCLAS). With members from both the Northern and Southern Hemispheres, the JCLAS aimed to create a distinctive regional studies association.

LASA was distinctive in 1966, a time when one of the much-debated issues in regional studies was what Edward Said (1978) later labeled "orientalism"—a general patronizing Western attitude toward societies outside of North America and Europe. In Said's analysis, the West views these societies as unchanging and underdeveloped. The implicit corollary to this conclusion is the view that Western society is developed, dynamic, and superior. Such Western patronizing was, in part, the residue of the fact that many of those societies had been parts of European colonial empires until the mid-twentieth century. Such patronizing was unacceptable to the members of JCLAS and the group of scholars it encouraged to form LASA. The leader among those scholars, a prime force in drafting its initial by-laws, was Silvert. He was persuaded by the JCLAS and the scholars it had assembled to serve as LASA's first president.

At the time of his death in June 1976, Silvert was serving as director of the Ford Foundation's Social Science Program for Latin America and as professor in New York University's Department of Politics. He had held both positions since 1967. The latter position gave him full and continuous access to the faculty and students of a great university; the former position made him central to the development of the social sciences in Latin America. At that time, no other individual had ever so fully and formally straddled the worlds of US universities and foundations as he did. This dual position allowed Silvert to immerse himself in the world of ideas, which he truly loved, and promote "the development of a social science that was both politically relevant and truly intellectual" (Jutkowitz 1977, p. viii) for the region to which he had devoted so much of his professional energies.

During Silvert's time at Ford, the foundation was one of the most important supporters of "modern" social sciences in Latin America. Its headquarters were in New York City, and it had field offices that directly supported local individuals and projects in Mexico City, Bogotá, Lima, Santiago, Rio de Janeiro, and Buenos Aires. It was an important supporter of the Consejo Latino Americano de las Ciencias Sociales (CLACSO), an incipient region-wide social science professional association and the Facultad Latino Americano de las Ciencias Sociales, a budding regional social sciences graduate-level research and teaching institution. In the United States, it provided virtually all of the support for the Latin American Foreign Area Fellowship Program and other graduate and postgraduate programs directed by the JCLAS. Ford's Social Science Program for Latin America was an important force attempting to create the modern empathic public policy–engaged individual that Silvert saw as essential for freedom and democracy in the region.

Silvert's time at Ford coincided with military takeovers of democratically elected governments in Peru (1968), Bolivia (1970), Ecuador (1972), Uruguay (1973), and Chile (1973) and had been preceded by coups in Brazil (1964) and Argentina (1966). These de facto military-dominated governments were the antithesis of his concept of democracies guaranteeing freedom to all of a nation's citizens. In fact, at the time of Silvert's death, all governments on the mainland of Latin America from Guatemala to Chile had been put in place by their nations' armed forces, with the exception of Colombia and Venezuela. These military governments greatly limited democratic freedoms and presented huge challenges to his work and that of the social scientists on the staff of the Ford Foundation.

The overthrow of the democratically elected government of Salvador Allende in Chile in 1973 was particularly traumatic for the mission of the Ford Foundation. Many of Ford's individual and institutional grantees were in jeopardy. Moreover, the brutality of the Chilean military establishing and sustaining its control over the country created grave concerns for broad sectors of Chilean citizens. Of special concern for Ford were the Chileans whose work it supported and the many refugees from other Latin American countries for whom Allende's Chile had become the last refuge for their efforts to build modern social sciences in Latin America. Chile had become the country of destination for thousands of Argentines, Brazilians, Uruguayans, Peruvians, Ecuadorians, Colombians, Bolivians, and Paraguayans who feared for their lives in their home countries or felt that their freedoms were seriously curtailed there. That the efforts of South American intelligence agencies were coordinating their surveillance and repression of individuals viewed as threats or potential threats to military regimes informally (and formally starting in 1975 through Operation Condor) was suspected and feared by many of these expatriates.

Ford received extremely alarming reports on the situation in Chile from the head of its Santiago office, Peter Bell, and dispatched senior Ford Latin American Program Officer Richard Dye to Argentina and Chile to report directly on conditions there. Dye's forty-four-page memorandum reporting on meetings with Ford Foundation staff and twenty-six "non-Foundation Persons" confirmed the worst reports.[8] As a result of this and other reports, Ford immediately began evaluating whether it should suspend or sustain its operations in Chile and other parts of Latin America. It strained to balance its goals of facilitating the development of politically relevant social science–based public policy with not appearing to support regimes that limited freedom and democracy with not abandoning or jeopardizing individuals who had been involved with Ford activities in the region.

Basic to the foundation's concerns was the urging of its local partners to "do what it can to help preserve, if possible, some significant portion of Chilean intellectual life"[9] and, as Dye reported, to assist people "who represent the potential future rebirth of Chilean intellectual life and stand to contribute the most generally wherever they end up."[10] In this regard, early on Dye and Bell recommended that Ford set a goal to "locate third party arrangements for the great bulk of assistance to individuals," thus removing the foundation from the role of decisionmaker on individual merits.

In New York Silvert was central to the coordination of efforts to deal with "the Chilean situation." On October 24, 1973, he reported to "WDC (Carmichael), RWD (Dye), et al," on "some highlights of the sessions" of "an *ad hoc* group" of twelve American and two Canadian scholars with whom he had met at the SSRC.[11] The import was that a mechanism needed to be created to find ways to assist "fellow academics and students" among "Chileans and other refugees in Chile" with finding positions in the United States and elsewhere. Silvert reported that the group suggested a base of operations be located in Chile, that coordinating functions in the United States should be centered in New York or Washington (he reported offering his own office at NYU as "temporary space in New York"), and that the group remain in existence. He also reported the recommendation of the creation of a small "steering committee," hiring an "executive secretary" who "should be a person of academic stature and respect," and locating an organization to administer the funds (LASA was suggested). His last paragraph began and ended as follows:

> Naturally, the Foundation was referred to on many occasions. I was
> very noncommittal except on one issue: ... the Foundation is not and
> should not be an operating agency except in the most abnormal situa-
> tion immediately affecting human rights and in the absence of other
> effective and more appropriate agencies. We shall be hearing in the
> normal course of events concerning expenses connected with this
> meeting, and with the establishment of a steering committee cum exec-
> utive director and staff.[12]

What was "heard" eventually came from a steering committee
involving the SSRC officer staffing the JCLAS (I had just become
JCLAS staff director) and faculty members from two universities—one
on each US coast (Riordan Roett of Johns Hopkins University and
Richard Fagen of Stanford University). Distinguished senior Latin
Americanist historian and former SSRC JCLAS staff director Bryce
Wood was hired to serve as executive director. The committee contacted
first a select group of presidents of colleges and universities throughout
the United States and then faculty members at institutions in Europe and
the Americas who they believed could provide "teaching, research, and
related academic positions for the many qualified scholars who may
wish to or may have to leave Chile." Based on Silvert's recommendation, funds were granted by Ford to the JCLAS through the SSRC to
finance the activities coordinated by Bryce Wood. Eventually that
resulted in a network of scholars, largely in the United States and also in
Canada, Mexico, and Europe, working pro bono to find professional
homes for refugee scholars from Chile and other South American countries with military governments.

Scholars in danger were identified through cooperation with CLAC-
SO, which relied in part on Ford Social Science funding. In addition,
thanks to the 1972 negotiations involving Wood and the JCLAS chair,
economist Joseph Grunwald, Silvert had recommended and Ford author-
ized that non-US scholars were able to receive Ford-funded JCLAS
grants. This allowed the economist Albert Hirschman,[13] who became
JCLAS chair in September 1973, to work with the Joint Committee
(whose members included Fernando Henrique Cardoso, Alejandro
Foxley, Osvaldo Sunkel, Julio Cotler, Franklin Knight, June Nash, and
Thomas Skidmore) to direct fellowship funds to Latin American scholars. The result was critical funding through the JCLAS starting with its
1973/1974 competitions to approximately twenty-five leading refugee
scholars per year (Adelman 1913, pp. 469–70). These funds, combined
with the positions secured by Wood's efforts and the network of volun-
teers he coordinated, rescued hundreds of refugees.[14] Many others were

supported without leaving their countries or while in exile by the operations of Ford's Latin American field offices, headed by the foundation's overall Latin American Program director William Carmichael, himself closely advised by Silvert.

Silvert's work at the Ford Foundation focused on building politically relevant social science for Latin America. It did so by attempting to construct inclusive institutions which could sustain the ideas of freedom and democracy and also by supporting (and rescuing) technically competent and interpersonally empathetic individuals to operate those institutions and produce the ideas that would drive them. Individuals supported by Ford programs, such as the Brazilian Fernando Henrique Cardoso, Chileans Ricardo Lagos and Alejandro Foxley, Uruguayan Carlos Filguera, and Argentines Elisabeth Jelin, Guillermo O'Donnell, and Tomás Eloy Martínez, are among the most visible. With these efforts at Ford, with his evocatively profound and humane AUFS and scholarly writings, with his mentoring of hundreds of students in the United States and in Latin America, with his *menschlich* relations with colleagues, Kalman Silvert aimed to create conditions for "life better and richer and fuller for everyone, with opportunity for each according to ability or achievement" (Adams 1931): the American Dream.

Notes

1. I was a student of Kalman H. Silvert at Dartmouth College from January 1963 to May 1964 and remained in close contact with him until his death in 1976. For some detail, see Goodman (2013).

2. The prologue to his posthumously published *The Reason for Democracy* (1977), suggestively starts, "In 1893 my parents came to the golden land. The metal they sought was not in mountains, in the beds of streams, or in banks" (p. xi).

3. One discussion of this phenomenon has been presented by Brzezinski (2012), esp. the chapter "The Impact of Global Political Awakening."

4. Emerson (1960) was Silvert's touchstone for discussing nationalism.

5. In his June 17, 1961, Farewell Address, Eisenhower warned against two threats to "our liberties or democratic processes...the acquisition of unwarranted influence, whether sought or unsought, by the military-industrial complex...[and]...that public policy could itself become the captive of a scientific-technological elite."

6. Silvert (1977), p. 81. Silvert based his assertion on arguments made in Huntington (1975).

7. In the Casseririan tradition, Silvert understood that each individual necessarily had a unique perspective and that understanding and action were processes of continual argumentation. Thus, he concludes the prologue to *The Reason for Democracy* with the words "Let us argue" (p. xiv).

8. See Ford Foundation Inter-Office Memorandum, Richard W. Dye to Dr. William D. Carmichael, October 11, 1973, Rockefeller Archive Center, Sleepy Hollow, New York.

9. Ford Foundation Inter-Office Memorandum, p. 2.

10. Ford Foundation Inter-Office Memorandum, "Chile Notes," p. 3.

11. Ford Foundation, Inter-Office Memorandum. I participated in the meeting. In addition to Kalman Silvert and me, the following individuals were present: Joseph Collins, Arthur Domike, Richard Fagen, Joseph Grunwald, Albert Hirschman, Henry Landsberger, June Nash, Michael Potashnik, Riordan Roett, Alfred Siemens, John Strasma, Brady Tyson, and Lionel Vallee.

12. Ford Foundation Inter-Office Memorandum, p. 2.

13. It is notable that Albert Hirschman in Marseilles in 1940 had worked incognito as Albert Hermant (nicknamed "Beamish" for his smile and can-do approach) with Varian Fry of the Emergency Rescue Committee to help more than 2,000 refugees from fascism leave France through Spain and Portugal to third countries.

14. Exact figures are not available as written records from Wood's operations are not available and many of the rescued scholars were placed through personal efforts initiated by Wood and completed by others.

11

Silvert as a
Public Intellectual

Morris Blachman and Kenneth Sharpe

On October 11, 1965, Kalman Silvert, then a professor of government at Dartmouth College, arrived on campus after a meeting at the State Department in Washington to address the college's Great Issues course. The scheduled topic was "Aspirations of Developing Nations." On the plane back from Washington, he ripped up his prepared talk. He was riled up and decided instead to talk about the justification the State Department and President Lyndon B. Johnson were giving for sending the Marines and troops from the 82nd Airborne to intervene in the Dominican Republic that past April. Officials still insisted that the intervention had been necessary to prevent the deepening of a civil war—and the dangers of establishing another communist foothold like Cuba in the Americas. Lists of communists supposedly involved on the rebel side were released by the State Department.

Silvert told the students that these official stories of a communist danger and another Cuba had no basis in fact. The list of communists released by the US embassy was largely false. He explained that in reality, this was an internal conflict between the traditional forces who had backed the brutal Trujillo dictatorship—a US-supported regime that ended in 1961 with the assassination of the dictator—and the supporters of Juan Bosch, an elected populist who took office in February 1963 only to be overthrown by a coup engineered by the old Trujillo military leadership seven months later. Silvert explained how the Dominican military itself was split and that the US intervention would prevent the defeat of the Trujillo loyalists by a more democratic coalition of Bosch supporters and progressive military officers. He said that the State Department refused to publicly recognize the facts of the case, that we

155

were not being told the truth by our own government, and that such lying corroded our democracy by making it difficult to hold our elected officials accountable or to trust them.

Such truths, alas, are not that surprising to hear today, but they were strong words in 1965. This was a time when the Vietnam antiwar movement was just beginning to get traction; many students were deeply skeptical of claims the protesters were making that our government was lying to us. For Ken Sharpe and many of Silvert's students in the audience, his claims were hard to dismiss, so rigorous and well-reasoned was his teaching. Silvert insisted that we carefully examine and learn how to critique the competing theories of political development. He also demanded careful attention to detail, facts, and history. He insisted, to use today's lingo, that arguments and policies be "evidence-based."

Here was this sober, deep-thinking, well-read prof standing in front of us, systematically demolishing claims made by our highest elected officials. You could feel the undercurrent of outrage that seethed beneath the logical, systematic, factual analysis. He was angry at officials not simply for what they had done but for their public lies and hypocrisy. For him, this was not just business as usual. This was unacceptable. Ken remembers thinking what was this smart and somewhat awe-inspiring academic—a person so comfortably at home in the halls of a university—what was he doing flying to Washington to talk to people in the State Department in the first place? To tell them what he thought? To challenge them?

Silvert had come to NYU from Dartmouth in 1967, and Moss Blachman arrived there that same year, before classes began. Moss first met this man who became his mentor and friend when Silvert invited him to his apartment to get to know him. Silvert sat him down and almost immediately launched into an intellectual tour de force explaining to his new graduate assistant his philosophical and theoretical roots. He began with the history of political and sociological thought and what he took as useful and what problematic in Aristotle, Machiavelli, Kant, Weber, phenomenology, Marx, Cassirer, Locke—all in about twenty minutes. Then he led Moss through his theory of knowledge and the central place of human choice in the construction of social reality. Man, he said, was a producer and consumer of symbols, a choice-making being, and social science had to help find where those choices were at any particular time. Silvert explained why general laws and deterministic social theories were limited and even destructive: they don't help us find where and when man has the power to make his social world, and sometimes they prevent the exploration of this question. He further argued that because man has power, he has a choice in how to use it—for good or for evil—or he could abnegate that power and try, for example, to live in the ivory tower of the academy. Moss nodded, but remembers that this experience was like drinking water through a fire hose. Over the next few years, he had the opportunity to grasp what Silvert was saying by working closely with him and watching what he did, not just what he said.

He regularly joined Silvert and his wife, Frieda, in the informal salons they hosted in their living room. This was the real classroom. Visitors to New York from Latin America—politicians, diplomats, party leaders, past and future presidents, scholars from all fields—would come to have dinner or a drink and talk late into the night about the current situation in their country or the region and beyond. They relished the interchange and often sought Silvert's counsel. They would analyze the current conjuncture, the new possibilities, the coming crises, the patterns that were not yet visible and, very important, the obstacles to and possibilities for action in pursuit of the public good, such as educational reform, social welfare, the inclusion of marginalized groups, tax policy, economic reform, and coalition building. Equally likely was some discussion of music and the arts or probing age-old philosophical questions. Everything had a purpose. Silvert believed the aesthetics and moral/ethical dimensions of life were as important to develop as was the intellectual—the use of reason and rationality and the pursuit of truth. Indeed, only by calling on all the aspects of being human could one begin to exercise the practical wisdom required to build and sustain democratic society.

What we both discovered learning from and working with Silvert was that he was quintessentially an academic. Learned. Theoretical. Analytical. A master of detail. Someone who was always putting things into an intellectual and historical context. But he was doing something that few professors did at the time. He did not want to live solely in the context of a small academic world. He wanted to engage actively in public life and was right at home doing so—not only as he traveled throughout Latin America but in his living room, where Latin America came to him.

We tried to make sense of the two seemingly contradictory hats that he wore. Silvert was not just a full-time NYU professor. When he moved to New York from Dartmouth he also took a full-time job at the Ford Foundation as the Social Science Advisor to the Latin American and Caribbean Program. Given his commitments, why had he not just left academia to work at Ford—to dedicate himself to doing the kind of development work a position there enabled? Why was being a scholar-teacher so important to him that he wanted to do both at the same time? What also seemed strange, at least at first, was the strategy Silvert undertook at Ford when faced by the truly momentous crises that the *dictaduras* had brought to the Southern Cone: the dictatorship in Brazil, the military regime in Argentina, and the overthrow of Allende and the Pinochet dictatorship that followed in Chile. Peter Cleaves carefully details the response Silvert led at Ford. He helped create a regional network of independent academic institutes so that the social scientists ousted from the national universities by the dictatorships had a place to work. He helped find positions for some in Europe and the United States. Quietly, he even helped rescue some of these scholars, enabling them to be whisked to safe havens.

Silvert's commitment to saving lives, his loyalty to those he knew and had worked with, was not surprising. But why respond to these dictatorships by creating social science institutes around the region? This was not a traditional human rights response, and it was certainly not a traditional political scientist's response. Neither was it the standard development work of the Ford Foundation. Silvert's response to the Dominican Republic crisis, his twin roles at NYU and the Ford Foundation, and his response to tyranny in Latin America were all of a piece. So were his earlier writings for the American Universities Field Staff reports and the advisory role he played on the Linowitz Commission. What Silvert modeled for his students and colleagues was the life of a principled scholar activist—a *public* intellectual. Deeply engaged in scholarship, theoretical and empirical, he felt obligated to use his knowledge, his position, and his power to repair or heal the world. "Tikkun olam" would be the expression in his Judaic tradition: to fix what is broken. In that tradition, he was a real mensch. He was a model for his time, and he is a model for our time.

The Vision

As an academic, Silvert believed that he and his students needed fidelity to the truth. In his vision, that required a deep knowledge of political theory and politics and history—social, cultural, political, and economic. This knowledge could throw light on the possibilities for change and continuity. If a central purpose of knowledge was to fix what was broken, what did that look like? Silvert held that no vision could transform the world, and transforming the world to make it fit a vision opened the door to tyranny. What could be done depended on what a particular historical context made possible, what kind of people lived in a society, and what their culture and values were. But what, in general, ought we to aim for?

Silvert's life as a public intellectual was informed by a vision of human flourishing and creating the kind of culture, class structure, and institutions (particularly political and educational) that enabled this flourishing. He knew that people's natural talents and potential skills were different, and he thought allowing those talents and skills to develop would enable each human being to be fulfilled—*eudemonia*, Aristotle would have said, the fulfilling of one's human capacities. Enabling such flourishing would also be good for society.

For him, individual flourishing could only happen in a social community in which there was a roughly equitable inclusion of all people—regardless of gender, race, or economic class—in the educational and economic institutions that would allow them to develop their reason, talents, and empathy for others. This was not about rugged individualism: he believed people were social animals and that democracy was the product of the mutual interactions within the social community. To the degree that anyone was excluded, the social community was impoverished and suffered. This was "the reason for democracy," the title of his book published posthumously in 1977. A society would flourish, argued Silvert, to the extent that it was inclusive: to the extent that it improved the life chances of all its citizens, allowing them to flourish independent of class or race or gender or ethnicity or religion. Inclusiveness—his way of talking about equality, of bringing everyone into the community—was a critical value for him. All deserved an equal life chance.

To analyze a particular society, Silvert first identified the particularities of the five major institutions derived from classical sociology: the family, religion, education, the economy, and the polity. One crucial characteristic of a democracy, he argued, was that decisions that affected all citizens were made in the public arena, which meant in the polity. No private groups or groupings should be empowered to control or determine public decisions. Religious leaders and economic entrepreneurs would have their say in public debate, but no group of religious leaders and no group of entrepreneurs should be able to have their words or their particular frames be the law or the public interest. Public decisions were made in the polity, by elected legislatures and executives, and by an independent judiciary. The takeover of the public space by religious institutions or by economic institutions was a kind of religious or economic imperialism: an invasion of what ought to be public by the private.

For Silvert, the queen of all the institutions was the polity: it was politics—good democratic politics, properly structured political institutions inhabited by good citizens and good politicians—that enabled the transformation in class and in educational and economic institutions that allowed this inclusion and flourishing. The kind of politics that was most likely to make this possible was democratic politics. Silvert was a modern Renaissance man: he believed in the possibility of the use of reason. He believed that man was always able to perfect himself, and you did this as a citizen who empowered both the self and others. Democracy, with all its warts, was the way to do this. The *public* sector *was* the public.

In a democracy the public space included *all* individuals—at least that was the promise of democracy. Silvert's critique of class was that class stratification risked excluding some from the public space: all people need to develop their talents and skills. The polis was the overarching institution because it had the role and responsibility of overcoming the accidents of birth so that all people could, in fact, be included in educational and economic opportunity. Down to every fiber in his body, Silvert believed you needed a system that allowed everybody to achieve their maximum.

Silvert was highly critical of social scientists who reified "value-free" social science because he feared that knowledge, reason, fact, and science could be disastrous to the human condition if not aimed at human flourishing. "Kal was passionate about values," remembers Peter Cleaves, a colleague of his at the Ford Foundation (and earlier a student of his at Dartmouth). "A question he raised in the classroom was telling: 'How is it that Germany—with its philosophical, musical, literary, scientific, and architectural accomplishments—being among the most advanced countries in the world, perpetrated the Holocaust?" (Cleaves 2013, p. 45).

Silvert was also critical of political scientists who saw democracy as merely a good compromise between the rule of the few who were rich and claimed to be wise, and the rule of the demos who threatened mob rule—a way to tame and channel humanity's animal instincts. Democracy was not just a practical system that created mechanisms for conflict resolution allowing interests to clash in nonviolent ways. It was not just a system for keeping leaders accountable, for checking tyranny with periodic elections or constitutional checks and balances. Nor was it just a system for allowing multiple voices to be heard and compromises reached. All true, Silvert thought. But democracy for him had a deeper promise and purpose. Democracy contained the seed for encouraging inclusion and human flourishing because it was built on the critical notions—often honored in the breach—of equality before the law, public education, popular participation by citizens, rational deliberation, and holding rulers accountable. The gap between that promise and the reality was what deeply concerned Silvert.

The United States has dedicated itself to the proposition of helping people become free as they attain competence. This vision, always difficult to define let alone realize, has ever been under attack. Never made real for everyone, it has still always been partially true for some. The rich successes of the United States have now brought this country to the point at which democratic freedoms can be extended to all members of society; the ethic of the American Revolution is ours to complete.

Silvert was not naive about the problems that human nature posed for democracy. Like Aristotle, Machiavelli, and Hobbes, he saw the dangers posed by people responding to their animal instincts. He witnessed, studied, and feared political systems that mobilized such instincts for national power, tyranny, and imperialism—as under Nazism, fascism, communism, or the authoritarianism of the Argentinian military or Pinochet's Chile. He believed that a democratic system made it possible to bring gradual improvement not only to tame these instincts but to spread reason, empathy, and national community in ways that would allow people to flourish on another basis beside their animal instincts— that could encourage the development of the kind of citizens who would express civic virtues like reason, deliberation, compromise, tolerance, respect, trust, and a desire to make their community inclusive. If you don't have democracy, people are not in a position to have the power to transform themselves into fully actualized human beings, to become empowered human beings. The reason for democracy is that without it, market forces become sovereign or political authority ends up in the hands of a few who become dominant or overwhelming and both threaten freedom and undermine human flourishing and could cause the kind of individualism and fragmentation that Hobbes predicted would lead to a war of all against all, which would necessitate a Leviathan.

Silvert was concerned about democracy everywhere, but he was especially focused on how to close the gap between the promise and reality of democracy here at home. Take educational institutions, for example. He saw the promise of a high-quality, inclusive public school system that could be a "crucial step in mitigating the effect of the accident of birth" on people's economic roles and life chances; it could sustain our competitiveness abroad. But it was a promise unfulfilled, he wrote in 1970, because of "opposition to taxes, misplaced political priorities and inattention" which "have contributed to a continuing decay of public education in the United States. The decline in quality of many grammar and high schools in American cities also underscores how a racial conflict concerning the extension of community affects institutions." The "extension of community" was his way of saying the inclusion of the excluded. This democratic promise of education was worth struggling for—and it's always under threat. Even Jean-Jacques Rousseau, who inspired many of our republic's founders, "would not have been at all surprised by the interplay between education and citizenship on the one hand, and incompetence and alienation on the other." Rousseau "saw it as in the nature of man to strive for reasoned understanding, and in the nature of social life as he knew it to attempt to deprive him of that understanding" (Silvert, *The Reason for Democracy*, p. 9).

Abroad, Silvert was a passionate critic of the role the United States played in undermining the promise of democracy. He believed democracy was organized and played out within the political boundaries of the nation-state. He also believed it was a universal good. Democratic nations had a responsibility to help other countries develop democracy and especially had a responsibility to act in international relations so as not to deter or harm the development of democracy elsewhere. In the early 1970s, for example, the Nixon administration responded to the election of socialist Salvador Allende as president of Chile by imposing severe economic and diplomatic sanctions and covert funding of opposition groups, all of which helped destabilize the country. When the military toppled the government in 1973—ending one of the oldest and most stable democracies in Latin America—the administration was willing to support the dictatorship of General Augusto Pinochet. "The Allende government," wrote Silvert, "was legally elected, even though by a minority of the voters, in a country that had practiced democratic forms for longer than any other Latin American state, and with less violence than the United States. Our actions helped destroy one of the world's few democracies" (Silvert, *The Reason for Democracy*, p. 59).

Such unchecked and unaccountable US power abroad undermined some of Silvert's optimism about the American dream, and led him to feel betrayed by the US government. At home, he criticized the leadership of US institutions "who seem neither to understand nor to respect the promise" of democracy but instead "deny the American ethic" by holding "the line against the process of completing our national community....Immobilism, hesitancy, and cautious tinkering no longer are acceptable ways of holding together a half-free, half-trammeled society." That failure of leadership to pursue the promise of democracy was "the essence of our contemporary crisis....Today accountability has broken down at all levels: the web of social life is weakened and in parts ripped. The corrosion affects us all." If the conflict persists, he wrote, "American life will continue to be severely perturbed—and our weakening will inexorably bring us down" (Silvert, *The Reason for Democracy*, p. 2). Silvert focused on the role of leadership—including the leadership of scholars as public intellectuals—because institutions and laws of history and culture would not automatically curb such corrosion nor fulfill the US ethic. Markets may be viewed as theoretically self-correcting, but he argued that mechanism has never operated fully in accordance with its theoretical design. Class conflicts and the contradictions of capital, some argued, theoretically will lead to revolutions and human improvement, but that general theory has also been challenged by history. There is nothing automatic about democracy improving itself. The collapse of the Weimar Republic into Nazism and the collapse of the longest standing democracy in Latin America, Chile, into Pinochet's authoritarianism are proof of that. Nevertheless, for Silvert there was a conjuncture here, full of potential for positive change: the very failure to live up to the democratic promise sat side by side with the promise, with a set of principles and often internal dynamics that might enable that promise to be fulfilled. But that fulfillment demanded wise leadership, dedicated to the promise of democracy.

This conjuncture created the space for ordinary citizens, politicians, civic leaders, and statesmen to act to encourage greater inclusion, greater flourishing, the fulfillment of the promise of democracy. In that space for action, academics as engaged citizens, as public intellectuals, could act to make a difference. Like a free press—that unofficial "fourth branch" of government—public intellectuals can help give the citizenry the knowledge to be empowered, help support a democratic civic culture, and provide the evidence and transparency to hold public officials accountable. They could help generate the knowledge, the free flow of ideas, the honesty, and the public transparency that were needed for democracy to fulfill its potential. Engaging citizens and leaders to act was crucial, argued Silvert in *Reasons for Democracy*:

> We will not move into a totalitarian dictatorship without breaking many heads and many institutions, nor will we deepen and extend our democracy without profoundly changing our system of rewards, our judgments of individual worth, and our ways of forcing accountability on public institutions. The only certainty is that we cannot choose to do nothing, for we are already in a pervasive irrationality that satisfies

neither the dark nor the light sides of our desires. We are not at a cross-roads where we can camp; we are on a freeway at rush hour. (pp. 11–12)

The Limits of Vision:
The Importance of Theory and Understanding

Silvert argued that to transform or to "repair the world," you first need to understand that world. You had to know what history taught and what theory enabled one to understand about the causes of our contemporary dilemmas and about the possibilities for creative human action. An activist-scholar could not be an activist without the scholarship; a public intellectual could not be effective in public without being an intellectual. The scholarship had to inform the activism—just like the vision informed the scholarship.

Because Silvert aimed to encourage political choices that would expand inclusion and human flourishing, he wanted to encourage scholarship that helped understand the spaces for human choice. That meant understanding how power was created and exercised, what caused conflict and change, what enabled conflicts to be resolved, and where human action—freedom, choice, empowered participation—fit into the larger social and historical structures that otherwise might seem causal and totally determining.

Understanding these social and historical structures demanded doing careful, empirically grounded fieldwork and the ability to tell a narrative. History, as he saw it, was not simply a chronicling of events; history involved identifying key characters, their intentions and aspirations, their capacities, their choices, the consequences of their mistakes, and how they dealt with them. Silvert's early work as a member of the American Universities Field Staff involved traveling to cities and villages in Latin America and writing detailed reports on topics like civilian–military relations in Argentina in the months before the overthrow of the Frondizi government. In these reports you can see Silvert bringing alive the rich context, the meaning that class and institutions and politics had for actors, and the choices these actors did or did not make. These were often woven together in narratives that brought the case to life for the reader. He encouraged his doctoral students to engage themselves deeply in this historically grounded and highly contextual fieldwork.

At the same time Silvert immersed himself and his students in theoretical debates. He emphasized the limited usefulness of any general theory that sought a universal law of social change or political power. He critiqued functionalist theories of then prominent sociologists like Talcott Parsons or political scientists like Gabriel Almond and Bingham Powell that sought to explain the nature of society's major institutions by pointing to the universal societal functions these institutions fulfilled. He questioned theories of capitalism or class conflict that sought to explain stability through false consciousness or explain change through inevitable contradictions built into the economic system. He challenged the equilibrium theories of economics that presumed there was a natural balance automatically achieved through the interaction of supply and demand. He was deeply skeptical of cultural theories that sought to explain the lack of democracy throughout Latin America by the hierarchical heritage of the Spanish Crown and the Catholic Church. Each drew attention to some important explanatory components, but none explained variation and change in particular contexts.

Silvert argued that "equilibrium theories"—particularly theories of economic man and his self-correcting market mechanisms—could falsely lead us to believe in a "tidy model" of change and cause like this one:

> False information given to policy-makers leads to false predictions; members of the policy then perceive a resulting failure of policy; they develop tensions caused by the discrepancy between anticipated and actual results, between the previous explanations and the new ones; action to alleviate the tension must occur; if all goes well, a new balance is attained. (Silvert, *Man's Power*, p. 46)

This kind of general theory, Silvert argued, failed to identify some of the most important things we need to know. We don't know, in a particular situation, whether policymakers will actually perceive a failure of policy. In the past four decades, this failure to perceive has been much in evidence. Failed attempts at using military force to do nation-building in third world countries have only occasionally led policymakers to perceive a failure in policy. Even if policymakers recognize the failure this may not lead "to subsequent action"—so we need to know "what influences affect the action." Furthermore, those who are supposed to "manage" the tensions "may well try to manipulate social 'facts' that exist only in their own fertile imaginations." How policymakers frame these facts—and the solutions—may have more to do with the lobbyists and deep pockets who fund them, with frameworks that blind them, or with the political expediency of the moment. At an even deeper level, such theories of equilibrium and self-adjustment "do not adequately account for the possibility that sometimes balance simply cannot be redressed within the existing system, that some social situations demand new and different systems to attain equilibrium" (Silvert, *Man's Power*, p. 47).

Silvert's critique of such general theories in *Man's Power* was quite concrete: they failed to provide adequate explanations. They could not explain why some democracies continue a politics of exclusion and others are more inclusive, or why a strong state can tame and regulate market capitalism in one country but not in another. Such theories failed because they fixated a priori on a single cause or were unconnected to the variable of context—they attempted, in his words, "to frame the whole of human experience...from an intellectual base somewhere outside of man's historical experience...they collapse when we apply them to particular cases." Keep in mind the universal, he argued in his classes and in his writings, but "think simultaneously of the universal and the unique, the generalizable and the particular, the variable and the invariable" (*Man's Power,* p. 9).

Silvert was particularly concerned about the failure of such theories when it came to questions about democracy: how do you explain the development of democracy, its maintenance, and its corrosion in actual historical cases? The design of constitutions and courts and representative legislatures and parties and educational systems is not like a skilled craftsman building a clock, a mechanism that can be left to work on its own with occasional winding or a battery replacement. Even in established democracies the institutions we live in always need care and improvement. This may seem obvious when said, but citizens and even scholars in long-standing democracies like the United States (and Chile until the early 1970s) take democratic institutions to be simply "background" conditions, the givens of our world: always stable, always reliable, always there to tame elites and protect us from the arbitrary use of power.

Parties and groups can battle out their competing interests within the assumed safety of their democratic institutions, with little thought given to the corrosive long-term effects of exclusion on the basis of class or race or gender or sexual preference and with little worry about the dangers that stalemate, gridlock, or vetoes or filibusters might have on the well-being or very existence of the democratic system itself.

The nurture and sustained care that democratic institutions need often goes unrecognized even in the United States, where our own history tells us better. Consider: the civil war; the failed efforts at inclusion for blacks in the aftermath of the failure of Reconstruction and the struggle almost a century later to fulfill the promise with the 1965 civil rights legislation; the dangers posed by McCarthyism; the growth of an unchecked presidency in foreign policy which in recent decades has become normalized and accepted; the ways that covert wars undermined congressional authority to declare war; state surveillance, repression, and the use of agents provocateurs by the Johnson and Nixon administrations to silence the free speech of antiwar protestors; the Nixon administration efforts to subvert the presidential elections in 1972 which the Watergate scandal revealed; the flouting of congressional legislation and its constitutional power of the purse in the Iran-contra scandal.

Many academic theories not only failed the test of "working" as explanations but failed a moral test, too: under the guise of being "value-free" and "scientific," they hid the way they framed the world. That was because "framing" was inevitable: every theory framed certain problems and left out others; every research project pointed to *this* as important to recognize rather than *that*. Even in the design of a survey there is an ethic, a morality in the very questions that are asked and how. He thought academics that talked about being "value-free" or "neutral" were talking nonsense: empirically speaking, every frame, every research project, has a built-in bias. Because scholarly work had a public impact—because it helped construct social reality in one way or another—he argued that academics needed to take public responsibility for the broader impact of their work. They did not spin their silk—or cotton—in an isolated academic cocoon.

While Silvert understood that all frameworks were biased, he was particularly concerned about one bias in many academic frameworks: their theories of causality were often deterministic, and that frame excluded the possibility of human action and choice in caring for democracy and transforming class structures, institutions, and cultures. Such frameworks blinded academics to the role that knowledge, ideas, and analysis played in sustaining or endangering institutions; and being so blinded it was easy for academics to abdicate responsibility. Such academic frameworks were disempowering, and produced fatalism. "The ideological effect of such views is to persuade us that the ways in which man can make his own world are depressingly limited" (*Man's Power*, p. 7).

Silvert was no Pollyanna: he knew that at some points in history the gateways for positive change were narrow or temporarily nailed shut. Academics needed the theoretical and analytical skills to figure out what was or was not open to choice in any particular context at *any* particular time. Where concretely did "causal" determination end and human choice begin? How could choices available now open up future possibilities for better choices in the future—how could politics increase the probability of the possibility? Academics needed to get this knowledge of possibility and danger into the public sphere. Silvert wanted them to be *engaged* academics, public intellectuals who empowered those seeking to protect and expand democratic institutions and through them, human flourishing.

Silvert did not eschew "theory." Quite the contrary, he argued that theory had to be informed by historical understanding and was critical to the intellectual work of the academy and public engagement by academics. As an alternative to general laws and abstract theories, he proposed a framework which identified key elements of politics that could explain power and change. Silvert argued that "if we want to diagnose and predict the behavior of political...men...we need to begin by learning the following [four things] about them":

1. Their "basic world views: their norms, religious beliefs, their most profound biases and prejudices."

2. "The potential power or effectiveness of individuals in groups," their "situations...within the stratification or class system of their society," "their potential ability to control goods and men on the economic marketplace, their power to command deference and prestige and to manipulate other institutional levers *if they so desire.*"

3. "Their institutional locations," the types of relations individuals and groups have to social institutions like family, religion, economy, education, and polity, and "ancillary structures as political parties [and] pressure groups."

4. The actors' personal characteristics: how "active and intelligent," "even-tempered, or irascible, possibly paranoid?" (*Man's Power*, pp.10–11).

How each element and the relationships among them were structured would be different in different historical contexts. The context told the theorists the content of each of these elements and how they were linked. It was the contextual and the theoretical insight of the analyst that created a good or bad explanation. Imagination, a knowledge of history and of the context, creativity, and good empirical fieldwork: these were the elements that would allow a good scholar to weave together an explanatory tapestry. An academic needed to understand theory and facts, and most of all needed to learn judgment: the kind of practical wisdom to interpret the facts in the light of theory, to put together the buzzing and blooming confusion of a particular context in a particular country into a plausible and useful interpretation.

What made that interpretation useful was not only its fidelity to the facts but also how accurately it portrayed the social meaning with which the context was imbued: to figure out how the social fabric could be repaired, the wounds healed, and the human condition improved in ways that nourished human flourishing and improved life chances.

Silvert as a Public Intellectual

It was no accident, then, that the last of the four "elements" of politics was personal behavior—the personal characteristics of actors. The subtitle of *Man's Power* was *A Biased Guide to Political Thought and Action*. Silvert's theoretical and intellectual approach sought to understand what could be changed by human choice and action recognizing that that would be different depending on the specific historical moment or context; his life as a public intellectual sought to transform that understanding into action.

It may seem obvious, Silvert said, "to say that events happen because men make them happen, whether consciously or not." Nevertheless "we excuse ourselves by turning technology, history, populations, communications and economies into blind forces through the simple device of putting our social eyes out." "The intellectually serious and difficult part of the matter," he said, "is to discover how much of what is made to happen is the result of rationality freshly applied, and how much is of rote response; how much it is possible at given times and places to submit to rational choice, all other things being equal" (*Man's Power*, pp. 42–43).

Among the "politically relevant aspects of personality" that he stressed were two that he strove to develop in his own life and in the lives of his students: "competence (interest, intelligence, energy level, and so on)" and "empathetic ability to see into the lives and thoughts of others who are removed by social distance." He modeled competence in his work and teaching; he insisted on competence among his students. Empathy, he taught, was not just a nice characteristic that good people ought to have. It was an essential virtue for the academic and intellectual to have: essential to teach well and essential to understand the world and improve it. An academic and an intellectual—in fact, a good citizen—must have the ability "to be sensitive to the worlds of others, to permit one's own world to be influenced by others, and to affect others in determinate and deliberate ways" (*Man's Power*, p. 36).

With a nod to Daniel Lerner, Silvert talked about empathy as "a person's ability to 'see' psychologically across social distance, to put himself in someone else's shoes." For him, empathy was a disposition and a skill that needed to be learned especially in complex and differentiated modern society, where "empathy is of great importance in overriding class and ethnic distinctions" and in new nations if leaders were to build "upon the variegated base of multi-tribal organizations" (*Man's Power*, p. 37). Empathy was particularly important for intellectuals: without it they could not understand how institutions and policies might succeed at encouraging inclusion, equity, and stability.

From the time we knew Silvert in the mid-1960s, he was dedicated to the American promise of realizing the benefits of democracy. The question for him was not whether to be publically engaged, but how? He did not run for office; he did not seek a political appointment. He wanted to inform and influence citizens, the press, and policy makers but he did not want to be a policy maker. Because he wanted his power and influence to be based on knowledge and understanding, it was important to keep one foot firmly grounded in the academic world. He wanted the integrity of what he did to be transparent, to be tested in the academic marketplace of ideas where the quality or veracity of one's ideas is always under the public scrutiny of other academics who could replicate or disconfirm his claims. Transparency and accountability were always under risk when one entered political life. He did not discourage his students from entering politics (far from it), but he warned us of how political life so often compromised academic integrity, truth telling, and reasoned choice.

Silvert's public engagement as a scholar was not common in the universities and colleges in the 1960s and 1970s. It is more common today to hear academics being interviewed and asked for their opinions in the press and on the Internet, but still not very common, at least in the United States, to see scholars actively playing a role in fighting to extend democratic principles or in helping society better understand how to make its choices or engaging in promoting institutional or policy changes aimed at human betterment. Silvert's stance on public engagement often confounded and even irritated his colleagues. On one hand he was a critic of the reigning view of "social science" as aspiring to be "value-free," which he thought was impossible, and that this belief was corrosive because it hid the inevitable biases in any framework and at the same time encouraged disengagement with politics. On the other hand, he held that direct involvement in politics destroyed the possibility of intellectual honesty and academic inquiry into the evidence base for policy. He could respect those who chose politics as a career—as long as they did not also pretend to be academics at the same time.

Being an engaged scholar-activist but not "in" politics was a difficult path to walk. It put Silvert at odds with both unengaged scholars and academics who had crossed the line into politics but still waved their academic bona fides. When the US Army began to secretly fund Latin American scholars to do research on the conditions conducive to internal revolt and the ways to curb it, Silvert's criticism was scathing about such research not only for its political consequences but because it threatened the independence and reliability of the scholars themselves. It undermined their accountability to professional academic standards by creating the image that they were beholden to military paymasters. It risked harming the legitimacy and trustworthiness of all US researchers in the region.

The fundamental importance of keeping a foot in academic life explains why Silvert was willing to work at the Ford Foundation while insisting on keeping his position as an active faculty member at New York University. His response at Ford to the threats posed by Latin American dictatorships also makes sense in light of his values, theory, and historical understanding. The politicization of the universities by the dictatorships closed the space for academics in the social sciences to do honest, probing intellectual work. The dictatorships were trying to shutter a window that could provide light and transparency on the government, its officials, and existing social conditions. The dictatorships were closing down the intellectual work that could help citizens understand what was happening, analyze the effects of government policies, and see alternative possibilities.

That is why Silvert put such great emphasis on building academic institutions in the dark times of the *dictaduras* in Latin America. He successfully urged the Ford Foundation to support social science institutes that could sustain or create the intellectual enterprise the tyrants found so dangerous. Creating a scholarly base throughout the region—and tying it to universities in the United States and Europe—was not simply an effort to save lives (although it was that) and not simply an effort to save social sciences for their own sake or because of loyalty to a "profession" (although it was that, too). Perhaps most important, Silvert wanted these institutes to advance the intellectual enterprise and lay the groundwork for the emergence of a viable and robust democracy in the region. The scholarly network would save the lives and work of people who could sustain the human capital needed to one day go back and help create better and more viable democratic institutions. He saw the institutes as keeping alive the free flow of ideas. The very value systems that were supportive of social science also nourished democracy. Silvert wanted to create a cadre of people—intellectuals—who could shine light on the forces of darkness. That's why—in the face of the coming of dictators like Pinochet—he wanted to ring Latin America with institutes, and why he also wanted to create places in the United States where Latin American intellectuals could wait out these times, a place that would be a haven for them.

Silvert might have been able to accomplish all this had he simply left academia and gone to work for Ford. The foundation would have been a power base to do a lot of things. But that was not his goal. Creating these options was part of a larger purpose and effort. NYU gave him his academic home, and the Ford Foundation gave him a venue for action. The intellectual part was a pillar of his own identity and for this he wanted, he needed, the academic home. He did not want a formal role in politics because that meant being accountable to other forces besides knowledge and truth and could thus easily distort them. Foundation life had its own temptations—minor compared to politics— to distort the truth to accomplish its goals and gain support: any institution does. That's why he wanted to keep one foot in the world of the university, a world that despite its foibles and hypocrisies made knowledge, understanding, and truth central. The academic world allowed him to take research and theory very seriously, to question approaches that mislead, to challenge frameworks that diverted attention from the key role of human choice in shaping the realm of what was possible.

In the way he embraced the academic world, Silvert was rejecting the idea of the solitary intellectual living in an ivory tower. A democratic society needed intellectuals who could not only provide the research and facts for evidence-based policymaking but do something even more important: use their writings and voice to help make the political and social world more transparent to citizens so they could speak truth to power and hold political leadership accountable. The knowledge of intellectuals could help preserve what was good about the existing public space, change what was bad, and transform and heal the world. In that world, no State Department could make false claims about the conditions in the Dominican Republic or elsewhere without a storm of counter-comment from the public intellectuals who would set the record straight. That was the world of an empowered public. That was the world Silvert aimed to create.

Silvert got together with Richard Morse and Richard Adams, historian and anthropologist, and a few others to found LASA. This was not merely the case of an academic wanting to create a new (professional) organization that would allow intellectuals to give academic papers, build their bona fides, prepare articles for journal publications, and look for academic jobs. These things, of course, come with the territory if you are creating a traditional academic organization. For Silvert, building LASA was an extension of his larger vision.

He saw it as a place where publicly engaged intellectuals could gather together to share equally, a place where Latin American scholars could meet as colleagues with North Americans: no more "the North" studying "the South." It was meant to be a place of synthesis, of interdisciplinary approaches to the big issues of the time and region. It was meant to be an antidote to the fragmentation of academia into warring subspecialties and fields; a place of enlightenment and empowerment. It was also a public space where intellectuals from the United States could leverage their freedom and resources to help expand academic freedom to parts of Latin America where truth seeking, intellectual work, and public engagement by academics were under attack. Truth seeking and research went hand in hand with human flourishing and human development and the flourishing of future democracies in the region. LASA was meant to be a public institution, a public space. It was meant to be an institution that could have a lasting impact through the intergenerational activity of scholars who would encourage the development of public intellectuals following the path that he initially blazed. That is why Kal Silvert, a public intellectual par excellence, invested his passion, skill, and political acuity in birthing it. It is a piece of his legacy that we all have been fortunate to inherit.

Note

The authors thank Max Cameron, Abe Lowenthal, and Victoria Chien Scott for their insightful critiques.

Epilogue

Kalman Silvert and Latin American Studies Today

Gilbert M. Joseph

As president of the Latin American Studies Association during its fiftieth anniversary year, I take great pleasure in contributing an epilogue to this rich, timely volume commemorating the life's work and legacy of Kalman Silvert, LASA's founding president. Forty years after Silvert's untimely passing, the institutional, intellectual, philanthropic, and ethical legacies he left still affect Latin American studies, even if many in the present generation of scholars and practitioners are largely unaware of them. To be sure, academe and area studies have undergone profound, paradigmatic shifts in recent decades, and Latin America has witnessed epochal transformations since the Cold War era that Silvert navigated for all of his extraordinary professional life. Still, the values that he stood for, the commitments he made, and the institutions he helped shape remain exemplary.

My own career bears witness to several of these legacies. I first heard about Kalman Silvert in passing, when as a college underclassman in the late 1960s I told my father about my plans to study Latin American history. He mentioned that he had an old college friend and formidable debating partner from the University of Pennsylvania—Silvert—who he thought had gone on to study the region, and perhaps someday I would learn more about him. Years later, as a doctoral student at Yale, I did. Shortly after my arrival in New Haven, one of my mentors, Richard Morse, introduced me to Silvert's letters for the American Universities Field Staff, which he rightly touted as models of engaged and engaging prose. Morse also encouraged me to join the fledgling Latin American Studies Association, which he and several others helped Silvert found in 1966. Several years into my graduate work, I was privileged to encounter my other mentor, Emilia Viotti da Costa, one of Brazil's greatest historians, who had been fired from her position at the Universdade de São Paulo during the most draconian days of military rule. Soon compelled to leave the country, Viotti da Costa found her way into the North American academy and New Haven with an assist from the Ford Foundation's Latin America program under Silvert's direction. In the years that followed, my training benefited from a Foreign Area Fellowship, a dissertation grant Silvert had helped create, one of his many initiatives to build the quality of research on Latin America at North American institutions, and do so by maximizing cross-talk among younger scholars across the hemisphere. Fifteen years later, now a mentor to my own international group of doctoral students, I joined the Social Science Research Council's Joint Committee on Latin America, where my colleagues included the members of a younger generation of Latin American social scientists who had been trained at the very institutions Silvert's Ford Foundation had helped nurture and support during the darkest days of the Southern Cone's dirty wars. Now, decades since, I regularly savor the distinguished lectures presented at LASA's annual congresses by the winners of the aptly named Kalman Silvert Award, LASA's highest recognition of lifetime achievement in Latin American studies. This year, at LASA's watershed fiftieth Congress in New York City, I will have the honor of presenting that award as president of the association.

The Silvert awardees embody the dedication, commitment, and broad-gauged intellectual contributions to Latin American studies that characterized Silvert's brief but consequential career. The core principles that guided him—a deep contextual understanding of the region's domestic affairs and international relations based on language, culture, and history; an openness to new forms of interdisciplinary and hemispheric collaborations; and a broadening of the processes of community building, social transformation, and of knowledge formation—guide LASA still. These were the staples of LASA's mission during its first half century, and a reengagement with these principles will help sustain Latin Americanists over the next fifty years.

Last year, for example, I returned from the international congress in Sun Juan, Puerto Rico, marveling at the potential for interdisciplinary renovation and innovation that LASA epitomizes. Deeply inspiring was the lecture by Silvert honoree, Chilean sociologist Manuel Antonio Garretón, himself trained in the social science tradition that Silvert did so much to promote and preserve during the Latin American Cold War. In a speech that would have made Silvert proud, Garretón discussed the disciplinary challenges that attend studying political parties and national political processes in a multidisciplinary and socially conscious context. He ended his lecture by expressing his commitment to the pluralism of LASA, especially the association's involvement with newer kinds of grassroots collaborations, many of which reflect a new generation of culturalist, gendered, subalternist, and postcolonial agendas that Silvert's post–World War II scholarly establishment would not have been exposed to. Nevertheless, from the inception of Silvert's founding presidency in 1966, LASA has always constituted a "big tent" for scholars and agents of social change. In recent years, the development of cultural and performance studies, studies of gender and sexuality, and the intersection of Latin American studies with Latino/a studies have become vital currents among LASA's membership, bringing fresh, often experimental methods and epistemologies to LASA's enterprise.

The institutionalization of the Otros Saberes (Other Knowledges) project, for instance, promotes collaborations with emerging constituencies around the kind of ethnoracial, environmental, and gender issues that preoccupy epistemic communities and grassroots movements and identities that Silvert's fledgling LASA did not encounter in the late 1960s and early 1970s. Silvert's founding generation committed itself, often in extreme circumstances of dictatorship and repression during the Cold War, to preserve and enrich social science scholarship in the hemisphere's cosmopolitan capital cities; in time, they hoped to diffuse rigorous methods throughout the hemisphere's secondary centers and provincial intelligentsias. By contrast, Otros Saberes seeks to strengthen intellectual collaborations and activist relationships between academic scholars and nonelite subaltern groups, expanding an appreciation of and a dialogue among different ways of knowing, as well as posing novel inquiries into the process of knowledge formation itself. Yet consonant with Silvert's abiding ecumenism, which has always guided LASA, the association continues to honor classical fields of social science scholarship as well as emerging fields of academic inquiry and social action. The social sciences and the humanities are equally represented in the research interests of LASA's members, and both the annual congresses and the association's flagship journal, the *Latin American Research Review*, remain committed to promoting the kind of rigorously engaged disciplinary scholarship and far-reaching interdisciplinary debates that marked LASA's founding by Silvert and his colleagues.

In other words, LASA and its affiliated centers and institutions are engaged in a variety of projects that distinguish an extremely vital moment of Latin American studies, one in which Latin Americanists are staking our own claims to appropriate and refashion area studies and global studies. For example, very much in the wheelhouse of the kind of rigorous social science research that animated so many of Silvert's comparative and interdisciplinary projects on the dynamics of democratic societies, Notre Dame's Kellogg Center has just publicly launched its Varieties of Democracy (V-Dem) project, complete with a democracy data set of some 15 million data points across 173 countries from 1900 to the present. According to one of its lead researchers Michael Coppedge, the data set promises to revolutionize the study of democracy in its breadth, depth, and precision. In the meantime, from the cultural studies/performance side of LASA's constituency, the Fiftieth Anniversary Congress features a Presidential Session, sponsored by Otros Saberes, to showcase the role of hip-hop artists and activists in diverse political, social, ethnic, racial, gender, sexual, and linguistic movements of the Global South (which also includes the immigrant imaginaries in the Global North). LASA's members received a pulsating demonstration of this vernacular musical genre at the welcoming ceremony of the 2015 San Juan Congress, when Oaxacan female hip-hop artist Mare Advertencia Lirika brought down the packed house and graphically underscored LASA's changing demographics.

The context and dynamics of LASA's watershed fiftieth Congress provide a revealing glimpse into how much the profile of Latin American studies has changed since Silvert's leadership of the association in the mid-1960s. LASA returns to New York for the first time since it held its inaugural meeting in 1966, when its members barely reached triple digits, the preponderant majority of them North American scholars. Now LASA is an organization of more than twelve thousand members, nearly half of whom reside in Latin America. Not only is "LASA at 50" the largest congress the association has ever sponsored, with well over a thousand panels and about six thousand attendees, it is also the most international in character, with more than 60 percent of the paper presenters residing outside the United States.

LASA's return to New York is particularly fortuitous, for reasons more profound than historical symmetry. Over the course of LASA's first half century, New York has become an important part of the field itself—a critical crossroads for the study of Latin America in its rich transnational and multilayered contexts. It is therefore fitting that two of the congress's thirty-nine program tracks privilege Latino/a studies, and many of the panels feature a continuing discussion of how specialists in that field might better communicate with those who work on what is traditionally regarded to be Latin America. A variety of panels engage

Latino New York, and one highlighted session links Cold War–era New York City and Latin America. That session also premiers an interdisciplinary, multimedia installation that interrogates conventional notions of north–south encounters, imperial core and periphery, and spatial concepts of interborough and outerborough. One of the Congress's presidential panels presents a timely interview, six months before the US presidential election, with Deputy Secretary of Homeland Security Alejandro Mayorkas, conducted by *New York Times* national immigration correspondent Julia Preston, regarding the dilemmas posed by international migration and border security and the prospects for comprehensive immigration reform. Another presidential panel features a high-profile dialogue among the leading Cuban and US diplomats and policymakers behind the normalization of relations between the two nations. Another plenary session, "Latin American Transformations," brings some of the most distinguished interdisciplinary thinkers in our field, including John Coastworth, Alejandro Portes, Maria Herminia Tavares de Almeida, Florencia Mallon, and Steve J. Stern, to assess changes over the past fifty years. The panelists focus on US power and hegemony, migration and demographic trends, democracy and dictatorship, economic paradigms and policies, and new grassroots constituencies—and speculate on what the decades ahead will bring. A companion presidential roundtable on fifty years of journalistic coverage of Latin America includes some of the hemisphere's most renowned reporters and photojournalists, an intergenerational cohort, all of whom seek to promote a deeper exchange with academic scholars. Finally, the fiftieth takes particular pride in fostering a dialogue on the achievement and prospects for democracy in the hemisphere between two of Latin America's most enduring statesmen and thinkers, Fernando Henrique Cardoso and Ricardo Lagos—two of Silvert's young colleagues and protégés decades ago—and a blue-ribbon panel commemorates Guillermo O'Donnell's classic work on democratic transitions (a magnum opus that likely benefited from conversations with Silvert).

Much of the program of the fiftieth congress resonates with Silvert's core interests and principles; much of it underscores his hemispheric, interdisciplinary, and comparative sensibilities. He would be pleased to know that Latin American historians and political scientists have of late returned to focus on civil society, reexamining public intellectuals, rationality, and the centrality of the public sphere—thereby deepening his own work and activism around these themes. Some of the new trends in Latin American studies—especially poststructural preoccupations with cultural studies, subaltern studies, transnationality, and the post-modern condition—would challenge him to stretch his thematic, disciplinary, and methodological comfort zones. He would welcome the increasing Latin Americanization of LASA's membership and be encouraged to know that about 20 percent of LASA's current members are students and have approached the association's receptive leaders about greater participation and representation. Similarly, he would be encouraged by the recent trend to nominate Latin Americans to serve as vice president, president, and treasurer of the organization.

Finally, Silvert would be surprised (and no doubt pleased) to learn that the vast majority of LASA's presidents in recent years, as well as a great percentage of its officers, are women, thereby redressing a notable imbalance. When I first was introduced to this collection, I was powerfully struck by the fact that all of the contributors were men, and that apart from Silvert's wife and colleague, Frieda, only a few women collaborators were even mentioned (e.g., Argentina's distinguished scholar of memory and repression during the dirty wars, Elizabeth Jelin). This should not be surprising, however. Silvert taught at Dartmouth when it was an all-male college, and he only taught grad students at NYU during the late 1960s and early 1970s, when few women were enrolled in graduate programs in political science or Latin American studies throughout the Americas. That is why the contributors to this volume, personally inspired and mentored so well by Kalman Silvert, are all male.

As this richly textured collection demonstrates so clearly, Silvert's ambitious career was inextricably bound up with crossing boundaries, increasing participation, and ensuring that individuals at every point in society fulfilled their individual potential, thereby enhancing the "social good" of their nations and of modern society more generally.

Bibliography

Adams, James Truslow. 1931. *The Epic of America*. New York: Little, Brown.

Adams, Richard N. 1976. "Kalman Hirsch Silvert, 10 March 1921–15 June 1976," *Latin American Research Review* 13, no. 1: 189–194.

Adelman, Jeremy. 2013. *Worldly Philosopher: The Odyssey of Albert O. Hirschman*. Princeton, NJ: Princeton University Press.

Almond, Gabriel A., and James S. Coleman, eds. 1960. *The Politics of Developing Areas*. Princeton, NJ: Princeton University Press.

American Universities Field Staff (AUFS). 1957. *AUFS Reports: West Coast South America Series*, vols. I–IV. Hanover, NH: AUFS.

American Universities Field Staff (AUFS). 1957. "Coda," KHS-11-1957, in *AUFS Reports*. New York: AUFS, 1957.

American Universities Field Staff (AUFS). 1957. "Elections, Parties, and the Law," KHS-4-1957, in *AUFS Reports*. New York: AUFS, 1957.

American Universities Field Staff (AUFS). 1957. "Other People's Classrooms," KHS-2-1958 in *AUFS Reports*. New York: AUFS, 1957.

American Universities Field Staff (AUFS). 1957. "Truancy and Illiteracy: Chilean Sociology Moves Toward Quantification," KHS-7-1957, in *AUFS Reports*. New York: AUFS, 1957.

American Universities Field Staff (AUFS). 1966. "Area Studies and Subject Areas: A Comment on Specialists, Generalists, and Disciplinarians in Foreign Area Studies," KHS-1-1963, in *AUFS Reports*. New York: AUFS, 1966.

American Universities Field Staff (AUFS). 1966. *AUFS Reports: East Coast South America Series*, vols. I–XI. Hanover, NH: AUFS.

American Universities Field Staff (AUFS). 1966. "The Meeting of North and South: Comments on Problems of Hemispheric Relations," KHS-2-1961, in *AUFS Reports*. New York: AUFS, 1966.

American Universities Field Staff (AUFS). 1966. "Political Universes of Latin America," KHS-5-1961, in *AUFS Reports*. New York: AUFS, 1966.

Anderson, Charles W. *Politics and Economic Change in Latin America*. Princeton, NJ: Van Nostrand, 1967.

Atwater, Verne S., and Evelyn C. Walsh. 2011. *A Memoir of The Ford Foundation—The Early Years (1936–1968)*. New York: Vantage Press.

Bell, Peter D. "Social Sciences," FXS History Project, Series VI, Box 61, Ford Foundation Archives (Sept. 1967): 17–21. Rockefeller Archive Center, Sleepy Hollow, NY.

Bemis, Samuel Flagg. 1943. *The Latin American Policy of the United States: An Historical Interpretation*. New York: Harcourt Brace and World.

Berger, Mark T. 1995. *Under Northern Eyes: Latin American Studies and US Hegemony in the Americas 1899–1993*. Bloomington: Indiana University Press.

Bonilla, Frank. "Notes on Social Sciences in Brazil," Folder 001972, Ford Foundation Archives (1971): 1–17. Rockefeller Archive Center, Sleepy Hollow, NY.

Bresnan, John. 2006. *At Home Abroad: A Memoir of the Ford Foundation in Indonesia, 1953–1973*. Jakarta, Indonesia: PT Equinox Publishing.

Brooks, David. 2014. "Introspective or Narcissistic," *New York Times* (August 8): A-23.

Brunner, José Joaquín. 1985. "La Participación de los Centros Académicos Privados (Chile)," *Estudios Públicos* 19 (Invierno): 1–12.

Brzezinski, Zbigniew. 2012. *Strategic Vision: America and the Crisis of Global Power*. New York: Basic Books.

Burr, Robert N. 1967. *Our Troubled Hemisphere: Perspectives on US–Latin American Relations*. Washington, DC: Brookings Institution.

Carmichael, William D. 1964. "The FLACSO Decision," Memorandum to Harry E. Wilhelm, Folder 008799, Ford Foundation Archives (July 17, 1964): 1:8. Rockefeller Archive Center, Sleepy Hollow, NY.

Casanova, José. 1994. *Public Religions in the Modern World*. Chicago: University of Chicago Press.

Cassirer, Ernst. 1946. *The Myth of the State*. New Haven, CT: Yale University Press.

Cleaves, Peter S. "Silvert Reminiscences Project at Dartmouth College," *LASA Forum* 44, no. 3 (Summer 2013): 43–51.

Cline, Howard F. 1966. "The Latin American Studies Association: A Summary Survey," *Latin American Research Review* 2, no. 1 (Autumn): 57–79.

Commission on United States–Latin American Relations. 1974. *The Americas in a Changing World*. New York: Center for Inter-American Relations.

Commission on United States–Latin American Relations. 1974. "Minutes of the Six Commission Meetings, 1974." Typed rapporteur's notes in the personal archives of Abraham F. Lowenthal.

Commission on United States–Latin American Relations. 1975. *The Americas in a Changing World*. Chicago: Quadrangle Press.

Commission on United States–Latin American Relations. 1976. *The Americas in a Changing World: Next Steps*. New York: Center for Inter-American Relations.

Cotler, Julio. 2014. "Kalman Silvert, Amigo y Compañero de Ruta," *LASA Forum* 45, no. 1 (Winter): 31–32.

Crozier, Michael, and Samuel P. Huntington. 1975. *The Crisis of Democracy: On the Governability of Democracies*. New York: New York University Press.

Delpar, Helen. 2008. *Looking South: The Evolution of Latin Americanist Scholarship in the United States: 1850–1975*. Tuscaloosa: University of Alabama Press

Dun, Doreen. 1979. Evaluation of FY 1974 Graduate Fellowship Program, "Microfilm PA 749-0010, Ford Foundation Archives (March 7): 1:4. Rockefeller Archive Center, Sleepy Hollow, NY.

Dye, Richard W. 1973. "Report on My Trip to Chile and Argentina, October 4–10," Bogotá Files on Southern Cone, Box 1, Confidential Folder 1973–1978, Ford Foundation Archives (October 11): 1–44. Rockefeller Archive Center, Sleepy Hollow, NY.

Emerson, Rupert. 1960. *From Empire to Nation*. Cambridge, MA: Harvard University Press.

Ford Foundation. n.d. "List of ECALAS Grantees through December 1975," Bogota Southern Cone Files, Box 2, Refugees, Ford Foundation Archives: 1–30. Rockefeller Archive Center, Sleepy Hollow, NY.

Ford Foundation. 1975. "Support to Assist Latin American Scholars Displaced by Political Events," Grants 74-364, 74-365, and 74-187, Ford Foundation Archives: 1–32. Rockefeller Archive Center, Sleepy Hollow, NY.

Geertz, Clifford. 1971. "A Program for the Stimulation of the Social Sciences in Indonesia," Report to the Ford Foundation, Asia and Pacific Office, Folder 011740, Ford Foundation Archives (August): 1–30. Rockefeller Archive Center, Sleepy Hollow, NY.

Gillen, John, and K. H. Silvert. 1956. "Ambiguities in Guatemala," *Foreign Affairs* 34, no. 3 (April): 469–482.

Goodman, Louis W. 2013. "Kal's Gift," *LASA Forum* 44, no. 2 (Spring): 24–27.

Harkavy, Oscar. 1995. *Curbing Population Growth*. New York: Plenum Press.

Hernandez, Oswaldo J. 2014. "Entrevista" (June 30). Retrieved from http://www.plazapublica.com.gt/ content/flavio-rojas-lima-o-el-ritual-de-la-resistencia.

Horowitz, Irving Louis. 1976. "Remarks at Memorial Service for Kalman H. Silvert," held at La Maison Française Faculty of Arts and Sciences, New York University, June 17. Philadelphia: ISHI—The Institute for the Study of Human Issues.

Huntington, Samuel P. 1975, "United States," in Michael J. Crozier, Samuel P. Huntington, and Joji Watanuki, *The Crisis of Democracy: Report on the Governability of Democracies*. New York: Trilateral Commission, pp. 59–118.

Huxley, Aldous.1934. *Beyond the Mexigue Bay*. New York: Harper and Brothers Publishers.

Jutkowitz, Joel M. 1977. "Foreword," in Kalman H. Silvert, *Essays in Understanding Latin America*. Philadelphia: ISHI—Institute for the Study of Human Issues.

Lagos, Ricardo, with Blake Hounshell and Elizabeth Dickinson. 2012. *The Southern Tiger: Chile's Fight for a Democratic and Prosperous Future*. New York: St. Martin's Press.

Langer, Suzanne K. 1996. *Philosophy in a New Key*, 3rd ed. Cambridge, MA: Harvard University Press.

Levine, Daniel H. 2012. *Politics, Religion and Society in Latin America*. Boulder, CO: Lynne Rienner.

Levine, Daniel H. 2014. "Surprises," in Robert Schramm, ed., *The Road Less Travelled, A Tradition of Leadership: Reflections of Dartmouth 64s on the Occasion of Our 50th Reunion*. Hanover, NH: Dartmouth College.

Levine, Daniel H. 2016. "On Mentors and Mentoring: A Memoir of Robert A. Dahl and Kalman H. Silvert," *PS: Politics and Society* (forthcoming).

López, Sinesio. 1997. *Ciudadanos Reales y Imaginarios*. Lima: Instituto de Diálogo y Propuestas.

Manitzas, Nita R. 1980. "Evaluation of the Southern Cone DAP," Folder 011879, Ford Foundation Archives (February): 1–37. Rockefeller Archive Center, Sleepy Hollow, NY.

Manitzas, Nita R. 1971. "Social Science Program, Argentina," Memorandum to Reynold E. Carlson, Folder 008437, Ford Foundation Archives (December 13): 1–37. Rockefeller Archive Center, Sleepy Hollow, NY.

Manitzas, Nita R., and Richard Fagen. 1973. "The Social Sciences in Chile," Folder 005920, Ford Foundation Archives (January): 1–32. Rockefeller Archive Center, Sleepy Hollow, NY.

Mills, C. Wright. 1959. *The Sociological Imagination*. New York: Oxford University Press.

Mitchell, Christopher M. 2013. "Kalman Silvert as Colleague at New York University," *LASA Forum* 44, no. 4 (Fall): 29–31.

Morse, Richard M. 1977. "Kalman H. Silvert, 1921–1976: A Reminiscence," *Hispanic American Historical Review* 57, no. 3 (August 1977): 504–510.

Navarro, Juan José. 2011. "Cold War in Latin America: The Camelot Project (1964–1965): Political and Academic Reactions of the Chilean Left," *Comparative Sociology* 10: 807–825.

Needler, Martin C. 1963. *Latin American Politics in Perspective*. Princeton, NJ: Van Nostrand.

Ollman, Bertell. 1971. *Alienation: Marxist Concept of Man in Capitalist Society*. New York: Cambridge University Press.

Organisation for Economic Co-operation and Development. 2014. *Education at a Glance 2014: OECD Indicators*. Paris: OECD.

OECD. 2013. *Colombia: Implementing Good Governance*. Paris: OECD.

Packenham, Robert. 1977. *Liberal America and the Third World. Political Development Ideas in the Third World*. Princeton, NJ: Princeton University Press.

Plotkin, Mariano Ben. 2015. "US Foundations, Cultural Imperialism and Transnational Misunderstandings: The Case of the Marginality Project," *Journal of Latin American Studies* 47, no. 1: 65–92.

Polanyi, Karl. 1957 [1944]. *The Great Transformation: The Political and Economic Origins of Our Time*. Boston: Beacon Press.

Puryear, Jeffrey P. 1982. "Higher Education, Development Assistance and Repressive Regimes," *Studies in Comparative International Development* 17, no. 2 (Summer): 3–35.

Rangil, T. T. 2013. "Citizen, Academic, Expert, or International Worker? Juggling with Identities at UNESCO's Social Science Department, 1946–1955," *Science in Context* 26, no. 1: 61–91.

Richardson, Heather Cox. 2014. *To Make Men Free: A History of the Republican Party*. New York: Basic Books.

Rodó, José Enrique. 1900. *Ariél*. Montevideo, Uruguay: Emprenta de Dornaleche y Reyes.

Said, Edward W. 1978. *Orientalism*. New York: Pantheon Books.

Sanders, Thomas G. 1982. *Colombian Politics in 1982.* American Series No. 25. Hanover, NH: AUFS.

Sarason, Seymour B. 1974. *The Psychological Sense of Community: Prospects for a Community Psychology.* San Francisco: Jossey-Bass.

Silvert, Frieda, and Marlis Krueger. 1975. *Dissent Denied: The Technocratic Response to Protest.* New York: Elsevier Publishing Co.

Silvert, Kalman H. 1954. *A Study in Government: Guatemala.* New Orleans: Middle America Research Institute, Tulane University, 1954.

Silvert, Kalman H. 1958. "Welcome to the fold, Mr. Nixon . . ." *AUFS Field Staff Reports* vol. 5 (East Coast South America Series). Hanover, NH: AUFS.

Sivert, Kalman H. 1960. "A Study of Mexico," Ford Foundation Archives, Report 000016, Rockefeller Archives Center, Sleepy Hollow, NY.

Silvert, Kalman H. 1961. *The Conflict Society.* New York: Hauser Press and AUFS. (Rev. ed., 1966; 1968).

Silvert, Kalman H, ed. 1963. *Expectant Peoples: Nationalism and Development.* New York: Random House.

Silvert, Kalman H. 1964. *Discussion at Bellagio.* New York: AUFS.

Silvert, Kalman H. 1965. "Academic Ethics and Social Research Abroad: The Lesson of Project Camelot," *Background* 9, no. 3 (November): 215–236.

Silvert, Kalman H., ed. 1966. *Churches and States: The Religious Institution and Modernization.* New York: AUFS.

Silvert, Kalman H., 1968. *The Conflict Society: Reaction and Revolution in Latin America.* Revised edition. New York: Harper Colophon.

Silvert, Kalman H. 1968. "An Essay on Interdisciplinary and International Collaboration in Social Science Research in Latin America," Discussion Paper, Folder 011937, Ford Foundation Archives (June 5): 1–21. Rockefeller Archive Center, Sleepy Hollow, NY.

Silvert, Kalman H. 1968. Social Science Research and Social Relevance." Inter-Office Memorandum to Country Representatives and Social Science Advisors, Folder 011937, Ford Foundation Archives (June 5, 1968). Rockefeller Archive Center, Sleepy Hollow, NY.

Silvert, Kalman H. 1969. "Area Studies Look Outward," Discussion Paper, Folder 002955 (February): 1–16. Rockefeller Archive Center, Sleepy Hollow, NY.

Silvert, Kalman H. 1969. "Draft of Policy Guidelines for Social Sciences in Latin America," Inter-Office Memorandum, Folder 008774, Ford Foundation Archives (January 27): 1–17. Rockefeller Archive Center, Sleepy Hollow, NY.

Silvert, Kalman H. 1970. *Man's Power: A Biased Guide to Political Thought and Action.* New York: Viking Press.

Silvert, Kalman H. 1971. "Distasteful Regimes and Foundation Policies Overseas," Inter-Office Memorandum to David E. Bell, Ford Foundation Archives (October 18): 1–3. Rockefeller Archive Center, Sleepy Hollow, NY.

Silvert, Kalman H. 1972. "Field Office Budget Proposals," Memorandum to William D. Carmichael, Folder 005848, Ford Foundation Archives (March 14): 1–17. Rockefeller Archive Center, Sleepy Hollow, NY.

Silvert, Kalman H. 1972. "'Population' as a Social Science 'Problem,'" Discussion Paper, Folder 009860, Ford Foundation Archives (May 30): 1–10. Rockefeller Archive Center, Sleepy Hollow, NY.

Silvert, Kalman H. 1974. "Budget Cuts Revisited: An OLAC Perspective on Adjusting to Reduced Spending Levels," Folder 007817, Ford Foundation Archives (May 29): 1–9. Rockefeller Archive Center, Sleepy Hollow, NY.

Silvert, Kalman H. 1974. "Chile," Ford Foundation Inter-Office Memorandum to William Carmichael, Ford Foundation Archives (March 26): 1–5. Rockefeller Archive Center, Sleepy Hollow, NY.

Silvert, Kalman H. 1975. "Rural Development as a Social Science Problem," Discussion Paper, Folder 004926, Ford Foundation Archives (April): 1–6. Rockefeller Archive Center, Sleepy Hollow, NY.

Silvert, Kalman H. 1977. *Essays in Understanding Latin America*. Philadelphia: ISHI—Institute for the Study of Human Issues.

Silvert, Kalman H. 1977. *The Reason for Democracy*. New York: Viking Press.

Silvert, Kalman H., and Frank Bonilla. 1961. *Education and the Social Meaning of Development: A Preliminary Statement*. New York: American Universities Field Staff.

Silvert, Kalman H., and Leonard Reissman. 1976. *Education, Class and Nation: The Experiences of Chile and Venezuela*. New York: Elsevier.

Staples, Eugene S. 1992. *Forty Years: A Learning Curve: The Ford Foundation Program in India, 1952–1992*. New York: Ford Foundation.

Stepan, Alfred. 2003. "The World's Religious Systems and Democracy: Crafting the Twin Tolerations," in Alfred Stepan, ed., *Arguing Comparative Politics*. New York: Oxford University Press, pp. 213–53.

Sutton, Francis X. 1961. *American Foundations in Non-Western Areas*. New York: Ford Foundation.

Tocqueville, Alexis de. 1990. *Democracy in America*, vol. 1. New York: Vintage.

Van Cott, Donna Lee. 2008. *Radical Democracy in the Andes*. Cambridge: Cambridge University Press.

Veliz, Claudio. 1980. *The Centralist Tradition of Latin America*. Princeton, NJ: Princeton University Press.

Weber, Max. 1949. *The Methodology of the Social Sciences*. Glencoe, IL: Free Press.

Weber, Max. 1966. *Politics as a Vocation*. Philadelphia: Fortress Press.

Wolf, Alfred, Kalman Silvert, and Reynold Carlson. 1959. "Ford Foundation Mission to Argentina," Folder 002814, Ford Foundation Archives (Aug–Sept): 1–32. Rockefeller Archive Center, Sleepy Hollow, NY.

Yashar, Deborah. 2005. *Contesting Citizenship in Latin America: The Rise of Indigenous Movements and the Post Liberal Challenge*. Cambridge: Cambridge University Press.

The Contributors

Abraham F. Lowenthal is Robert F. Erburu professor of ethics and development and professor of international relations, emeritus, University of Southern California, as well as founding director of the Latin American Program at the Woodrow Wilson International Center for Scholars and of the Inter-American Dialogue.

Martin Weinstein is professor emeritus of political science, William Paterson University of New Jersey. He is also founding member of the advisory board for ReachingU, a foundation for Uruguay.

Jorge Balán is senior research scholar at the School of International and Public Affairs, Columbia University, and former senior program officer, International Education Policy, at the Ford Foundation (1998–2006).

Morris Blachman is clinical professor in the Department of Neuropsychiatry and Behavioral Science and assistant dean for Continuing Medical Education and Faculty Development in the School of Medicine, University of South Carolina.

Peter S. Cleaves is president of DRG International, former program officer at the Ford Foundation, and former director of the Institute for Latin American Studies and of the Center for the Study of Western Hemisphere Trade, University of Texas, Austin.

Julio Cotler is senior research fellow at the Instituto de Estudios Peruanos and emeritus professor of San Marcos University. He received the Kalman H. Silvert Award from the Latin American Studies Association in 2012.

Richard W. Dye is president and senior associate, International Education Solutions; former foreign service officer, US Department of State; former program officer at the Ford Foundation; and former executive vice president and chief operating officer at the Institute of International Education.

Louis W. Goodman is professor and dean emeritus, School of International Service, American University, and former senior associate, Social Science Research Council.

Gilbert M. Joseph is Farnam Professor of History and International Studies, Yale University, and president of the Latin American Studies Association (LASA) (2015–2016).

Joel Jutkowitz is senior technical director, Management Systems International, Washington, DC.

Ricardo Lagos is former president of Chile (2000–2006) and former secretary general of the Latin American Faculty of Social Sciences (FLACSO), Buenos Aires (1973–1974).

Daniel H. Levine is professor of political science emeritus, University of Michigan.

Christopher Mitchell is professor emeritus of politics, New York University.

Kenneth Sharpe is William R. Kenan Professor of Political Science, Swarthmore College.

Index

Adams, James Truslow, 143
Adams, Richard, 7, 85, 172
Afghanistan: conflicts in, 70
Ahumada, Jorge, 138
Alienation: Marxist Concept of Man in Capitalist Society (Ollman), 78–79
Allende, Salvador, 4, 66, 101, 116, 138, 162
Almeida, Tavares de, 179
Almond, Gabriel, 56, 165
American Council of Learned Societies(ACLS), 149
American Dream, 143, 144–145
American Universities Field Staff (AUFS), 10, 17, 41, 80, 85, 95, 111, 148
Anderson, Charles, 26, 39n1
Arab Spring, 65
Árbenz, Jacobo, 17, 33, 94, 95
Argentina: academic culture, 87; democratic transition, 126; military coup, 82; nationalism, 22; political development, 117, 132n21; Silvert's letters about, 18; social science, 20
Armas, Castillo, 85

Batlle y Ordóñez, José, 39n1
beliefs: typologies of, 58
Bell, Peter, 3, 116, 123, 151

Bentham, Jeremy, 27
Betancourt, Rómulo, 137
Beyond the Mexique Bay (Huxley), 19
Bitar, Sergio, 126, 132n23
Blachman, Morris, 75, 156
Bonilla, Frank, 138
Bordaberry, Juan María, 116
Borlaug, Norman, 115
Brazil, 57, 115, 126
Brooks, David, 76
Bundy, McGeorge, 3

Cardoso, Fernando Henrique, 79, 116, 126, 141, 152, 153, 179
Carlson, Reynold, 81, 99, 109, 111, 130n2
Carmichael, William, 113, 124
Carter, Jimmy, 103
Cassirer, Ernst, 27, 41, 143
Castro, Fidel, 96, 99
CEBRAP (Center for Analysis and Research), 3, 126, 131n18
CEDES (Centro de Estudios de Estado y Sociedad), 3, 119, 126, 133–134n28, 138, 139
Center for Inter-American Relations, 101, 102
Chile: democratic transition in, 5, 67, 73n9, 126; as destination of refugees, 150; D'Hondt system of proportional representation, 18;

189

Tannenbaum, Frank, 98
theories: of causality, 167, 169; critique of general, 166; importance
  to academic work, 168; moral test
  for, 167
theory of understanding, 164–165
Tocqueville, Alexis de, 48, 121–122
*To Make Men Free: A History of the
  Republican Party* (Richardson),
  147

Ubico, Jorge, 16
United States: civil war in, 166–167;
  foreign policy, 162, 163, 167;
  intervention of Dominican
  Republic, 101, 140, 155; promise
  of democracy in, 161–162
Uruguay, 80, 116
US–Latin American relations: characteristic of, 92, 96, 104, 125;
  Kennedy administration initiatives, 99; Latin American Studies
  and, 75; Linowitz Commission on,

102–104, 105n4–5; role of governments in, 92; scholarship on, 93–
  95; Silvert's impact on, 95, 100–
  102

values: conflicts of, 65–68; political
  behavior and, 57
Varieties of Democracy (V-Dem) proj-
  ect, 178
Venezuela, 29, 52, 59, 72–73n6, 140
Videla, Jorge, 117

Weber, Max, 27, 42, 48, 81
Weinstein, Martin, 11
Wieschhoff, Heinrich Albert, 84
Wilhelm, Harry, 109, 111, 113
Wipfler, William, 118
Wolf, Alfred, 81, 111
Wood, Bryce, 7, 141, 152
World University Services (WUS), 4,
  118, 119
world views: topology of, 59–60

About the Book

Kalman Silvert highlights the extraordinary career of an extraordinary man—one of the founding architects of Latin American studies in the United States, a major builder of the inter-American scholarly community, and an influential figure in US–Latin American relations.

Thirteen distinguished Latin Americanists discuss Silvert's role as scholar, teacher, mentor, colleague, public intellectual, institution builder, and philanthropist. They also emphasize his contributions at the Ford Foundation, where he served as senior program adviser from 1967 until his death in 1976. Coeditors Abraham F. Lowenthal and Martin Weinstein frame the retrospective, underlining the integration of Silvert's multiple contributions and the continuing relevance of his legacy.

Abraham F. Lowenthal is professor emeritus of international relations at the University of Southern California. He was the founding director of both the Wilson Center's Latin American Program and the Inter-American Dialogue. **Martin Weinstein** is professor emeritus of political science at William Paterson University of New Jersey.